START WITH THE SUN

UNIVERSITY OF NEBRASKA PRESS

Lincoln, 1960

What we want is to . . . re-establish
the living organic connections
with the cosmos, the sun and earth,
with mankind and nation and family.
Start with the sun, and the rest
will slowly, slowly happen.

D. H. LAWRENCE
Apocalypse

By JAMES E. MILLER, JR.

KARL SHAPIRO, *and*

BERNICE SLOTE

START

WITH

THE

SUN

Studies in Cosmic Poetry

Copyright © 1960 by the University of Nebraska Press
Library of Congress Catalog Card Number 60-5493
MANUFACTURED IN THE UNITED STATES OF AMERICA
No part of this book in excess of 250 words
may be reproduced in any form without per-
mission in writing from the publisher.

Acknowledgment is made to the Viking Press, Inc., for permission
to reprint material from *Sons and Lovers*, *The Rainbow*, *New Poems*,
The Lost Girl, *Psychoanalysis and the Unconscious* and *Fantasia of
the Unconscious*, *Aaron's Rod*, *Studies in Classic American Litera-
ture*, *Kangaroo*, *The Boy in the Bush*, *Collected Poems*, *The Letters
of D. H. Lawrence*, *Apocalypse*.
Quotations from *The White Peacock* (first published 1911), *The
Trespasser* (first published 1912) and *Pansies* (privately printed 1929)
reprinted by permission of the Lawrence estate.
Howl! copyright 1956 by Allen Ginsberg, published by City Lights
Books 1956.
Quotations from *The Collected Poems of Hart Crane* by permission of
Liveright, Publisher, N.Y. Copyright, 1933, Liveright, Inc.
Quotations from *The Collected Earlier Poems of William Carlos
Williams* (copyright 1938, 1951 by William Carlos Williams); Henry
Miller: *The Books in My Life* (all rights reserved); Henry Miller:
Big Sur and the Oranges of Hieronymus Bosch (copyright © 1957 by
New Directions); *The Collected Poems of Dylan Thomas* (copy-
right 1939, 1942, 1946 by New Directions, copyright 1952, 1953 by
Dylan Thomas); and Dylan Thomas: *Letters to Vernon Watkins* (©
1957 by New Directions) reprinted by permission of New Directions.

Foreword

A three-headed book may need some explanation.

This study of the Whitman tradition began during a poetry program at the University of Nebraska in 1955, when both Miss Slote and Mr. Miller (who had recently finished his *Critical Guide to Leaves of Grass*) began to detect that below the unlikely surface of Dylan Thomas's poetry there lay the vigorous ghost of Walt Whitman. They decided to collaborate on an article (which, after editorial excursions that would have given Captain Ahab pause, was published as "Of Monkeys, Nudes, and the Good Gray Poet" in *Western Humanities Review*, Winter 1959). Mr. Miller and Miss Slote continued to work on Whitman and other modern writers—Hart Crane and D. H. Lawrence emerging in clear relationships. When they met Karl Shapiro in 1957, they learned that by some cosmic chemistry he had, on his own, been looking into the same subject. His article on Whitman and Lawrence, "The First White Aboriginal," was appearing in a Japanese magazine, *The Rising Generation* (reprinted in the *Walt Whitman Review*, Sept. 1959). The result was a planned collaboration by the three of us on a book which would combine individual essays focused on a central theme. Our subsequent

Foreword

articles on the Whitman tradition were therefore designed for the development of *Start with the Sun*—an organic attempt to define unity through diversity.

We continued to try out separate articles in the critical journals, staking out claims to our idea. Mr. Miller's "The Poetics of the Cosmic Poem" appeared in a slightly different form as "Four Cosmic Poets" in the *University of Kansas City Review*, Summer 1957; "Walt Whitman and the Secret of History" in *Centennial Review*, Summer 1959. Miss Slote's "Views of *The Bridge*" developed from two articles: "Transmutation in Crane's Imagery in *The Bridge*," *Modern Language Notes*, January 1958; and "The Structure of Hart Crane's *The Bridge*," *University of Kansas City Review*, Spring 1958. We thank the original publishers of the articles for their permission to use the material reshaped in this one body.

During the progress of the work, we were given some valuable assistance. In particular,

THE AMERICAN COUNCIL OF LEARNED SOCIETIES awarded James E. Miller, Jr. a grant-in-aid which provided opportunity for a firsthand look at Lawrence and Thomas country in Great Britain.

THE UNIVERSITY OF CINCINNATI invited Karl Shapiro to deliver the Elliston Lectures for 1959. The essays "Cosmic Consciousness," "The Greatest Living Patagonian," and "The True Contemporary" are based on three of these lectures.

THE RESEARCH COUNCIL OF THE UNIVERSITY OF NEBRASKA gave Bernice Slote assistance in the preparation of the book.

MR. CHARLES FEINBERG, who has given generous support and constant encouragement to Whitman scholarship, not only has extended his warm personal interest but has put at our disposal his personal collection of valuable unpublished manuscripts.

In general, all of our colleagues in the Department of English at the University of Nebraska have, over countless cups of coffee, forced us to clarify our ideas by challenging them at every turn.

The three of us who wrote this book do not agree on every point, nor do we wish to. We have not said all that might be said —and that fact, we hope, will open other roads in a way of seeing, a way of writing, that has been too long an unrecognized living way of art in our time.

THE AUTHORS

Contents

vii

Contents

The WHITMAN TRADITION

The Whitman Tradition

IF one were asked to draw the face of twentieth-century poetry, he would very likely describe its intellectual complexity, its concentration into cubicles of wit, its wasteland derogation of possibilities, its lack of physical joy. He would, in fact, be describing the New Puritanism—that tradition of rigorously honed intellectualism in which the old worship of the soul has been replaced by the worship of the mind, but in which the same sort of exile is imposed on the body. The New Puritanism has been the dominant face in modern poetry, from the negation of *The Waste Land* through several poetic generations of a tradition focused in the theory of Ezra Pound, the performance of T. S. Eliot. It includes such diverse figures as Wallace Stevens, caught on an island of images; and Robert Lowell, revolving in a seventeenth-century sense of sin. And the New Puritanism is fortified in the pulpit of nearly all contemporary criticism. While many readers have admired the classic excellences of the Eliot tradition, they have also viewed modern poetry (which is considered one and the same thing) with a vague sense of estrangement, of loss. Where is the song, the incantation, the magic, the passion of poetry? These seem to be sacrificed, like the body, to metrical essay, analysis, and exposition. And modern poetry (which is the poetry of the New Puritanism) takes on connotations of harsh-

3

ness, obscurity, dogma; it is colored by intellectual pride and a wry despair.

And yet, a fair examination of all the contemporary scene will trace quite a different design. There are two main streams of poetry in our time, not one. Both are reputable. The Eliot tradition is, in fact, only the more vocal half of modern poetry; and the other tradition, though generally unrecognized, is a definable force, different from but equal to its companion way of poetry. I shall call it the Whitman tradition, from the poet who is its focal point—though it would be a fair comparison to call it the New Paganism. This tradition does have the pagan joy and wonder in the natural world, the living cosmos. It believes in the body *as well as* the soul, both in a unified duality that also combines emotion and intellect, good and evil. It is religious, physical, passionate, incantatory. It is affirmative in its constant sense of life. Where the New Puritanism has its affinities with the scholastics, the seventeenth-century verbal dramatists, and the eighteenth-century reasonable wits, the other tradition has its origin in the Romantics of the early nineteenth century—Blake and Wordsworth; a little of Shelley and Keats; Emerson and Thoreau. In the twentieth century, the strongest figures in the tradition are D. H. Lawrence, Hart Crane, and Dylan Thomas. We may add Vachel Lindsay, Carl Sandburg, William Carlos Williams, perhaps Theodore Roethke. (Yeats straddles the two traditions; Frost detours.) There is also the closely related prose of D. H. Lawrence, Henry Miller, and—surprisingly—James Joyce. For although a favorite of the New Puritan intellectuals, Joyce, ironically, was himself an admirer of Whitman and "influenced" by him.[1] Between the two groups of older and younger writers is the magnetic, complete figure of Whitman, who in *Leaves of Grass* fused the diverse elements of the tradition so organically that those who followed him found a world in which they could meet. Their cause was the celebration of life, not of course without some of the darkness and the sense of tragedy that are parts of the whole.

Conrad Aiken wrote in 1940 that a revival of romanticism was long overdue.[2] The fact is that it was here all along, but no one seemed to recognize it. And why not, when the catalogue of poets in such a tradition is full and strong? One may well wonder

4

why modern poetry has been so long and completely identified with the other stream—the Eliot tradition. One reason is that most of the writers *about* poetry have been themselves a part of the New Puritanism, and the circle of critical journal to critic to poet to journal has been unbroken. The intellectual and literary tradition is proudly and naturally given to exegesis, explication, and the manipulation of theory. Poets of the cosmos (as Whitman called them) are not naturally given to writing close analysis and criticism. They are likely to be expansive, rhapsodic, impressionistic. But perhaps the least admitted barrier to critical recognition is simply that "life poetry" is more difficult. It is difficult because it requires the reader to be personally and completely involved, not with the mind alone (though the demands of intellectual understanding may be severe), but with the whole emotional, even physical, self. And the most difficult of all things in poetry— when the poetry demands it—is the necessary engagement with mystery. It is a part of the letting-go that man finds so terrifying —what Keats called negative capability. A truthful account of twentieth-century poetry *as it was written* (not as it has been critically propagandized) must show two main traditions, not one. A revaluation, with some attention to definitions and relationships in the Whitman tradition, is long overdue.

Some poets and close readers have always seen what Whitman was about, but just as his tradition has not fallen into the canons of current orthodoxy, so his real nature as a poet has long been misunderstood, a misunderstanding which becomes both cause and effect. It is almost a literary axiom that any cosmic or prophetic poetry must be related to Blake, even when the poets themselves pronounce Whitman. The reason is that Blake is critically respectable; Whitman is not. For Blake's excessiveness and passion can be excused by his religion. Whatever in Blake is irreverent in the Christian tradition can be ignored as cabalistic or occult, and not really for general human consumption. It is seen that Whitman, if he has any religion, does not talk about it very much. But since his tone of exaltation and expansiveness *must* be attached to something unusual, he is then seen as the poet of what to some is a legitimate religion—the worship of country, nationality, patriotism. Whitman is thus made the poet of American democracy. But Whitman is *not* the jolly chauvinist, the champion of America, the wild-eyed gusty busy formless citizen-poet. Far from it. That the real Whitman was a mystic, a poet of cosmic consciousness and the life-force in all of nature; that he was primarily a religious poet (priest of the New Paganism, perhaps); and that he was a poet of artful control—these things recent criticism is beginning to make clear.* Writers who feel themselves bound to Whitman, who look to him as the spokesman of a tradition, do so because more than anyone else he has given this particular mysticism an effective body and voice.

Readers of the real Whitman first of all listen to the sound of the leaves. Whitman is primarily the bard of the immortal mysteries, strong and certain in his singing. His voice is rolling, hypnotic, incantatory. It has rush and flow, the shock of harshness, a delicate precision. For one thing, Whitman was master of his line. Giving the impression of careless freedom, his verse is actually an artfully handled, intricately composed music. It is molded into subtleties of tone and meaning that are possible only with skill, care, and an immensely knowing ear. This artistry of language and rhythm and sound, designed literally to enchant, is perhaps the immediate cause of his attraction.

The next appeal of Whitman is that he gives *full* expression to the cosmic, physically generative, sense of life. In this, he contrasts with earlier writers who were only partly involved. Blake, for example, was physical, but he thought the world a shadow. Wordsworth was a nature mystic, but he preferred the literal to the rhapsodic tone, and his physicality was limited to nature. Shelley was rhapsodic and prophetic, but he sometimes wrote in air. In prose, although Emerson had the oversoul and Thoreau was at least a reprobate transcendentalist, both may have found more good than evil in their cosmos. It was Whitman who wrote the poetry that made the catalogue complete.

And finally, Whitman more than most poets can capture the

* Even as we surrender this book to the press, Malcolm Cowley's significant article on Whitman's mysticism, especially as it is related to Eastern thought, has appeared (*Saturday Review*, 31 Oct. 1959). "Whitman's Buried Masterpiece," written as an introduction to the Viking Press reissue of the 1855 edition of *Leaves of Grass*, makes a strong case for both the mysticism and the artistry of "Song of Myself" and the original *Leaves*.

imagination through the body of his beliefs, ideas, themes. I would suggest one way to account for his effectiveness: that he uses striking, organic paradoxes to form the structure of his thought, paradoxes that may in their very poise and balance take dramatic hold on the imagination. Although paradox is implicit in a tradition concerned with life and the cosmos (birth is death is birth, the many and one), Whitman heightens it with his own emphasis, makes it more particular and full. He begins with the individual, who contains all ("I am an acme of things accomplish'd, and I an encloser of things to be"), and with the moment which contains the past and future. But both moment and man are alive only when in the stream of motion, or of consciousness. This is the principle of procreation, and the paradox is that the fulfillment of the moment can come only in mystic evolution. The individual, too, must be attached in union to others. This is the principle of adhesiveness, and the paradox is that the fulfillment of selfhood can come only in response to other selves. Whitman develops the themes of procreation and adhesiveness in space-time relationships. Procreation (demonstrated most vividly in the "Children of Adam" poems and his sexual imagery) is, in space, the intensity of creative experience in physical fact; in time, it is the sequential life-force. Adhesiveness (demonstrated most directly in the themes of "Calamus") is, in space, the touch and attachment of brotherhood; in time, it is the sense of reality of past and future, in which the personality of an older poet has immediacy for a present reader. To amplify the themes further, Whitman uses two significant streams of symbol: For procreation and its associated themes of mystic evolution and movement, he uses the motifs of exploration—sky-sea imagery, the open road, the journey, the voyage. For adhesiveness he uses the motif of discovery—the constant sense of the immediate physical world, the direct contact with the poet through his type-figure of human identity, the speaking voice and the live presence that inhabits *Leaves of Grass*. (Who touches this book touches a man.) It is the personal voice with the universal meaning, the individual identity and the merge into wholeness. So he begins the book:

> One's self I sing, a simple separate person,
> Yet utter the word Democratic, the word En-Masse.

7

With such interrelation of themes, Whitman gives a structural tension to the body of *Leaves of Grass*. The imagination is arrested by intensity, held through dramatic variations.

Whitman's distinction is therefore not the central core of his belief, but the fantastic detail, complexity, and completeness of its embodiment in his work. The whole is made whole. All is bound in an absolute logic, but each individual point of view or development seems fresh and new, is given intensity. He does little by exposition, much by demonstration. All comes alive. And the poet speaks with a voice so clear and direct, so engagingly human, that it is easy to call him Walt.

In this collection of essays, the Whitman tradition is examined in some particular relationships. The key figures are Walt Whitman (1819–1892), D. H. Lawrence (1885–1930), Hart Crane (1899–1932), and Dylan Thomas (1914–1953). Here it is necessary to say that we do not mean that Whitman "influenced" Lawrence, Crane, and Thomas in the sense that he told them through *Leaves of Grass* what they must think and write. It is true, of course, that in each of these poets some specific admiration of or engagement with Whitman is expressed, directly or indirectly. In each we may find obvious resemblances—not only with Whitman but with each other. Yet we must discount any feeling that a tradition is necessarily successive instruction. No doubt all who admire Whitman learn from him, but we may better call the relationship an affinity rather than an influence. A statement by Waldo Frank in regard to Hart Crane and Whitman is pertinent. He writes,

. . . the node of continuity was there, because of Crane's own mystical vision. Whitman's writing, and the others, 'influenced' Crane, in the sense of a corroboration; of a substantiation. 'The Bridge' comes out of Whitman's work, essentially because of the consanguinity of their experience of life.

Only because this inward harmony of views was already there could the literary 'influence' take place. This is the normal process of the artist. His vision is pristine, but inchoate. He seeks kindred formulations; finds them in the works of earlier, older artists, and builds upon them.[3]

The choice is made: afterwards the enrichment; the revisions of attitude; the phrase half-quoted, comfortable on the tongue.

Sometimes two walk in the same way without knowing. Henry Treece tells how he and others thought Dylan Thomas must have been influenced by Hart Crane because of similarity in sound and phraseology. Thomas said that he had never read Crane, but admitted the likeness.[4] Hart Crane knew the poetry of D. H. Lawrence, and he found a particular pleasure in D. H. Lawrence's last story, *The Man Who Died:* "Lawrence never wrote a greater story, nor one which provoked less divided feelings. It was a great revelation to me. . . . it has more to tell me—at least in my present state of mind—than any book in the Bible."[5] Occasionally, resemblances in the work of two poets are more than curiosities or coincidences. One may illuminate the other, and both held in the mind will give further dimensions of meaning. One example is Lawrence's use of Whitman's "Sparkles from the Wheel," in which

> A knife-grinder works at his wheel sharpening a great knife,
>
> .   .   .   .   .
>
> . . . as he presses with light but firm hand,
> Forth issue then in copious golden jets,
> Sparkles from the wheel.

In the early version of Lawrence's "Corot" (as it first appeared in *Love Poems and Others*), the striking wheel-and-spark image gains a particular vividness when one recalls the Whitman poem. Lawrence's lines:

> For what can all sharp-rimmed substance but catch
> In a backward ripple, God's purpose, reveal
> For a moment His mighty direction, snatch
> A spark beneath His wheel.

That Lawrence uses the wheel and spark in a cosmic sense suggests symbolic possibilities for Whitman's vignette of a city street. It recalls that Whitman did use the wheel image for the universe. And for another example of interfusion: If one has been reading Lawrence's intensely physical poems in *Birds, Beasts and Flowers,* he will come upon Dylan Thomas's opening lines in "A Refusal to Mourn the Death, by Fire, of a Child in London" with fresh awareness. Thomas must have been thinking of Lawrence:

> Never until the mankind making
> Bird beast and flower
> Fathering and all humbling darkness
> Tells with silence the last light breaking. . . .

There is no trouble, then, in interpreting "darkness" as the creative mystery, the god-force, the dark sun of imponderable origins which is so particularly Lawrence's image. To associate with "A Refusal to Mourn" the elemental oppositions of fire and water, and the cyclic phoenix-creation that are thematic in Lawrence is to comprehend more completely the fire which has preceded Thomas's poem, and the "burning of the child's death," with its phoenix-like return by the waters of the Thames to the grains and veins of the earth-mother. Thomas, like Lawrence, turns to sexual images of genesis: the "darkness" is the male principle, "fathering" bird, beast, and flower.

Studies in the Whitman tradition must be of relationships, affinities, definitions, rather than influences. The tradition is made when several on the open road nod in recognition; when all make poems out of the wholeness of man and reject the broken halves of the New Puritanism. The credo is given in Whitman's epigraph to *Leaves of Grass*:

> Come, said my soul,
> Such verses for my body let us write, (for we are one,)
> That should I after death invisibly return,
> Or, long, long hence, in other spheres,
> There to some group of mates the chants resuming,
> (Tallying earth's soil, trees, winds, tumultuous waves,)
> Ever with pleas'd smile I may keep on,
> Ever and ever yet the verses owning—

Whitman would be the last to call himself the originator of a tradition. "I charge that there be no theory or school founded out of me," he wrote in "Myself and Mine." "I charge you to leave all free, as I have left all free." Yet he knew the kind of poet he hoped would follow him. "By Blue Ontario's Shore" gives his invocation: "Bards of the great Idea! . . ./ Bards with songs

as from burning coals or the lightning's fork'd stripes!" For, as he
well knew (in "Poets to Come"),

I myself but write one or two indicative words for the future,
I but advance a moment only to wheel and hurry back in the darkness.

Mine is a brief encounter, he said,

> Leaving it to you to prove and define it,
> Expecting the main things from you.

Whitman saw a possible continuity in the kind of poem he made
out of leaves of grass—the generative life-poem, the sun-poem.
It is this continuity that must be defined as a living way of poetry
in the twentieth century.

BERNICE SLOTE

Part I

THE ELEMENTS

The poets of the kosmos advance through all inter-
positions and coverings and turmoils and stratagems
to first principles.

WALT WHITMAN
1855 Preface to *Leaves of Grass*

Walt Whitman and the Secret of History

The force that through the green fuse drives the
  flower
Drives my green age.　　　　—DYLAN THOMAS

WALT WHITMAN has always seemed to evoke from his passionate readers responses remarkable in their intensity. From the fanatic loyalty of W. D. O'Connor, who wrote *The Good Gray Poet*, to the deep-seated revulsion of John Greenleaf Whittier, who threw his copy of the 1855 edition of *Leaves of Grass* into the fire, few poets have elicited such impassioned gestures of approval or disapproval from their readers.

The history of Whitman's reputation is filled with fascinating accounts of passionate attachments, explosive reprovals, denials and reversals. So much smoke has been produced by the heated controversies that it has been almost impossible to see distinctly what fed the flames. But it has always been clear that the passions of the participants have been deeply and directly involved.

A re-examination of the startlingly varied responses to Whitman of a select few nineteenth-century poets, together with a close look at the odd, seemingly irrational responses of a number of twentieth-century poets, might reveal, in some small measure

15

at least, that enigmatic element in *Leaves of Grass* which has both attracted and repelled with such radical force. In tracking this element, we shall, perhaps, discover what one responsible and perceptive reader called the lost secret of history.

I. THE MODERN IMAGE

Although Whitman warned against movements in his name, he has been repeatedly hailed as a symbolic leader and sometime saint. The most recent canonization has taken place in San Francisco, where the high priests of the beat generation have issued their manifestoes, read their poetry to jazz, and muttered their enigmas into their cool cups.

The celebrated poet of this beat generation is Allen Ginsberg, whose book, like Whitman's, became involved with the law over alleged obscenities. There are additional and deeper resemblances. We are told that Ginsberg's book was first to have been called *Yawp!*, after Whitman's primitive outcry in "Song of Myself," but that instead the beat poet finally settled on *Howl!* His instinct was right. His poems are not so much a barbaric yawp as an agonizing howl.

Ginsberg's specific tribute to Whitman appears in a short poem, "A Supermarket in California" (dated 1955), which opens:

What thoughts I have of you tonight, Walt Whitman, for I walked down the sidestreets under the trees with a headache self-conscious looking at the full moon.

In my hungry fatigue, and shopping for images, I went into the neon fruit supermarket, dreaming of your enumerations!

What peaches and what penumbras! Whole families shopping at night! Aisles full of husbands! Wives in the avocados, babies in the tomatoes!—and you, Garcia Lorca, what were you doing down by the watermelons?

I saw you, Walt Whitman, childless, lonely old grubber, poking among the meats in the refrigerator and eyeing the grocery boys.

I heard you asking questions of each: Who killed the pork chops? What price bananas? Are you my Angel? [1]

The lines recall, in a bizarre way, Whitman's line in "Song of Myself"—"I reach to the leafy lips, I reach to the polish'd breasts of melons." There is, running through the Ginsberg lines, as through many of the most brilliant passages of Whitman, a sexual symbolism and sexual identification that seems constantly on the verge of becoming embarrassingly explicit. In spite of the image of Whitman as the "lonely old grubber," Ginsberg's portrait of the poet ("dear father, graybeard, lonely old courage-teacher") is basically sympathetic, and as they wander (in Ginsberg's poetic imagination) out of the supermarket into the night, they seem drawn together in a lonely communion derived from a secret understanding: they "stroll dreaming of the lost America of love."

Ginsberg's image of Whitman is a far cry from the image of the Good Gray Poet, or of the Poet of Democracy, or of the Singer of America. But the beat generation was not the first to envision an off-beat image of Whitman. Dylan Thomas, in a poem only recently published (in *Letters to Vernon Watkins,* 1957) but contained in a 19 March 1940 letter, sketches an unusual Whitman. Thomas explains in his letter: "I've got very little to say about it [the poem] myself: you'll see the heavy hand with which I make fun of this middle-class, beardless Walt who props humanity, in his dirty, weeping, expansive moments, against corners & counters & tries to slip, in grand delusions of all embracing humanitarianism, everyone into himself." In the poem ("The Countryman's Return"), Whitman's long line with its majestic sweep of all-inclusiveness is reduced to an absurd brevity and Whitman's ecstatically sung catalogue is turned into a halting and niggling list of the ludicrous:

> Beggars, robbers, inveiglers,
> Voices from manholes and drains,
> Maternal short time pieces,
> Octopuses in doorways,
> Dark inviters to keyholes
> And evenings with great danes,
> Bedsitting girls on the beat
> With nothing for the metre,
> Others whose single beds hold two
> Only to make two ends meet,
> All the hypnotised city's
> Insidious procession
> Hawking for money and pity
> Among the hardly possessed.

Thomas is not writing a parody of Whitman so much as a parody of himself imitating Whitman: "And I . . ./Conjured me to resemble/ A singing Walt." This singing Walt does bear some resemblance to Ginsberg's Walt poking among the pork chops at the supermarket: both Whitmans are reduced considerably in size and rendered less mythic, more human. Indeed, Thomas's identification with the poet, like Ginsberg's communion, suggests an intimacy which the reader can observe but cannot share. Thomas, too, seems to have his secret with Walt, a secret which runs much deeper than the jumbled surface of his poem.

A comparable tone of intimacy, which seems to derive from similar depths of secret familiarity, is found in the Spanish poet Federico Garcia Lorca's "Ode to Walt Whitman" (a part of his *Poet in New York*, written in 1929–30).[2] We do not read far into this modern vision of a spiritually desolate city before we discover a Whitman of extraordinary attributes:

> Not for one moment, Walt Whitman, comely old man,
> have I ceased to envision your beard full of butterflies,
> your corduroy shoulders, worn thin by the moon,
> your chaste, Apollonian thighs,
> your voice like a pillar of ashes;
> patriarch, comely as mist,
> you cried like a bird
> whose sex is transfixed by a needle;
> satyr's antagonist,
> grapevine's antagonist,
> and lover of bodies under the nap of the cloth.

With his "beard full of butterflies," his "chaste, Apollonian thighs," and his "transfixed" sex, Whitman is the symbol of agonized purity opposed in the poem to the "perverts of the cities," the "mothers of filthiness, harpies, sleeplessly thwarting/the Love that apportions us garlands of pleasure." As the poem increases in bitter condemnation of the perverts and "toadies," it increases in intensity of shared feeling with "handsome Walt Whitman." As in Ginsberg's and Thomas's Whitman, there seem to be lurking in Lorca's image of the poet enigmatic qualities which only Lorca fully and sympathetically comprehends.

Hart Crane, in the "Cape Hatteras" section of *The Bridge* (1930), may seem on first glance to present a more conventional Whitman than Lorca's, Thomas's, or Ginsberg's. Crane seems to invoke Whitman as his and the nation's creative daemon or divinity:

> Our Meistersinger, thou set breath in steel;
> And it was thou who on the boldest heel
> Stood up and flung the span on even wing
> Of that great Bridge, our Myth, whereof I sing!

But this "national" Whitman is not the conventional, yawping American chauvinist; he is the maker of a complex myth of possible future fulfillment. A note of intimacy is introduced early in "Cape Hatteras":

> Or to read you, Walt—knowing us in thrall
> To that deep wonderment, our native clay
> Whose depth of red, eternal flesh of Pocahontus—

Basic to Whitman's myth (as delineated by Crane) is his sexual insight into man's thralldom to his "native clay," a fundamental element of man's nature celebrated elsewhere in *The Bridge* in the figure of Pocahontus as emblem of the eternal female principle. But also basic to the myth is Whitman's spiritual insight into man's adhesive attachment to his comrade, the Whitman of "Recorders Ages Hence" in "Calamus." Crane continues in "Cape Hatteras":

> . . . in pure impulse inbred
> To answer deepest soundings! O, upward from the dead
> Thou bringest tally, and a pact, new bound,
> Of living brotherhood!

Though Crane's Whitman is elevated to a national mythmaker, he is not inflated into a gaseous, windy orator. Indeed, that suggestion of a complex vision intuitively shared, present in Ginsberg, Lorca, and Thomas, runs through all Crane's lines, including the closing:

> Yes, Walt,
> Afoot again, and onward without halt,—
> Not soon, nor suddenly,—No, never to let go
> My hand
> in yours,
> Walt Whitman—
> so—

II. THE BEWILDERING RESPONSE

Crane, Thomas, Lorca, and Ginsberg all participate in the creation of a twentieth-century Walt Whitman who was relatively
unknown in the nineteenth. This lonely old grubber, with butterflies in his beard, expansively singing as he strolls hand in hand
with his comrade-poets, is something of an eccentric and an
exile—but mystically appealing and containing unplumbed depths
of human understanding.

During Whitman's own time, two images of him warred with
each other, neither ever quite firmly established, but both so
strongly asserted that subtle composites or radically new charac-
terizations seemed impossible. The poet's friends and the poet
himself promulged the image of the Good Gray Poet—an image
so inhumanly pure and innocent that even Whitman's strongest twentieth-century admirers reject it. The poet's enemies,
abetted by the tight-lipped disapproval of the genteel tradition,
painted a picture of sexual indecency and moral depravity
that can only draw a smile from the sophisticated modern
reader.

The nineteenth century's insistence on a Whitman absolutely
pure or totally depraved resulted in some curious and revealing
incidents in the erratic growth of the poet's reputation. As there
was no middle ground to which to retreat, nineteenth-century
readers, when they did not simply ignore Whitman, usually became deeply involved, either as disciple or enemy. Some, like
W. D. O'Connor and Horace Traubel, made up the band of hot
little prophets that seemed to fight for Whitman's deification.
Others, who generally preferred the anonymity of such organiza-
tions as Anthony Comstock's Society for the Suppression of Vice,
denounced, sometimes violently, the obscenity of both the poet
and his book.

In the midst of this strange struggle, it should not be surprising
to find curious ambivalences and even sudden reversals in the
nineteenth-century response to Whitman. Many commentaries
could be cited, but three important ones should suffice to illustrate
the pattern: those of Ralph Waldo Emerson, Sidney Lanier, and
Algernon C. Swinburne. Each of these writers reacted to Whitman in a special way. Emerson's initial enthusiastic letter was

followed by a long silence. Lanier attempted to explain the conflict in his emotional and intellectual response. Swinburne began in adulation and ended in vilification.

In many ways Emerson's brief letter,[3] properly titled the most significant letter in American literature, contains some of the most astute criticism of Whitman ever written, and it was apparently dashed off in the first flush of a strong, sympathetic response to that 1855 edition: "I am very happy in reading [*Leaves of Grass*], as great power makes us happy. . . . I give you joy of your free and brave thought. . . . I find the courage of treatment which so delights us, and which large perception only can inspire. . . . the solid sense of the book is a sober certainty." *Solid sense, courage of treatment, free and brave thought*—these are not the casual phrases of a polite thank-you note, but the profound tribute of a deep, spontaneous impression. Whatever the ethics involved in Whitman's unauthorized use of the letter to publicize his book, Whitman was certainly right in gauging the success of his poetry by this one intelligent and unsolicited reaction. Emerson's closing sentence—"I wish to see my benefactor, and have felt much like striking my tasks and visiting New York to pay you my respects" —suggests that same desire to stroll hand in hand expressed by Crane and Ginsberg. Indeed, that personal note of intimate and even exhilarated understanding dominates Emerson's letter. The reason for Emerson's subsequent silence, even to the exclusion of Whitman from his 1874 anthology of American poetry, will probably remain obscure. But we may guess that Emerson felt the Victorian necessity of atoning for the "sin" of this one indecent exposure of his raw, instinctive response. The feelings called forth by Whitman's powerful poetry might prove troublesome, even if one attempted to clothe their nakedness in the garments of gentility.

Sidney Lanier, in a confession of his honest response to *Leaves of Grass*, began with a staggering series of qualifications which Emerson probably wished he had made in his 1855 letter—and which he might have made had he expected publication. But Lanier apparently felt the strong necessity of bringing his imprecise emotional involvement into some kind of intellectual focus, and as a result tripped himself up in one of the oddest—and funniest—commentaries ever made on Whitman:

Here let me first carefully disclaim and condemn all that flippant and sneering tone which dominates so many discussions of Whitman. While I differ from him utterly as to every principle of artistic procedure; while he seems to me the most stupendously mistaken man in all history as to what constitutes true democracy, and the true advance of art and man; while I am immeasurably shocked at the sweeping invasions of those reserves which depend on the very personality I have so much insisted upon, and which the whole consensus of the ages has considered more and more sacred with every year of growth in delicacy; yet, after all these prodigious allowances, I owe some keen delights to a certain combination of bigness and naïvety which makes some of Whitman's passages so strong and taking, and, indeed, on the one occasion when Whitman has abandoned his theory of formlessness and written in form he has made *My Captain, O My Captain* [*sic*] surely one of the most tender and beautiful poems in any language.[4]

Surely very few paragraphs in all of criticism begin with such a bang and end with such a whimper. After the considerable build-up to Whitman's *bigness and naïvety*, we are offered not a "strong and taking" example—possibly one of those "sweeping invasions"—but the flat and jingling *My Captain, O My Captain:* the very mistitling suggests the violent application of the brakes on an untraveled sideroad and a sudden return to the public highway. But in spite of Lanier's shifting directions, he gives us a momentary glimpse, in acknowledging "some keen delights," of a personal Whitman related to Emerson's or Ginsberg's.

Unlike Emerson, Swinburne wrote his first, enthusiastic praise of Whitman for publication. In his essay on Blake, Swinburne selected Whitman as the measure of comparison:

The points of contact and sides of likeness between William Blake and Walt Whitman are so many and so grave, as to afford some ground of reason to those who preach the transition of souls or transfusion of spirits. The great American is not a more passionate preacher of sexual or political freedom than the English artist. . . . To each all sides and shapes of life are alike acceptable or endurable. From the fresh free ground of either workman nothing is excluded that is not exclusive. The words of either strike deep and run wide and soar high.[5]

This bold, daring praise, with emphasis on the *fresh free ground*, the deep striking and the high soaring, recalls the exhilarated response of Emerson and the reluctant response of Lanier. But

Swinburne adds a touch of casual defiance in his admiration for the *passionate preacher of sexual freedom*. These words must have burned in his mind when, some twenty years later, Swinburne in "Whitmania" recanted with the same intense energy of his earlier praise.

But under the dirty clumsy paws of a harper whose plectrum is a muck-rake any tune will become a chaos of discords. . . . Mr. Whitman's Eve is a drunken apple-woman, indecently sprawling in the slush and garbage of the gutter amid the rotten refuse of her over-turned fruit-stall . . . Mr. Whitman's Venus is a Hottentot wench under the influence of cantharides and adulterated rum.[6]

Twenty years can make a lot of difference, especially in one's sexual views. But there seems to be an unreasoned hostility, perhaps based on fear, in Swinburne's vitriolic attack. We can only exclaim with Whitman (when he was informed of Swinburne's switch from prophet to enemy), "Ain't he the damndest simulacrum."

III. VIRGINS, DYNAMOS, AND SEX

In reading Emerson, Lanier, and Swinburne, we recognize, if but fleetingly, a common ground with Crane, Lorca, Thomas, and Ginsberg. But the chasm that separates the previous age from the present cannot be easily bridged.

In search of a link, we might well begin with a nineteenth-century figure who lived on into the twentieth. Henry Adams's search for the secret of history took him far beyond both of the centuries in which he lived. But it was the powerful dynamo of his own industrial age that gave him the clue he sought. The clue led back to the thirteenth-century Virgin. Having identified history as sequence, Adams examined and rejected in turn the sequence of men, the sequence of society, the sequence of time, the sequence of thought. He came around finally to the sequence of force, which yielded a logical connection between the thirteenth century's Virgin and the nineteenth century's Dynamo.

Upon discovering this connection, Adams next raised the question of sex as force:

. . . any one brought up among Puritans knew that sex was sin. In any previous age, sex was strength. Neither art nor beauty was needed. Every one, even among Puritans, knew that neither Diana of the

23

Ephesians nor any of the Oriental goddesses was worshipped for her beauty. She was goddess because of her force; she was the animated dynamo; she was reproduction—the greatest and most mysterious of all energies; all she needed was to be fecund.

Observing in passing the significant creative link between Lucretius' invocation of Venus and Dante's invocation of the Virgin, Adams turned finally to the American mind and American art (he refers to himself in his *Education* in the third person):

On one side, at the Louvre and at Chartres [art and architecture inspired by the Madonna], as he knew by the record of work actually done and still before his eyes, was the highest energy ever known to man, the creator of four-fifths of his noblest art, exercising vastly more attraction over the human mind than all the steam-engines and dynamos ever dreamed of; and yet this energy was unknown to the American mind. An American Virgin would never dare command; an American Venus would never dare exist. . . . Adams began to ponder, asking himself whether he knew of any American artist who had ever insisted on the power of sex, as every classic had always done; but he could think only of Walt Whitman. . . . All the rest had used sex for sentiment, never for force.[7]

There seems to be, in this one casual reference to Whitman, more revealed insight than in many a full treatise on the poet. Whitman emerges as neither the Good Gray Poet nor an obscene old man, but as the poet of sexual force, the poet of procreation. It was this fresh wind blowing through his *Leaves* that Emerson and Lanier and Swinburne felt but could not or would not identify. It is this enduring, magnetic energy in his work that constitutes the secret shared by Crane, Lorca, Thomas, and Ginsberg.

As Adams speculated on the relevance of the sexual force to history, Sigmund Freud explored the central significance of the force in the psyche, and, later, Alfred Kinsey discovered the intricate omnipresence of the force in society. It is time that criticism caught up with history and evaluated Whitman not with nineteenth-century reticence but with twentieth-century reality —a reality he prophetically anticipated.

If, as Adams suggests, *Leaves of Grass* is one of those rare classics containing the lost secret of history, Whitman's sexual vision might well come under a fresh and frank scrutiny. Though that vision comes into precise focus in the "Children of Adam" cluster, where Whitman declares himself singer of "the song of procreation," it pervades the whole of *Leaves of Grass* so as to become impossible of disentanglement from the book's total meaning. If by some intricate method the sexual content of *Leaves* were to be expurgated, the book would lie maimed and impotent before us, its strength and its vitality obliterated. As well castrate a man as bowdlerize *Leaves of Grass.*

Whitman envisioned man's sexual energy as primal, creative energy, a simple extension of a creatively evolving natural world. When Whitman loafed at his ease and observed a spear of summer grass, he saw more than an isolated green blade. He saw himself and the grass impelled to growth and reproduction by an identical creative force. Whitman repeatedly dramatized the natural world in sexual terms, constantly exploring the intimate kinship of nature and man. Such subtly sexual lines recur throughout *Leaves:*

> Smile O voluptuous cool-breath'd earth!
> Earth of the slumbering and liquid trees!
> Earth of departed sunset—earth of the mountains misty-topt!
> Earth of the vitreous pour of the full moon just tinged with blue!

Indeed, Whitman might best be described as a "sexual pantheist," envisioning the world and man as infused by an identical, creative sexual vitality.

Whitman's sexual vision was comprehensive and shaped the opening sections (after the introductory cluster and poem) of *Leaves:* "Song of Myself," "Children of Adam," and "Calamus." These poems give *Leaves of Grass* its substantial sexual foundation. Freud later was to identify the three sexual stages of man as auto-, homo-, and hetero-sexual. Whitman has reversed the order of these last two stages, probably for programmatic purposes: he dramatizes in succession the relationship of man to self, of man to woman, of man to man: identity, love, and friendship.

Invariably in Whitman's sexual vision the physical vitality is prelude to the spiritual. The sexual awakening or the achievement of sexual identity comes in the middle of "Song of Myself," in the celebrated passage on touch, which appears largely auto-erotic:

Is this then a touch? quivering me to a new identity,
Flames and ether making a rush for my veins,
Treacherous tip of me reaching and crowding to help them,
My flesh and blood playing out lightning to strike what is hardly
   different from myself,
On all sides prurient provokers stiffening my limbs,
Straining the udder of my heart for its withheld drip. . . .

This passage continues developing in intensity until, with the cry,
"Unclench your floodgates," a climax is reached, followed by the
calm retrospect and a return to the poem's dominant image: "I
believe a leaf of grass is no less than the journey-work of the
stars." This entire passage represents the marvelous achievement
of sexual identity through experiencing directly the sense of
touch. This development of an acute physical self-consciousness
is, in the poem's drama, one of the major stages on the way to
spiritual identity and the mystic merge.

In "Children of Adam" Whitman turns from man alone to man
and woman. The poems of this cluster were to "Celebrate you
act divine and you children prepared for,/And you stalwart
loins." In one of these poems of procreation, "I Sing the Body
Electric," the sexual drama is extended to the rhythmical flow
of time itself:

Ebb stung by the flow and flow stung by the ebb, love-flesh swelling
   and deliciously aching,
Limitless limpid jets of love hot and enormous, quivering jelly of love,
   white-blow and delirious juice,
Bridegroom night of love working surely and softly into the prostrate
   dawn,
Undulating into the willing and yielding day,
Lost in the cleave of the clasping and sweet-flesh'd day.

The vivid celebrations of heterosexual love in "Children of
Adam" are accompanied by an insistence throughout on the spiritual innocence of the physical act. "I Sing the Body Electric"
concludes: "O I say these are not the parts and poems of the body
only, but of the soul,/O I say now these are the soul!" The dominant metaphor of the cluster of poems, suggested by the title,
is the Garden. The poet calls for a return to the innocent sexual
existence of Adam and Eve in Eden before the Fall.

From man-woman love in "Children of Adam" Whitman turns finally to man-man love in "Calamus," pairing, as many essayists (including Emerson) had done before him, his concept of love with his concept of friendship. And like previous writers relating these two themes, Whitman uses some of the same terms of passion for the two relationships. He is concerned with drawing a clear distinction:

Fast-anchor'd eternal O love! O woman I love!
O bride! O wife! more resistless than I can tell, the thought of you!
Then separate, as disembodied or another born,
Ethereal, the last athletic reality, my consolation,
I ascend, I float in the regions of your love O man,
O sharer of my roving life.

The "Calamus" cluster may be interpreted variously as a homosexual proclamation, a confession, an inadvertent revelation, or a sublimation—depending on one's psychoanalytical bent. But the poems' intensity of emotion strikes home as entirely honest. And the intensity is matched by an impressive breadth. Whitman ranges from the complexity of the single relationship to the vision of a democratic brotherhood based on a multiplicity of such relationships. In these poems Whitman explores and celebrates friendship in all its democratic possibilities and religious implications— as well as its Freudian subtleties.

No poet before Whitman had been so bold or so deep in his insight into the sexual intricacies of man. In vividly dramatizing the emotional complexity of man's sexual nature, Whitman was bound, naturally, both to attract and to repel. Hence that ambivalence in such nineteenth-century readers as Emerson, Lanier, and Swinburne—drawn by the fresh honesty of the vision, but frightened by its naive boldness. Sensitive twentieth-century readers, like Crane, Lorca, Thomas, and Ginsberg, have taken the honesty and the boldness as their private secret. They respond to the emotional validity of the sexual vision and accept that personal invitation to intimacy that seems to emanate from every page of *Leaves of Grass*.

Whitman was one of those "Beginners" he so knowingly described—"How dear and dreadful they are to the earth . . ./How people respond to them, yet know them not." After Whitman, the sexual force achieved solid recognition in clinic and laboratory through the investigations of such imaginative scientists as Freud and Kinsey. It came to play a central role, too, in a considerable body of literature produced by some major talents—notably Lawrence and Joyce. One wonders, even, what obscure debt Vladimir Nabokov and his nymphet owe to that lonely old Beginner, Walt Whitman.

At the end of his poetic career, in "A Backward Glance O'er Travel'd Roads," Whitman reaffirmed the sexual bias of his book: " 'Leaves of Grass' is avowedly the song of Sex . . . . the espousing principle of those lines so gives breath of life to my whole scheme that the bulk of the pieces might as well have been left unwritten were those lines omitted . . . . the lines I allude to, and the spirit in which they are spoken, permeate all 'Leaves of Grass,' and the work must stand or fall with them. . . ." Whitman surely knew, as Henry Adams recognized, that in his sexual vision he had focused on a neglected historical force that was central to the human experience.

JAMES E. MILLER, JR.

Cosmic Consciousness

IT appears that in the twentieth century we have reached the point at which Oriental "ways of life" are about to penetrate the West. At the same time it appears that science has reached that frontier at which it meets up with art and what is called mysticism. We can see this in the reaction of Jung against Freud (cosmic versus rationalistic psychology), in the tremendous spurt of creative activity the world over, and in the speculations of cosmic scientists—which I know about mostly from rumor. Civilization is no more the concern of the poet than it is of the scientist and the mystic. Nature consciousness or cosmic consciousness is being forced upon the attention of the world from every side; the deep vein of mysticism has been opened again and the age of pure rationalism seems to be on the wane. In this there can be little advantage to science except on those shadowy borders where knowledge of the mind can help the scientist to apprehend his own material. "Science," says the religious philosopher Von Hügel, "is but part of a whole, but a function, a necessary yet preliminary function, of the whole of man . . . . Crush out, or in any way mutilate or de-autonomize, this part, and all the rest will suffer." A tremendous synthesis is in the making between modern science, the ancient psychologies of the past, and what we call poetry or art. The good will is all on the side of the scien-

29

tists; and the *rapprochement* must come from the artists. The artist seems to be the nexus between the scientist and the mystic.

I will attempt an inquiry into the "cosmic consciousness" of the poet or artist, the object being to show a certain unity of aim between poetry, mysticism, and science. (When I use the word "science" I exclude all sciences of man—social sciences—especially psychology. Our inquiry into cosmic consciousness *is* in fact psychology, but it is psychology based upon the works of poets, mystics, ecstatics, and those writings which are incorporated into the scriptures of every people. This kind of psychology also touches all those forms of protoscience such as alchemy, astrology, and magic.)

I choose the term "cosmic consciousness" because it was used in the nineteenth century in reference to Walt Whitman. It is as good a name as any. By cosmic consciousness is meant the capacity of the individual consciousness to experience a sense of total unity with all Nature, or the universe, or some degree of that experience. Whether this capacity is pathological or "normal" makes no difference; what is important is the fact of its existence and its significance. The literature of cosmic consciousness is, as I have mentioned, very wide and is possibly the largest body of written matter in the world—or was before the age of mass printing. In a sense, all literature of any kind before modern science is related to the literature of cosmic consciousness, whether poetry or magic (early experimental science or consciousness psychology). The works at the center of this literature are, however, those usually classed as mystical writings.

Whitman was the chief modern exponent of cosmic consciousness, as Blake was a half-century before him. We must admit at once that we cannot know Whitman through modern criticism. Eliot called *Leaves of Grass* claptrap; Pound, the rationalist poet, could see only politics in Whitman; Williams was steered carefully away from Whitman by his contemporaries. The scholar and historian F. O. Matthiessen could not, writing in the Thirties, Forties, and Fifties, see anything more in Whitman than a political visionary, which was only a minute fraction of Whitman's vision. Recently, the scholar James E. Miller, Jr. published perhaps the first full-scale study of *Leaves of Grass* as a mystical document; this book may mark a turning point in our attitude toward Whit-

man. It ignores the rationalist sociological view of Whitman and
plunges into the central mystical experience of Whitman's poetry,
even outlining the stages of the revelation or psychological breakthrough in Whitman's case. I would like to go back, however,
to an older book, one written at the turn of the century, the book
called *Cosmic Consciousness*, by Richard M. Bucke.[1] Bucke was
a doctor and medical superintendent of asylums for the insane in
London, Ontario, Canada; he was a friend of Whitman's and once
had to write a defence of Whitman's sanity. (One of the contemporary views of Whitman was that he was mad.) I am not
recommending Bucke's book as any sort of definitive work or even
as a good study, but as an example of the kind of interpretation
which lies closer to the meaning of this kind of poetry than our
criticism can deal with. Bucke's book is only partly about Whitman, and it is in most respects a very quaint study.

Bucke gives the following instances of cosmic consciousness:
Gautama, Christ, Paul, Plotinus, Mohammed, Dante, Las Casas
(the fifteenth-century Spanish-American who fought against Indian slavery); St. John of the Cross, Jacob Behmen, Blake, Balzac
(on the basis of *Seraphita*); and Whitman. Among imperfect instances of cosmic consciousness he treats Moses, Isaiah, Socrates,
Pascal, Spinoza, Swedenborg, Wordsworth, Pushkin, Emerson,
Tennyson, Thoreau, Ramakrishna, and a score of persons identified by initials (more or less contemporary case histories). It
might clarify matters if we said that Bucke today would probably
place Mahatma Gandhi in the first category as a true case of
cosmic consciousness and Dylan Thomas in the second as a doubt-
ful case.

Cosmic consciousness differs from human consciousness in that
human consciousness is ordinarily consciousness of oneself as distinct from all other objects and beings in the universe. In cosmic
consciousness there is a sense of identification with the universe,
an intellectual enlightenment or illumination which may last only
briefly but which (according to the testimony of all illuminati)
places the individual on a new plane of existence. According to
Bucke and other commentators, the man of cosmic consciousness
is in effect a member of a new species of the race. He is character-
ized by a state of moral exaltation, enhanced intellectual power,
a feeling of elevation, elation, and joyousness, and a conviction

of immortality. To the mystic (which is the ordinary name for this kind of consciousness) the world and the universe are indeed paradise; this is in direct opposition to the religious view that the world is an illusion, a vale of tears, or perhaps Hell itself. There is an incurable optimism in this position which is repellent to both the rational and the religious mind. The Americanism of Whitman is neither political nor philosophical, though it implies a philosophical optimism, perhaps. To the man of cosmic consciousness all things are purposeful, innately and extrinsically perfect. "Divine am I, inside and out," says Whitman, which is usually misconstrued as an egotistical poeticism when it is something quite different.

There is a *basic* relationship between poetry, mystical writings, and science, namely, the expression of the principle of unity in all things. I know nothing about science, but it is apparent that underlying all scientific inquiry is the *belief* in this unity. It is belief in precisely the same way that the mystic believes in his perception of unity. Without this belief in a total interrelationship of things science would be powerless to add one construct to another. Psychologically it would have no motive. Mystical writings, however, are not a search for this unity but a record of it. And poetry, all art, is a more formal and immediate expression of the same principle.

Neither science, mysticism, nor poetry need articulate this principle. It is taken for granted; it is a kind of intuitive knowledge which can be erased only by the more rigid forms of thought, those in which a sterile logic is allowed to operate at the expense of experiential or subjective knowledge.

The poet does not know the difference between subjective and objective knowledge. He is a poet partly because he doesn't. Nor does he know the difference between sacred and secular knowledge: that is a theological distinction which lies outside his sphere of interest. As far as one can tell, poetry is not a metaphorical or symbolic version of the world but an actual representation of reality. Given the condition of art—that it materializes from the emotional centers of the mind—it yet belongs to the same world of reality as the mathematical formula. We are all under the influence of the mechanistic psychologies of the nineteenth and twentieth centuries, and our terminology is clumsy to begin with. But as far as poetry is concerned, objective and subjective do not exist. (Modern poetry succeeded in destroying the natural poetic impulse in our time by evolving a theory of "objective" poetry and even a theory of personality to go along with it. Naturally, this objectivity theory used Whitman and Blake as the first point of attack.)

Our education tells us that the reasoning faculties are the highest faculties of man. Poetry tells us that the reasoning faculties are only equal to and perhaps even inferior to the emotional and instinctual faculties as powers of perception. The kind of consciousness I am talking about does not appear in Freud or in measurement psychology; it appears in all those works I mentioned, those of the mystics, illuminati, poets, and magicians (pre-modern psychologists), certain philosophers, and, I am sure, scientists.

Higher consciousness, in fact, results from a unification of the reasoning centers with the other centers of the mind and body. A purely reason-bound science shortly finds itself confronted with disturbing and inexplicable phenomena, or with contradictions which upset the applecart. In speaking of the unification of other "centers" in the mind and body, I am paraphrasing certain of the ancient psychologies which are far more sophisticated than any we know in our time and which are rejected by contemporary psychology—the official psychologies in our schools and hospitals. Most, but not all, of these psychologies I am speaking of are Oriental and are just beginning to make their way into the West.

The chief authority on magic at the present time, Lynn Thorndike, mentions a Chinese work called the *I Ching* (*Book of Changes*) as an ancient work of divination. Thus he gives the typical rationalist view of what is thought by other scholars to be one of the world's most important books. Jung, in writing an introduction to this work, notes first that both branches of Chinese philosophy, Confucianism and Taoism, are rooted in it.[2] Hence its historical importance, if nothing else. The *I Ching* or *Book of Changes* is more than three thousand years old, in all likelihood much older. To Western eyes it has always appeared as a collection of spells for the purpose of fortunetelling, and in a sense that is precisely what the *I Ching* is! When writing his introduction to the book, Jung himself asked the *I Ching* (as one

asks a human being) its judgment about its present situation—
that is, Jung's intention to present the book to the Western world.
The answer he received was highly intelligent. We cannot go into
this here.

I want to quote a few observations of Jung's about this book
and its relation to "consciousness" psychology.

It is a curious fact that such a gifted and intelligent people as the
Chinese has never developed what we call science. Our science, however, is based upon the principle of causality, and causality is considered to be an axiomatic truth. But . . . the axioms of causality are
being shaken to their foundations [by modern physics]: we know
now that what we term natural laws are merely statistical truths and
thus must necessarily allow for exceptions. . . . We need the laboratory with its incisive restrictions in order to demonstrate the invariable
validity of natural law. If we leave things to nature, we see a very
different picture: every process is partially or totally interfered with
by chance, so much so that under natural circumstances a course of
events absolutely conforming to specific laws is almost an exception.[3]

Here I may interject the commentary that poetry and all art
are natural in precisely this manner, the staggering phenomenon
of individuation (chance) being the starting point of poetry.
Western science is unable to cope with the fact, for instance, that
every biological event is unique. Notice how the poet D. H.
Lawrence says the same thing. "There is in the nature of the infant something entirely new, underived, underivable, something
which is, and which will forever remain *causeless*." Lawrence
underlines "causeless."

Jung goes on to say that the Chinese mind as seen through the
I Ching is exclusively preoccupied with the *chance* aspect of events
and not the causal aspect. Causality is hardly noticed. "While the
Western mind carefully sifts, weighs, selects, classifies, isolates,
the Chinese picture of the moment encompasses everything down
to the minutest nonsensical detail, because all of the ingredients
make up the observed moment." This "upside-down" Chinese
view Jung calls "synchronicity," the opposite of our law of
causality. In synchronicity there is "a peculiar interdependence
of objective events among themselves as well as with the subjective (psychic) states of the observer. . . . The ancient Chinese
mind contemplates the cosmos in a way comparable to that of the

modern physicist, who cannot deny that his model of the world is a decidedly psychophysical structure." [4]

I will leave the *I Ching* at this point except to add that the *I Ching* "fortunetelling" method follows upon a throw of coins or a throw of a bundle of yarrow sticks, the configurations of which are interpreted in the text of the book in answer to a question asked. Only one throw is permitted. As Jung says: "If a handful of matches is thrown to the floor, they form the pattern characteristic of that moment. But such an obvious truth as this reveals its meaningful nature only if it is possible to read the pattern and to verify its interpretation, partly by the observer's knowledge of the subjective and objective situation, partly by the character of the subsequent events." [5]

The "one chance" is similar to Lawrence's "one chance" of being born in a particular form. And "reading the pattern" of events is, of course, a fair definition of the creative act of the artist. The *I Ching* is thus an oracular interpretation of reality based on the actual observation of the subjective-objective event.

I am not trying to make a parallel between the *I Ching* and the poetic process; I mean only to point out the similarity between "synchronicity" in this ancient system of thought and in all creative activity. The psychological process is the same; the awareness of chance on a cosmic scale is the same. We get this awareness in all great Western literature. Tolstoy, writing of the Napoleonic Wars, says: "Nothing is the cause."

The difference in attitude toward Nature or the cosmos in the East and in the West is best seen in Zen Buddhism. (The present interest of poets in this Japanese "way of life" is a reaction against the rationalistic poetry and criticism of the whole Modernist school.) The exercises, quips, and disciplines of Zen attempt to abolish dualities of every description. It opposes symbolism and draws the attention to what it calls "direct pointing" to the truth. Immediacy in Zen is not unlike synchronicity in the *Book of Changes*. A Zen saying goes:

> No thought, no reflection, no analysis,
> No cultivation, no intention;
> Let it settle itself. [6]

35

The high aim of Zen is a perfect awakening of consciousness without ignoring the immediate situation: "to enter into awakening without exterminating the defilements" (that is, without ignoring what is unpleasant to recognize; this is the poetic of William Carlos Williams). Zen instruction is a maze of paradoxes all designed to destroy the false rationalism of logic, classification, and symbol. Zen sayings and Zen "problems" belong to nothing comparable in Western thinking except poetry, writings of the mystics, and, it may be, certain phases of modern science. Even the dualism of good and evil is eradicated in Zen, just as it is in all successful works of art. "The conflict between right and wrong / Is the sickness of the mind," says one of the oldest Zen epigrams. Zen also gets rid of the distinction between "me" and "my experience." This entire philosophy or way of life claims that it has nothing to teach, that its truth is self-evident and so obvious that it is, if anything, concealed by explaining it. But this truth is self-evident only to the awakened, to the absolutely conscious. Its object is to waken higher consciousness.

Zen Buddhism has had a profound impact upon the arts as well as upon the social life and history of the Japanese people. The Noh drama, one of the highest reaches of dramatic art, is founded upon the Zen paradox of naturalness in extreme control. The terrific formality of Japanese art is not based upon the false dualism of form-content but upon the noncausal idea of immediacy and spontaneity in all works of nature. To be able to perceive the formality in chance and the chance in formality calls for a conditioning of consciousness which is familiar to artists everywhere, as well as to mystics and to the great scientific discoverers. Western scientists are fully aware of the play of "intuition" in discovery and the phenomenon of coincidental discovery, recognized even by Freud as a manifestation of Psi activity.*

It is quite obvious that causal science has achieved all its successes independent of these synchronistic psychologies of the Orient and of the European past. Similarly, all the failures in Western science occur in the realm of human events (social science). Science seems incapable of dealing with problems of civilization. But the question whether science is a deterrent to

---

* *Psi phenomena* is a term that refers to such data as extrasensory perception, telepathic communication, mediumism, etc.

civilization is absurd. Science claims no such ambition in one direction or the other. Once it does it ceases to be science.

The modern physicist has a much greater tolerance for the mystical view than the nineteenth-century scientist. The Austrian physicist Erwin Schrodinger, in a book called *Mind and Matter*, discusses the modern scientific idea of what Jung calls synchronicity: he calls it "potential simultaneity." [7] Because of the discoveries of Einstein, Lorentz, Poincaré, Gibbs, and others, the physicist no longer takes causality as the basic mechanical law. "Event A causes Event B" is no longer the rule. A and B may occur together or even in reverse, as in the events in *Through the Looking-Glass* (Lewis Carroll was, of course, a mathematician who was dealing with what we call relativity). Schrodinger says this of the modern physicist's conception of time: "To be allowed to play about with such a master's programme believed unassailable . . . , seems to be a great relief, it seems to encourage the thought that the whole 'timetable' is probably not quite as serious as it appears at first sight. And this thought is a religious thought, nay I could call it *the* religious thought." And this scientist even points to the reason for the obscurity of such a notion to most people, namely, that language is so imbued with the idea of time that we cannot use a verb *without using it in one or another tense*.

I maintain through this fog of references that modern science, mysticism, and poetry occupy the same ground, which may be called, for want of a better phrase, cosmic consciousness.

There is an intermediate stage to be included as well. It is the stage that can accommodate, at least temporarily, the writings of the modern science-mystic (to coin an expression). There is, in fact, such a thing as science-mysticism which should be the concern of every scientist and every poet, if only as bedside reading. Poets gravitate toward this kind of literature in the same way that Yeats gravitated toward medieval magic—partly in revulsion against religion but still searching for the truth lying back of religion. I will cite two modern "science-mystics": P. D. Ouspensky and Wilhelm Reich. I first came upon Ouspensky through reading about the American poet Hart Crane. Reich came to my attention through a personal friend, a Freudian psychologist who became a Reichian. Reich himself died in prison after the police ordered his books burned in New York City. A truckload of Reich's works were destroyed by court order; most of his books are under ban of publication in the United States. Reichian psychologists, doctors, and technicians have been driven from hospitals and persecuted in the same way that the Nazis and Communists dealt with people who did not fit in with the system.

Ouspensky's interest was consciousness discipline. His aim was to discover such a discipline suitable for modern twentieth-century man. Previous disciplines of consciousness meant renunciation of the world. The Hindu fakir undergoes fantastic physical suffering in order to rise to a higher stage of consciousness; in so doing, his emotional and intellectual faculties atrophy. The monk follows a path of faith and religious sacrifice in order to expand consciousness; in his case the physical and intellectual centers tend to atrophy. The Yogi follows a way of knowledge at the expense of the body and of the emotional faculties. Ouspensky posits a fourth method to attain superior consciousness which will not exclude any of the psychophysical "centers" nor the day-to-day element of chance. The object, as with all mystics, is to rise above the confused states of consciousness and living sleep which characterize nearly all men. According to Ouspensky, there are three types of men we know of, the lowest type motivated by the physical centers, the second by the emotional centers, and man number three by the intellectual centers. But four other higher types can be hypothesized, the seventh or highest being the one which can account for such figures as Jesus and Gautama, the founders of religions. These men did not intend to found religions; it is the misinterpretation of their teachings to their students which were eventually written down and turned into systems of action which we know as Hinduism, Buddhism, Christianity, and so on. According to this view, all religions are debasements of esoteric teaching and mystical instruction. Ouspensky calls them pseudo-religions. For instance, Ouspensky and Gurdjieff, one of his teachers, expound the New Testament as a system of consciousness knowledge in which the expression "the Kingdom of Heaven" is a gloss for "esoteric knowledge" of higher consciousness. The entire Testament suddenly becomes intelligible according to a few such glosses. (A glimmering of this knowledge creeps through in the recent discussion of the Dead

Sea Scrolls and the Essenes. Mystics have always been familiar with the Essenes and their relation to esoteric Judaism and Christianity; in rational scholarship it is something new.) Whether Jesus and the Buddha were "divine" is a matter of terminology; both had attained the "seventh" stage or "heaven" of consciousness. "The Kingdom of Heaven is at hand" does not mean the end of the world but final illumination. It is a parallel to the Hindu saying: "When the student is ready the master arrives."

Religion, in short, is debased psychology, just as psychoanalysis is debased religion. Freudianism tries to displace the old pseudo-religions; but it is itself a pseudo-pseudo-religion.

Ouspensky's system is only a modern version of dozens of ancient consciousness systems; he was certainly not trying to start a cult. His objectivity repels me considerably; he has nothing to say about art or literature, and his works are full of mathematical formulae and diagrams which I cannot understand. Yet when he explains the phenomenon of the Gothic cathedral not from the "history of art" but as the geometrical model for the occult teaching of cosmic consciousness, I begin to understand these fantastic monuments. The science-mystic is always looking for the context, the wider context, the still wider context, ad infinitum. This is good "poetry"; I assume it is good science as well.

The objective scientific validity of the findings of Wilhelm Reich is not for me to decide. If you mention the name of Reich to anyone at random, people will dig around in their memory and perhaps come up with a terrified leer. "Oh, Reich, the orgone-box man." Reich broke with official psychoanalysis and founded a school of his own based upon the concept (according to him, the physical existence) of a universal cosmic energy which he named "orgone" energy. Evidently Reich was highly respected in some circles before his crash; at least the Atomic Energy Commission backed him and his laboratories in experimenting with this energy, medically and theoretically. During the Korean War, Reich and his workers experimented with the effects of radio-active fissionable matter on orgone-active materials. The clash of the two "energies" produced its own kind of radiation sickness with such dangerous consequences that the experiments were abandoned and the AEC withdrew its support.

Orgone energy (or cosmic energy) was originally used by Reich for medical therapy and psychotherapy. Later it was used for cancer treatment, evidently with favorable results. Reich, however, was ostracized from the medical profession; at present, he is considered as evil as those anatomists who robbed graves in the Dark Ages under pain of death.

The basis for the hatred of Reich is, of course, his use of sex therapy and his theory of the orgasm, which were as offensive to psychological "science" as to the police and the clergy. Reich nevertheless speaks to the poet and the mystic as well as to the scientist. The feeling of having one's roots in nature, he says, is common to all great poets and writers, thinkers and artists, just as it is always felt in true religion though never concretely realized. And because this sense of being rooted in nature either has been experienced mystically or attributed to the eternally unknowable regions beyond human ken, the search for knowledge, according to Reich, has always turned into superstitious, irrational, metaphysical beliefs.

Reich observes that modern man as chemist will regard his writings as a return to the "phlogiston theory" or to alchemy, while the religious fanatic will regard him as a criminal blasphemer. To the poet and mystic it will be evident that what Reich calls the cosmic-energy ocean in which all things exist is indeed what others call God.

And having gone so far with the mention of esoteric, unknown, and even disreputable books, I will close with mention of one or two more. One is the recent "grammar of poetic myth," as its author calls it, the book being Robert Graves's *White Goddess*. His work is based on the belief that true poetry is a magical language bound up with popular religious ceremonies in honor of the Moon-Goddess or Muse. This magical poetry was rejected by the early Greek philosophers, who substituted the religion of logic and a rational poetic (Classicism) for the poetry of poetic myth. Graves's book, in short, is a bible of "Romanticism" encompassing the secret Mystery—cults of Eleusis, the ancient poetic colleges of Ireland and Wales, and the witch-covens of Western Europe. This poetic tradition survived until the close of the seventeenth century, after which it was driven so far underground that true poetry from that time on results from only inspired or even pathological states. According to Graves, nineteenth-century poetry is melancholic and degenerate on the whole, with notable exceptions. Throughout European history, we can trace the inner struggle of the poet between worship of the goddess and the official religions. In the ancient rite the poet and priest were one; in modern Europe the poet must choose between poetry and religion, as we know from the works of Skelton, Donne, Crashaw, Herbert, Herrick, Swift, Crabbe, Kingsley, and Hopkins.

The poet survived in easy vigour only where the priest was shown the door; as when Skelton . . . wore the Muse-name 'Calliope' embroidered on his cassock in silk and gold, or when Herrick proved his devotion to poetic myth by pouring libations of Devonshire barley-ale from a silver cup to a pampered white pig. With Donne, Crashaw and Hopkins the war between poet and priest was fought on a high mystical level; but can Donne's *Divine Poems* . . . be preferred to his amorous *Songs and Sonnets?* or can the self-tortured Hopkins be commended for humbly submitting his poetic ecstasies to the confession-box? [8]

And John Clare worshipped the White Goddess as did Keats in *La Belle Dame sans Merci,* and Coleridge in *The Ancient Mariner.* Blake was a bardic college unto himself. The Goddess, among other things, is a lovely, slender woman who may suddenly transform herself into sow, mare, bitch, vixen, she-ass, weasel, serpent, owl, she-wolf, tigress, mermaid, or loathsome hag. She is, of course, the Moon, the object of all fertility ritual. But the poet concerned with this theme cannot draw distinctions between "sacred history" and "profane myth," says Graves. Graves sees no reason to reject the scriptures as irrelevant to the theme of the White Goddess. Pure mysticism he rejects for poets "since poetry is rooted in love, and love in desire, and desire in hope of continued existence. However, to think with perfect clarity in a poetic sense one must first rid oneself of a great deal of intellectual encumbrance, including all dogmatic doctrinal prepossessions: membership of any political party or religious sect or literary school deforms the poetic sense . . . . [The poet] must achieve social and spiritual independence at whatever cost . . . ." [9]

I have chosen, more or less at random, a few examples from

the "poet's library." Another poet would provide ten or twenty or a hundred other studies, perhaps from astrology or alchemy. Poe was a phrenologist, Hopkins a Scotist, but these particular beliefs signify nothing. Whether the poet becomes a student of flying saucers or of the mystical doctrine of correspondences is all one; so long as he steps across the line from Reason to Intuition he is safe. Dr. Bucke's old-fashioned work on cosmic consciousness is as valid for the poet as Professor Schrodinger's account of noncausality or Jung's explanation of oriental "synchronicity"; Lawrence's blood religion or Graves's ritual of goddess worship are not, to the poet's mind, categorically different from Reich's theory of the orgone energy of the universe. And the psychological disciplines of Ouspensky, based upon Hindu and Christian exercises, point to the same phenomena we find in Bucke or in Whitman, and so forth. All of this literature is "poetry," that is, irrationally true. And were all such literature lost to the world overnight it would almost immediately reappear of itself, because it exists outside time and beyond reason. I imagine that every poet who ever lived had as his motto in one form or another the saying of Tertullian: *Credo quia absurdum.* "I believe it because it is absurd." The truth of the absurd lies beyond reason, beyond science, and beyond poetry itself. That is the meaning of Wordsworth's line "Enough of Science and Art":

> Our meddling intellect
> Mis-shapes the beauteous forms of things:—
> We murder to dissect.
> Enough of Science and Art;
> Close up those barren leaves;
> Come forth, and bring with you a heart
> That watches and receives.*

KARL SHAPIRO

* I ran across this quotation from "The Tables Turned" not in Wordsworth but in a very strange and wonderful book called *Zen in English Literature,* by a British scholar, R. H. Blyth (Tokyo: The Hokuseido Press, 1942).

The Poetics of
the Cosmic Poem

The poetic quality is not marshalled in rhyme or uniformity or abstract addresses to things nor in melancholy complaints or good precepts, but is the life of
these and much else and is in the soul.

WALT WHITMAN
1855 Preface to *Leaves of Grass*

IT is surely no surprise that alongside the poetry of the cosmic
consciousness has developed a related poetics. Walt Whitman,
D. H. Lawrence, Hart Crane, and Dylan Thomas, though they
constructed no philosophical systems, did remark now and
again on the art of poetry. And these sometimes sustained, sometimes random remarks, when brought together, reveal a remarkable coherence. The resemblances are great enough to suggest a fundamental approach common to all—a cosmic poetics:
a poetics which is, naturally, intimately rooted in the cosmic
vision. A brief reconstruction of that vision will illuminate the
origins and the nature of the poetics.

From the poetry of our four cosmic poets emerges a coherent
view of the universe and of man's place in it—the "myth" which
constitutes the materials of their poetry. This "myth" may be

formulated: The universe is not chaotic but schematic, the scheme best defined by Whitman's term, Mystic Evolution—a coherent, rhythmical, and purposeful unfolding of time; impelling Mystic Evolution onward is the mystic life-force, primal, elemental, inexplicable, inexorable; man's and the world's body constitutes a mystical materialism, the paradoxical infusion of the material by the spiritual; man's participation in Mystic Evolution in the ritualistic acts of life places supreme importance on the mystic *here* and *now*, the focal point of all time past, the origin of all time future; in the ritualistic act of reproduction man symbolically *becomes* the eternal, infinite life-force, itself *constituting* time and space; each man's potential contribution to Mystic Evolution constitutes his supreme, divine individuality, his separateness, while the acts of contribution themselves are acts of merging, acts which unite the individual to the Divine One; death, like birth, is a ritualistic act, neither to be courted nor abhorred, but accepted when inevitable as a contributory and mystically meaningful event.

Whitman, Lawrence, Crane, and Thomas thought of themselves as deeply religious poets, but they would be the first to deny allegiance to institutional religion, made and governed by man. Their religion was not made by the mind but discovered by the instinct, not embodied in a dogma, but embraced by life, nature, the universe. Singing the inspiration of this myth, these poets have left an affirmative, essentially joyous poetry in direct contrast to the negative, gloomy poetry of *The Waste Land*. From this myth these poets have drawn a faith in the "act" of art as a direct participation in the mystical progression of the universe: creation of a poem is one of the infinite acts in the continual creation of the world.

Whitman's chronological position renders him the fountainhead, the prophetic source. Lawrence, Crane, and Thomas are among the few poets who penetrated far below the "democracy and science" surface of Whitman and by their penetration discovered a good deal more than a mere barbaric yawp. In aligning themselves with Whitman, as each of them at one time or another did, they discovered a view of poetry—a theory of the art process—which flowed naturally out of their basic beliefs and attitudes: they discovered that not only is there a mystic evolution of the universe but a mystic evolution of the poem. In spite of the distinctive and unique styles of each of them (and in poets of their rank, such divergence is inevitable and welcome), they spring from a luxuriant poetic root whose soil is too rich for the spare, lean root which nourishes the *Waste Land* writers.

These poets might be called poets of the solar plexus (Lawrence's term) whose chief reliance in the poetic process is on the "mystic" instinct or the "divine" spontaneity. Poetry of the ordered emotions—the unfrenzied fit—suggests the essence of their poetic belief. Whitman once said of one of his works that though it seemed "let loose with wildest abandon, the true artist can see it is yet under control." [1] "Controlled abandonment" describes the poetic ideal of these cosmic poets. Theirs is a poetry steeped in the emotions but not the emotions brought to a hysterical boil. The emotions flow not just from the personality but from dark, mystic sources, involving, ultimately, the cosmic order both of the man and of the universe. Perhaps the central position of these poets emerges most clearly in contrast with the basic view of the *Waste Land* poets. Theirs is a poetry of the "cerebral plexus," a poetry which relies chiefly on the mind, a poetry of the ordered intellect, invoking no fit, frenzied or unfrenzied. Most characteristic in the thinking of these poets is the celebrated concept of the "objective correlative," a term which T. S. Eliot exploited in his attempt to demonstrate the deficiency of *Hamlet*. The "objective correlative" is the *formula* which is arbitrarily designated as the "only way of expressing emotion" in art, and it is the formula intellectually calculated to *evoke* the emotion. As Eliot says elsewhere, "Poetry is not a turning loose of emotion, but an escape from emotion." [2] It has not been sufficiently noticed that Eliot distorts the position of others in order to justify his own: nobody—not even the wildest Romantic—has held that poetry is merely the emotions turned loose. Perhaps the most revealing gesture of the *Waste Land* poets has been their frequent celebration of *wit* in all of its intellectual complexity as the essence of great poetry.

It is characteristic of the cosmic poets that they would speak not of the *creation* of a poem but of the *growth* of a poem: a true poem is not made but creates itself. This idea takes its origin, of course, in the Romantics' concept of organic form. In his famed 1855 Preface to *Leaves of Grass*, Whitman made organic form an important part of his poetics: "The rhyme and uniformity of perfect poems show the free growth of metrical laws and bud from them as unerringly and loosely as lilacs or roses on a bush, and take shapes as compact as the shapes of chestnuts and oranges and melons and pears, and shed the perfume impalpable to form." Hart Crane, in his essay on "Modern Poetry" (which he concludes in qualified tribute to Whitman), quotes Coleridge as authority: "No work of true genius dares want its appropriate form, neither indeed is there any danger of this. As it must not, so genius cannot, be lawless: for it is even this that constitutes its genius—*the power of acting creatively under laws of its own origination.*" Dylan Thomas seems to be attempting to give voice to a similar idea when he comments, "Poetry is the rhythmic movement from an overclothed blindness to a naked vision. My poetry is the record of my individual struggle from darkness towards some measure of light." [3]

If the *organic* method (the process of "independent" growth) were no more complex than these statements suggest, one might easily conclude with Eliot that the theory is inadequate and misleading, merely another romantic concept more ideal than real. But Whitman and the others realized that the mystery of art was not readily penetrated, that the nature of the poetic genius was not easily explained. That their position can be quickly reduced to oversimplified absurdity (cf. Yvor Winters on Whitman and Crane as "automatic men" [4]) no more invalidates it than does a like vulnerability disqualify Eliot's.

Whitman's prose becomes tortured in its attempts to hint at the complexity of the poetic mystery. He writes in *Democratic Vistas:* "The [artistic] process, so far, is indirect and peculiar, and though it may be suggested, cannot be defined. Observing, rapport, and with intuition, the shows and forms presented by Nature . . . out of these, and seizing what is in them, the poet . . . by the divine magic of his genius, projects them, their analogies, by curious removes, indirections, in literature and art . . . . This is the image-making faculty, coping with material creation, and rivaling, almost triumphing over it." Where does the poet acquire this complicated faculty for "image-making"?

At one point in the 1855 Preface, in a kind of poetic anticipation of Jung, Whitman asserts that the attributes of the poet are "called up of the float of the brain of the world" and that they are "parts of the greatest poet from his birth out of his mother's womb and from her birth out of her mother's." Such remarks suggest an embryonic concept of the racial memory, the collective unconscious, as the deep source of all genuine poetry.

When Jung formulated the theory explicitly in this century, he made it immediately available, directly or indirectly, to critics and poets. Lawrence's quarrel with Freud, written with poetic fervor if not with logical order, resulted in a formulation of a concept similar to Whitman's and Jung's. He charged, "The Freudian unconscious is the cellar in which the mind keeps its own bastard spawn." The Laurentian unconscious, on the other hand, is the unconscious *pristine*, primitive, elemental, unsullied by mind: this unconscious, asserts Lawrence, *is* the soul. Physically embodied in the solar plexus, this soul-conscious lies "beneath the burning influx of the navel," [5] physical (even literal) symbol of the *blood* connection, the blood brotherhood of all mankind. Out of this pristine unconscious rises man's purest instincts and his genuine poetry.

Hart Crane once described the creative process as an act not willed but observed by the poet (italics mine): "One must be drenched in words, literally soaked with them to have the right ones *form themselves* into the proper pattern at the right moment. When they come . . . they come as things in themselves; it is a matter of felicitous juggling!; and no amount of will or emotion can help the thing a bit." [6] Crane here assumes the role of the naive and innocent poet surprised at the creative achievements attributed to him: his poems are not *caused* but *happen*. Dylan Thomas has suggested a similar contribution of the unconscious processes to the substance of poetry: "It [poetry] must drag further into the clean nakedness of light more even of the hidden causes than Freud could realise." [7] Poetry here appears as an independent force bringing itself into being from the unprobed, unknown inner darknesses of the poet. Common to all of these poets is the belief in the poetic process as a veiled mystery, as an act begun if not completed in the mystic unconscious. Antithetical to their concept of the poetically functioning unconscious is Eliot's theory of the objective correlative, an idea involving for Whitman, Lawrence, Crane, and Thomas too intimately and directly the poet's rational faculty.

But these poets were not opposed to the poet's application of his intellect to his poems. Although the intellectual application comes late in the poetic process and is a kind of fatherly scrutiny of the newborn poem, it is nevertheless important, if not actually essential. It is well known that Whitman, over a large number of years, diligently revised even his most seemingly "frenzied" and "spontaneous" poems, and his revisions were frequently for the purpose of making the poems appear more frenzied and spontaneous. Sometimes even in the immediate inspiration of poetic composition (as a few surviving original manuscripts attest), Whitman's critical faculty came into play. The recently published manuscripts of a previously unnoted poem, "Kentucky" (*Prairie Schooner*, Fall 1958), effectively demonstrate Whitman's tortuous search for the right word, the exact phrase, in the very act of the poem's birth. In a meditative mood Whitman once wrote in *Specimen Days:* "The play of Imagination, with the sensuous objects of Nature for symbols and Faith—with Love and Pride as the unseen impetus and moving-power of all, make up the curious chess-game of a poem." No poet could conceive of the poetic process as a "curious chess-game" without involving the intellect somehow in his conception.

Perhaps the most deliberately "abandoned" of these poets of the mystic unconscious, D. H. Lawrence, has pointed out (in his Preface to *New Poems*) the necessity of the function of the intellect: "Free verse toes no melodic line, no matter what drill-sergeant. Whitman pruned away his clichés—perhaps his clichés of rhythm as well as of phrase. And this is about all we can do, deliberately, with free verse. We can get rid of the stereotyped movements and the old hackneyed associations of sound or sense." To get rid of such associations is about all any poet can hope for in the cold light of intellect after the emotional "flash" of the poem. The revisions through which Crane took *The Bridge* are so well known as to become classroom exercises in the functioning of the poetic mind. Crane had no hesitation in extensively tinkering with the poems which emerged from him in an "unfinished" state. Thomas, too, labored to bring to a state of perfection his rough-born verse. John Malcolm Brinnin reports seeing "two hundred separate and distinct versions" of "Fern Hill," and notes that "its process of growth was like that of an organism." [8]

Closely associated with this basic concept of the uninhibited flow of the mystic unconscious followed by the deliberate scrutiny of the "pruning" intellect is the theory of the "breeding" metaphor. This technique of composition was described by Thomas, practiced by Crane, admired by Lawrence, and "originated" (though not perfected) by Whitman. The technique exists in embryo in Whitman's famous catalogues. These "lists" have been more frequently condemned than praised, and such condemnation has obscured certain possible virtues. Frequently a dramatic procession of substantives, sharply and individually vivid but with no logical syntactical connection, the catalogues seem, superficially, chaotic or frenzied—a meaningless *naming* of all the objects in the universe. What has too often gone unnoticed is that in place of a surface syntactical logic frequently appears a subterranean emotional logic. The images, related subtly one to another, flow in a pattern which is no less valid for being extremely complex.

Whitman's use of the catalogue is the natural result of one of his main tenets of poetic theory. After *Leaves of Grass* had gone through nearly all of its "lifetime" editions, the poet asserted in "A Backward Glance," "The word I myself put primarily for the description of them [the *Leaves*] as they stand at last, is the word Suggestiveness." This term did not mean for Whitman, as it did for Poe, mere vagueness and a deliberate blurring of meaning. As Poe's use of the word is typically romantic, so Whitman's is characteristically contemporary. In his defense of his poetry (in *Democratic Vistas*), Whitman talks in the language of the poet of today: "In certain parts in these flights [*Leaves of Grass*], or attempting to depict or suggest them, I have not been afraid of the charge of obscurity." It is the practice arising from the doctrine of *suggestiveness* that calls forth the familiar charge of obscurity, and such a charge is based upon a misunderstanding of the nature of words and the nature of the mind. Whitman says, "Human thought, poetry or melody, must leave dim escapes and outlets—must possess a certain fluid, aerial character, akin to space itself, obscure to those of little or no imagination, but indispensable to the highest purposes." This statement represents Whitman's concept of the logic of poetry as a logic of the imagination, in which certain faculties, emotional or mental— the "dim escapes and outlets"—play complex roles. The catalogue is only one of several devices Whitman uses which through suggestiveness discover their logic in the intricate emotional response of the reader.

It may seem strange that the diffuse style of Lawrence and the highly concentrated styles of Crane and Thomas are conceived as partaking of a common origin. But the truth is that these two apparently opposed styles are actually two sides of the same coin. All of these poets depend upon the "inherent" psychological or mystical logic of the unmolested flow of the unconscious. In Crane and Thomas there is the tendency to selectivity and even compression; in Lawrence there is the opposite tendency to "embody" copiously. But the role of the reader in each case is the same as the Whitmanian-reader's role: to reconstruct emotionally the context of feeling of the successive images in order to supply, where no logic exists on the surface, a complex of subterranean, instinctive connections.

In one of the most revealing of his essays, the Preface to *New Poems*, Lawrence demanded of the poet: "Tell me of the mystery of the inexhaustible, forever-unfolding creative spark. Tell me of the incarnate disclosure of the flux, mutation in blossom, laughter and decay perfectly open in their transit, nude in their movement before us." This poetry Lawrence called the "seething poetry of the incarnate Now" or poetry of the "sheer present." For Lawrence, Whitman's poetry was the finest example of the ideal he described: "Whitman truly looked before and after. But he did not sigh for what is not. The clue to all his utterance lies in the sheer appreciation of the instant moment, life surging itself into utterance at its very well-head." If poetry is "life surging itself into utterance," the poet's intellectually conscious role in what he produces appears small. Indeed, Lawrence's language—"surging," "well-head"—seems to suggest that the creative act is compulsive, imposed without regard to the desires of the poet. Out of an individual's instinctive, primitive response to the living moment springs the poetry. It is not difficult to see that the impulse behind these remarks—and, indeed, behind much of Lawrence's poetry—is closely related in kind and in quality to the impulse behind Whitman's creation of the catalogues.

And these impulses are in turn similar in nature to that underlying Hart Crane's theory of the metaphor as he defined it in his well-known letter to Harriet Monroe in *Poetry* (Oct. 1926) defending his poetic technique. The distinction crucial to his argument is the distinction between "ordinary logic" and the "logic of metaphor." He asserted that as a poet he is more concerned with the "illogical impingements of the connotations of words on the consciousness" than with "the preservation of their logically rigid significations." This concept gives rise to the terms "dynamics of metaphor" or "logic of metaphor," by which Crane means the metaphorical language charged by a complex of "emotional connectives" that are not grasped by the intellect but felt in the depths of the mind where "thought" becomes "feeling." If Whitman expected his reader to discover an emotional progression (or "logic") in his catalogues which connected one line (or image) to another and one group of lines (or cluster of images) to another, Crane in like manner expected his reader to discover emotionally the relationship of one word to another— words which "logically" might seem unrelated. Whitman and Crane use identical principles but on different scales. Crane's concept of the "illogical impingements of the connotations" is but a contemporary translation of Whitman's concept of the necessity for "dim escapes and outlets." Both poets are intensely aware that the "meaning" of poetry cannot be "logically" controlled.

Dylan Thomas too is in this same tradition, but of course more closely related to Crane than to either Lawrence or Whitman. In one of the few statements on poetic method he made, Thomas revealed his reliance on a subterranean creativity which takes place deep within: "I make one image—though 'make' is not the word; I let, perhaps, an image be 'made' emotionally in me." The self-conscious discarding of the active voice of the key verb reveals Thomas's allegiance to the tradition we are defining as opposed to the so-called "objective correlative" tradition (which would certainly insist on the active rather than the passive role of the poet). Thomas's metaphor, designed to suggest the self-originating and self-sustaining poetic process, is brilliantly conceived. He envisions the metaphor as endowed with an independent life and a capability of reproducing its own kind: "Let it [the first metaphor] breed another, let that image contradict the first, make, of the third image bred out of the other two together, a fourth contradictory image, and let them all, within my imposed formal limits, conflict." [9] Thomas does not deny the poet an active role; he asserts, indeed, not only that he imposes "formal limits," but that throughout this "breeding" process he applies "what intellectual and critical forces" he possesses.

But clearly Thomas's idea of the self-made and generative metaphor is related to Crane's "illogical impingements," to Lawrence's "incarnate Now," and to Whitman's "dim escapes and outlets." Involved in all these concepts is a mystic view of the complex interrelationship of language and man, words and emotion. Thomas once wrote as advice to a fellow poet: ". . . you must endeavor to feel and weigh the shape, sound, content of each word in relation to the shape, sound, content etcetera of the words surrounding it. It isn't only the *meaning* of the words that must develop harmonically, each syllable adding to the single existence of the next, but it is that which also informs the words with their own particular life; the noise, that is, that they make in the air and the ear, the contours in which they lie on the page and the mind, their colours and density." [10] Thomas, along with the others, saw the poem as endowed with a life that lay far deeper than the collective meaning of the individual words, that was much more than the mere sum of the separate parts—just as human life is much more than a mere assemblage of the individual parts of the human body.

All of these poets, holding the views they do of the poetic process, necessarily must agree that the reader as much as the poet creates the poem. If the process of creation is not re-enacted in the reader, if the subterranean links and connections do not link and connect, the poem fails. Surely Thomas, Crane, and Lawrence would subscribe to Whitman's austere demands of the reader. He writes at the close of *Democratic Vistas:* "Books are to be call'd for, and supplied, on the assumption that the process of reading is not a half-sleep, but, in highest sense, an exercise, a gymnast's struggle; that the reader is to do something for himself, must be on the alert, must himself or herself construct indeed the poem . . . —the text furnishing the hints, the clue, the start or framework." If in creation the metaphor assumes an independent life in the poet, it must be resurrected and given new life by each reader. To give it a fair chance for renewed life, the reader must be prepared, both mentally and emotionally, both in the conscious and the unconscious, for a "gymnast's struggle" for resuscitation, for a creative struggle as profound and moving as the poet's.

The major elements in the poetic theory of the poets of the cosmos grow naturally out of their common view of man and the universe. As Whitman, Lawrence, Crane, and Thomas are "religious" poets in the sense that they envision the universe as pervaded by "mystic evolution," so they are "instinctive" poets in the sense that they envision poetry as impelled by a kind of "emotional evolution." Both evolutionary processes are outside the control but not entirely outside the understanding of man, and both processes have an inherent, self-generating, if obscure, order. Poetry of the cosmos, unlike *Waste Land* (or "objective correlative") poetry with an imposed form, realizes its latent order in the emotional reconstruction provided by the responding and "participating" reader.

JAMES E. MILLER, JR.

Part II

WHITMAN *and* LAWRENCE

I am part of the sun as my eye is part of me.
That I am part of the earth my feet know perfectly,
and my blood is part of the sea.

D. H. LAWRENCE
Apocalypse

The First White Aboriginal

D. H. LAWRENCE has more in common with Walt Whitman than with any other man, and it was Lawrence who called Whitman the first white aboriginal. Coming from Lawrence, who felt unable to pay an unequivocal compliment, the epithet was the highest praise. Lawrence's quest was for the aboriginal, the pure energy of the soul. Being an Englishman, he fled from the white man and his white religions and the terrible whiteness of consciousness (which he called mentality) and raced with all his strength to the dark races and beyond, to the blood religions, the spirit of the serpent, and all that. Lawrence made a magnificent leap across civilization into the aboriginal darkness. He is one of the supreme heretics of white, modern civilization. And so for him to bless Walt with the title of the first white aboriginal is a matter of tremendous import. Lawrence is one of the great spirits of our age, as Whitman is, although from Lawrence stems a good deal of the negativity of modern intellectual life. From Whitman stems much of what there is of the opposite. Lawrence sprang from a modern industrial hell which he never forgave and was never far enough away from to understand. Whitman did not have to spring; he sprouted, he vegetated, he loafed out of nowhere into the role of prophet and seer. At a single stroke, apparently without preparation, he became the one poet of America and Democracy. He is the one mystical writer of any consequence America has produced; the most original religious thinker we have; the poet of the greatest achievement; the first profound innovator; the most accomplished artist as well —but nobody says this nowadays. For in the twentieth century Walt Whitman is almost completely shunned by his fellows. He has no audience, neither a general audience nor a literary clique. Official criticism ignores him completely; modern neo-classicism, as it calls itself, acknowledges him with embarrassment. (Ezra Pound "forgives" Whitman because "he broke the new wood," meaning he broke iambic pentameter.) And scholars nowadays, happily confused by the scholarly complexities of contemporary poets, look upon Walt as a grand failure and an anachronism.

Lawrence, in his search around the world for a pure well of human energy, acknowledged Whitman with love. It is a rare thing for Lawrence. He says:

> Whitman, the great poet, has meant so much to me. Whitman, the one man breaking a way ahead. Whitman, the one pioneer. And only Whitman. No English pioneers, no French. No European pioneer-poets. In Europe the would-be pioneers are mere innovators. The same in America. Ahead of Whitman, nothing. Ahead of all poets, pioneering into the wilderness of unopened life, Whitman. Beyond him, none. His wide, strange camp at the end of the great high-road. And lots of new little poets camping on Whitman's camping ground now. But none going really beyond.

But at this point Lawrence changes his tune and explains how Whitman failed. He says that Whitman fell into the old fallacy of Christian love, confusing his great doctrine of Sympathy with Love and Merging. Nothing was more loathsome to the puritanical Lawrence than Merging, and when Whitman merged Lawrence disgorged. How Lawrence longed to merge! And how the mere shake of the hand horrified him! Lawrence in thousands of passages obsessively records his tabu against touching. *Noli me tangere!* It is the opposite of Whitman's obsession *for* touching:

Is this then a touch? quivering me to a new identity,
Flames and ether making a rush for my veins,
Treacherous tip of me reaching and crowding to help them,

My flesh and blood playing out lightning to strike what is hardly differ-
ent from myself,
On all sides prurient provokers stiffening my limbs,
Straining the udder of my heart for its withheld drip,
Behaving licentious toward me, taking no denial,
Depriving me of my best as for a purpose,
Unbuttoning my clothes, holding me by the bare waist. . . .

(This is the passage in "Song of Myself" which, after a paren-
thesis—"What is less or more than a touch?"—leads into "I think
I could turn and live with animals, they're so placid and self-
contain'd,/I stand and look at them long and long." It is one of
the greatest moments of poetry.)

Lawrence, with his deep love of animals and his irritable sus-
picion of mankind, was the inferior of Whitman. Whitman had
the natural love of man which Lawrence, rightly, called American. Lawrence was fascinated, hypnotized, and slightly sick in
the stomach. Lawrence says if Walt had known about Charlie
Chaplin he would have assumed one identity with him too. What
a pity, Lawrence sneers. He'd have done poems, paeans, and what
not, Chants, Songs of Cinematernity. "Oh, Charlie, my Charlie,
another film is done—"

But in the end Lawrence gives in; he knows a kindred spirit
when he sees one. He looks down his nose at Whitman's paeans
upon Death—Lawrence, who is one of the true poets of Death—
and then adds:

> But the exultance of his message still remains. Purified of MERG-
> ING, purified of MYSELF, the exultant message of American Democ-
> racy, of souls in the Open Road, full of glad recognition, full of fierce
> readiness, full of joy of worship, when one soul sees a greater soul.
> The only riches, the great souls.

That is the last line of Lawrence's book called *Studies in Classic
American Literature*, and I submit that it is a fine concession to be
wrung from Lawrence, the archetype of tortured modern man,
the man without heroes. Lawrence and Whitman are two modern
poets with the deepest concern for mankind, the farthest insight,
the widest sympathy, the simplest and best expression. They are
scriptural writers in the long run, despising professionalism and
current fashions. But Lawrence fails to do more than pose the

59

problem of modern civilization versus the individual intelligence. He has no answer. He half invents fascism; he is torn between the image of the free natural male (the father who is always leaving home to become a gipsy) and the image of the leader, the aristocrat. He had it both ways: he remains unresolved. But he also had the vision. He became, in effect, an American, an American among Red Indians and rattlesnakes, close to that darker America betrayed by the white religions, Mexico, which he also loved. But it was Whitman's America that he held out for, "the true democracy [as Lawrence said], where soul meets soul, in the open road. Democracy. American democracy where all journey down the open road. And where a soul is known at once in its going." Strange words coming from the author of *Kangaroo* and *The Plumed Serpent*.

Lawrence suffers somewhat the fate of Whitman today. He is declassed. He enjoys a kind of underground popularity among writers, but he is outside the pale of the Tradition. He is too violent, too special, too original. And he is too outspoken. But Lawrence could never survive within a tradition, any more than Whitman. He has, at his best, a style so lean it matches the burnt-away clean language of prophets. Most of Lawrence's disciples, it seems to me, misunderstand him; but at least he has disciples. Whitman has no disciples and practically no living literary reputation. He is only a name.

What has happened to Whitman in the century since *Leaves of Grass* was published? It matters very little what happened historically. There were the usual false praises and the usual false deprecations, and enough of the true acclaim to give us faith in the history of criticism. There has never been anything we could call popularity for Whitman. Publishers are inclined to prepare elaborate editions of *Leaves of Grass*, in the same way that they release erotic editions of the Song of Songs: in a wrong-headed way, it is a compliment to Whitman. But the famous minds of the present century have not closed with Whitman, in my opinion. And the leading poets of the twentieth century have coolly and with relentless deliberation suppressed Whitman and kept him from exerting his force. Any Whitman advocate of great talent, for example Hart Crane, is forced to apologize for this allegiance before he is admitted to the company of moderns. There is no question that an Act of Exclusion has been in perpetual operation against Whitman since 1855 and is carried on today by the leading "classicists" of English and American poetry. Walt just won't do. He is vulgar; he is a humbug; he copies the names of rivers out of the sixth-grade geography book; he is an optimist; he is unlettered; he is a theosophist; he abhors institutions; he is auto-erotic; he loves everybody; he is a Rotarian; he goes to the opera; he can't distinguish between good and evil; he has no sense of humor; he cannot solve his own paradox about the greatness of the individual and the greatness of the En-Masse; he has no style—etc., etc.

All such accusations are true, and one could multiply them for pages and pages. Yet in the last analysis, they do not matter. Emerson saw humor in Whitman, though he called it wit. But Whitman thought he was writing a kind of bible. And it is the biblical quality of Whitman (as with Lawrence) that is so offensive to lovers of literature. What insolence! they say, and they are right. For neither Whitman nor Lawrence were "writers"; they were prophets. Literature makes it its business to stone prophets.

Whitman is indeed full of humbug, as when he talks about his experiences as a wound-dresser.

One night in the gloomiest period of the war, in the Patent Office hospital in Washington city, as I stood by the bedside of a Pennsylvania soldier, who lay, conscious of quick approaching death, yet perfectly calm, and with noble, spiritual manner, the veteran surgeon, turning aside, said to me, that though he had witness'd many, many deaths of soldiers, and had been a worker at Bull Run, Antietam, Fredericksburg, etc., he had not seen yet the first case of man or boy that met the approach of dissolution with cowardly qualms or terror. . . . Grand, common stock! to me the accomplish'd and convincing growth, prophetic of the future; proof . . . of perfect beauty, tenderness and pluck, that never feudal lord, nor Greek, nor Roman breed, yet rival'd. Let no tongue ever speak disparagement of the American races, north or south. . . .[1]

This sounds like Churchill at his worst.

It does not seem to me that Whitman is a complicated case of poor manners, confusions, and paradoxes; of philosophical muddle and literary naïveté; of good intentions, high passages, and bad dreary bogs. But even if I exaggerate his achievement, I maintain

61

that he is the one and only poet of America who has ever attempted to adumbrate the meaning of America. The twentieth-century American poet avoids this commitment, by and large: he considers it fitting and proper to take refuge in History against the horrors of progress; or in pure dialectic; or in the catacombs of established faith; or, failing that, in what is called the Language. Whitman's vision has degenerated into a thing called the Language; that is, the American Language, the natural nonhieratic language out of which a mythos might germinate. But Whitman contended that the mythos was at hand. He defined it; he sang it; he argued it; he poured it out. To no avail.

Twentieth-century poetry is a poetry of perfections. It is the least spontaneous poetry since—whatever date for the birth of artificiality you call to mind. It is the pride of twentieth-century poetry that even Yeats was brought to heel by critics who called for a "hard brittle technique." It is the pride of twentieth-century poetry that one publishes a poem once a decade. It is the boast of our poetry that it is impersonal, and that it can mean more or less what you think it means, and be right in the bargain. Whitman subscribed to—in a sense he invented—the philosophy of personalism. Lawrence too spoke with his own mouth and took the consequences. It was not for either to duck back into the Tradition. Yet Whitman did not repudiate the past; nor did he look with any pleasure upon the present, the America of a hundred years ago. He wrote in *Democratic Vistas:*

Never was there . . . more hollowness at heart than at present, and here in the United States. Genuine belief seems to have left us. The underlying principles of the States are not honestly believ'd in . . . . The spectacle is appalling. We live in an atmosphere of hypocrisy throughout. The men believe not in the women nor the women in the men. A scornful superciliousness rules in literature. The aim of all the littérateurs is to find something to make fun of. A lot of churches, sects, etc., the most dismal phantasms I know, usurp the name of religion . . . . The depravity of the business classes of our country is not less than has been supposed, but infinitely greater. The official services of America, national, state, and municipal, in all their branches and departments, except the judiciary, are saturated in corruption, bribery, falsehood, maladministration; and the judiciary is tainted. . . . In business (this all-devouring modern word, business), the one sole object is, by any means, pecuniary gain. . . . I say that our New World democracy . . . is, so far, an almost complete failure in its social aspects, and in really grand religious, moral, literary, and aesthetic results . . . .

Whitman sees the corruption and persists in his faith that the principle of democracy will overrule the corrupt. Let us call it the romantic position. But Whitman (like Jefferson) does not feel that the written word of democratic principle is sacrosanct. He goes to the heart of the matter. Man must do good, he says, because that is his ultimate nature. The man who falls a prey to corruption, dandyism, superficiality, selfishness, is a fallen man. Whitman despises him. He believes it natural to be pure: nature purifies. He has a kind of worship of chemistry, shared by his countrymen, an animal faith in the god of the sun and the god of water. It is precisely his contempt for ideas of sin and evil which places him among the great teachers of mankind.

What chemistry!
That the winds are really not infectious,
That this is no cheat, this transparent green-wash of the sea which is
    so amorous after me,
That it is safe to allow it to lick my naked body all over with its tongues,
That it will not endanger me with the fevers that have deposited them-
    selves in it,
That it is all clean forever and forever,
That the cool drink from the well tastes so good,
That blackberries are so flavorous and juicy. . . .
That when I recline on the grass I do not catch any disease . . .

He did not have a simple faith in the frontiers of knowledge; on the contrary, he held a limited belief in physical achievements.

> Not you alone proud truths of the world,
> Not you alone ye facts of modern science,
> But myths and fables of eld, Asia's, Africa's fables,
> The far-darting beams of the spirit, the unloos'd dreams,
> The deep diving bibles and legends,
>
> .   .   .   .   .
>
> You too with joy I sing.

America to Whitman was not a laboratory, but a place in the journey of mankind where the best in man might flower. America was not the goal; it was a bridge to the goal. In "Passage to India" he says of Columbus:

> (Ah Genoese thy dream! thy dream!
> Centuries after thou art laid in thy grave,
> The shore thou foundest verifies thy dream.)

But the dream is not satisfying enough. We must steer for the deepest waters and take passage to the skies themselves. We must go where mariner has not yet dared to go, risking the ship, ourselves, and all. It is not a geographical poem or a historical poem, although when Whitman talks about the Atlantic cable and its eloquent gentle wires, he sounds silly. But the physical achievement is his symbol of not progress but goodness. It is axiomatic to Whitman that we shall lay cables, build the Union Pacific Railroad, and fly airships to Jupiter. That is the childlike and wonderful faith of the ordinary modern man who is not thrown into reverse by the terror of it all. Whitman is not even talking about that. It is the twentieth-century "classical" poet who is materialistic and who writes scathing books of poems against the electric toaster. For Whitman says in the same poem that the seas are already crossed, weathered the capes, the voyage done. Everything is known already. The advancement of man physically seems to him good but only a trifle. What really concerns him is that man shall explore the soul.

> Passage indeed O soul to primal thought,
> Not lands and seas alone, thy own clear freshness,
> The young maturity of brood and bloom,
> To realms of budding bibles.
>
> . . . . .
>
> Back, back to wisdom's birth, to innocent intuitions,
> Again with fair creation.

Whitman is a mystic and he admits it. This is one more reason for his unpopularity. The best modern poets are allowed to admire a mystic but aren't allowed to be one. Whitman is too close for comfort. Furthermore, he had no theology worth sorting out, except a kind of Quakerism, and religion wasn't his concern. Man was his concern. And not American man. Whitman is not only the first white aboriginal; he is the first American; or that may be the same thing. When I read Whitman, good or bad, I always feel that here is first and foremost an American. I feel that the fundamental religiosity of Whitman plus the contempt for religion is American.

Whitman dissociated himself from mere poets and other writers. Who touches his book touches a man, he said in "Song of Myself":

I do not despise you priests, all time, the world over,
My faith is the greatest of faiths and the least of faiths,
Enclosing worship ancient and modern and all between ancient and
    modern,
Believing I shall come again upon the earth after five thousand years,
Waiting responses from oracles, honoring the gods, saluting the sun,
                    .   .   .   .   .

Helping the llama or brahmin as he trims the lamps of the idols,
Dancing yet through the streets in a phallic procession, rapt and
    austere . . .

and so on, down to the Mississippi Baptists with the jerks and spasms.

Whitman is too faithful in his belief in man to lay down the rules for a creed. It is unnecessary. If man is of Nature, and Nature is good, good will triumph. Evil is the failure of man to be as good as he can. For man to become all that is utterly possible is divine. And as every man is divine, inside and out, even the lowest are divinities. What is commonly looked down on nowadays in Whitman's talk about the divine average, is the average. Whitman would have emphasized the *divine*, rather than the average. Each person to him possessed divinity, and to repudiate that divinity was criminal. It is the god in each man and woman (which Lawrence called the Holy Ghost) that we can communicate with. I have rapport with you (Whitman's hieratic terminology is always couched in some kind of American French)— I have rapport with you because my divinity, my true personality, has a mouth to speak with. My lower self cannot speak; it can only commit acts of instinct. Yet there is a hierarchy of acts. Each thing to its nature:

(The moth and the fish-eggs are in their place.
The bright suns I see and the dark suns I cannot see are in their place,
The palpable is in its place and the impalpable in its place.)

65

And Whitman says he is not stuck up and is in his place. Being "in place," of course, is not humility; nor is it a sign of any known orthodoxy.

Whitman asserts his divinity and he cannot evade it, despite a passing show of humility. He has the vision of himself as well in the scale of things. But he acknowledges the god in oneself; and here he makes a break with conventional poetry and conventional thought which is the core of his philosophy.

Divine am I inside and out, and I make holy whatever I touch or am touch'd from.

It is Whitman's creed of the equality of the body and the soul. The body is not cursed; it is the miraculous materialization of the soul. The origin of this body-soul Whitman does not explain; he merely states that it is holy and the holy of holies. If he can find any object of worship more worthy than another it shall be his body or a part of his body. And while he is doting on himself he slips without warning into sun-worship, nature-worship, love-worship, and then back to himself. It goes like this:

If I worship one thing more than another it shall be the spread of my
    own body, or any part of it,
Translucent mould of me it shall be you!
Shaded ledges and rests it shall be you!
Firm masculine colter it shall be you!
Whatever goes to the tilth of me it shall be you!
You my rich blood! your milky stream pale strippings of my life!
Breast that presses against other breasts it shall be you!
My brain it shall be your occult convolutions!
Root of wash'd sweet-flag! timorous pond-snipe! nest of guarded
    duplicate eggs! it shall be you!
Mix'd tussled hay of head, beard, brawn, it shall be you!
Trickling sap of maple, fibre of manly wheat, it shall be you!
Sun so generous it shall be you!
Vapors lighting and shading my face it shall be you!
You sweaty brooks and dews it shall be you!
Winds whose soft-tickling genitals rub against me it shall be you!
Broad muscular fields, branches of live oak, loving lounger in my
    winding paths, it shall be you!
Hands I have taken, face I have kiss'd, mortal I have ever touch'd,
    it shall be you.
I dote on myself, there is that lot of me and all so luscious.

He begins with his own corpus, which he finds so luscious; he forgets himself and begins looking around the park, then he recalls the amorous uses of parks; and after a breath, he comes back to himself and "the lot of him." It is all very simple but it is anything but trivial. If you read on and on you see that Whitman is not talking about himself at all and acting like a baby discovering its toes—but that is the superficial trick of it; he is talking about the primal discovery of self. He is talking about consciousness in the only way it can be talked about: physically. I do not think for a second that Whitman was either narcissistic or egomaniac; he was trying to obliterate the fatal dualism of body and soul. All this monotony about keeping as clean around the bowels ("delicate" was the word he used) as around the heart and head is not a swipe at Victorian convention; it was his way of acknowledging the physicality of the soul, or the spirituality of the body. Lawrence shied away; and most American writers in more or less the same puritan tub get the backwash of revulsion about this physical "obsession" of Whitman's.

But this is only the beginning. Whitman wanted first to create the full individual, the full person, and this he did by tearing away the draperies. His wish was to form the complete person, the free man, the man free in himself, *in order to put this free man into the world.* The dialectical conflict in Whitman, as in everyone else I suppose, is the free individual versus the crowd of mankind. The twentieth-century poet slinks into his study and says, No crowds for me. But Whitman took it on. He is the only modern poet who has the courage to meet the crowd. And, falling back into his demotic French, he delivers the abstraction En-Masse. "Endless unfolding of words of ages! / And mine a word of the modern, the word En-Masse." This becomes one of the most ridiculed passages in Whitman, in which he drunkenly chants: "Hurrah for positive science! long live exact demonstration!" and "Gentlemen, to you the first honors always!" But these funny passages of Whitman, I must repeat, are there, not because he is a fool, but because he has the courage of his convictions. For just after this idiotic hurrahing for exact demonstration comes another of the great bursts of poetry, the one beginning "Walt Whitman, a kosmos, of Manhattan the son,/ Turbulent, fleshy, sensual, eating, drinking and breeding . . . ." (Whitman is always aware of the comic possibilities of his position

67

like most prophets. Imagine the jokes that Jesus told!) The balanced man, the free man, the man who meets his potentiality, is a fit man for the new world, the democracy he envisions.

The purpose of democracy [says Whitman in prose] . . . is, through many transmigrations and amid endless ridicules, arguments, and ostensible failures, to illustrate, at all hazards, this doctrine or theory that man, properly train'd in sanest, highest freedom, may and must become a law, and series of laws, unto himself, surrounding and providing for, not only his own personal control, but all his relations to other individuals, and to the State; and . . . *this*, as matters now stand in our civilized world, is the only scheme worth working from, as warranting results like those of Nature's laws, reliable . . . to carry on themselves.

The concept of En-Masse is not absurd and not laughable, as other expressions of his certainly are, such as Democracy, Ma Femme. But even Whitman's tendency to view Democracy as feminine is penetrating. He would not be surprised to discover in modern America that woman is slightly out of harness; he would approve it. Whitman was the first great American feminist.

A great poet is not merely a poet of his nation but a poet of all peoples. Whitman, who had little enough reward for his book, and has little enough today, looked beyond literature and beyond the greatness of art. His true personality went out beyond America, beyond religions, and even beyond mankind. His poems about the self and the mass of America were written before the Civil War, but the war between the North and South brought everything home to Whitman. His vision might well have been destroyed, but with his natural passion for unity he embarked on a new discovery, not of the body and soul, or rapport, or the En-Masse, but of the exploration of Death. Whitman had always believed in Death as the purposeful continuity of existence, but he had had no significant experience of it. One can barely imagine what the Civil War was to Whitman, this fanatically intense American, this New World man, the first white aboriginal, with his lusty physical joy of life, his love of comrades, his genius for poetry, and his natural mysticism. Whitman was stricken by the War but he was recreated by it. Columbus had been a rather nebulous hero; Lincoln was the reincarnation of the American god to him.

Half of Whitman's great poetry is war poetry and poetry upon
Lincoln and his death, and death poetry, though it cannot all be
dated from the War. Whitman accepted death as he did sex and
otherness, self and not-self. The War returned to him the particu-
larity of death, and it produced in him not bitterness but love.
He triumphed over it. He saw beyond history and beyond America. But what he saw was with the American vision: in Whitman's
dialectic, you do not give up the past for the vision: the past is of
the vision as much as the future. In the open air "a great personal
deed has room" and it is such a deed that seizes upon the hearts of
the whole race of man. And this deed is not discovery or triumph
or a formula of belief: it is the giving oneself—the Whitman in
oneself—to the other, the comrade. Whitman knew that giving in
the past had always been a form of taxation and protection. This
new kind of giving is reckless and mystical, differing from the
old giving because Whitman gives body and soul without sacrific-
ing one to the other. Whitman is no humanist and no ordinary
libertarian but a seer who dreams of free individuality in a world
of free souls. The open road may be a commonplace symbol, but
it is a deliberate symbol, and it stands for an actuality. That actuality is America as Whitman sees America in himself. The anti-
Whitman party of our time is an attempt, of course, to deny the
vision of the new world with its physical materialism, experi-
mentalism, and the whole concept of man for the world. It turns
out that Whitman is not for the "people" and not for the impres-
sively learned poets of our time. He is for man who begins at the
beginning—all over again. There is more to poetry than books,
he says in "Song of the Open Road."

I think heroic deeds were all conceiv'd in the open air, and all free
    poems also,
I think I could stop here myself and do miracles . . .
Here a great personal deed has room . . .
Here is realization . . .
Here is adhesiveness . . .
Do you know what it is as you pass to be loved by strangers? . . .
These are the days that must happen to you:
You shall not heap up what is call'd riches . . .
What beckonings of love you receive you shall only answer with
    passionate kisses of parting,

Start with the Sun

You shall not allow the hold of those who spread their reach'd hands
    toward you.
Allons! after the great Companions, and to belong to them!
They too are on the road—they are the swift and majestic men—
    they are the greatest women . . .
They go! they go! I know that they go, but I know not where they go,
But I know that they go toward the best—toward something great.

It is all there: the greatness of the body and the greatness of the
soul; the touching of the world and the heroism of departure; the
magnificent motion of death; the expanding cycle of consciousness; the essential holiness of all things. And always at the center,
the self, the moment of incarnation, the Walt Whitman of oneself.
The aboriginal or, if you like, the American.

The power of Whitman in the world is incalculable. In literature it has long been calculated as nothing. It is because of poets
like Whitman that literature exists, but it is always literature that
determines to exterminate its Whitmans, its Blakes, its Lawrences,
its Henry Millers. The probability is that Whitman will never be
"accepted" as one of the great writers of mankind; acceptance is
always a function of the writers who assume the power of literature, for whatever reasons, and who make literature one of the
arms of the law. Because Whitman is beyond the law of literature,
and beyond all law, he is condemned to extinction from generation to generation. Whitman is one of those poets who hate religion and who eventually become a religion. To prevent this
happening is forever the mission of his best disciples.

KARL SHAPIRO

The Leaves *of D. H. Lawrence*

WHAT does Whitman have to do with the poetry of D. H. Lawrence? Not much, imply some later critics, who have a tendency
when considering Lawrence's poetry to subtract Whitman and
add Blake. For example, F. R. Leavis notes "a significant parallel"
between Blake and Lawrence, but omits Whitman,[1] as does Harry
T. Moore in his careful attempt in *The Life and Works of D. H.
Lawrence* to place Lawrence in relation to other writers.[2] Yet
Blake has hardly an allusion in Lawrence's hand. There is mention of the satanic mills of Blake ("Dark Satanic Mills"), and a
poem reminiscent of "The Tyger" ("Michael Angelo"); "The
Evangelistic Beasts," however, is really more Bible than Blake. I
have found no acknowledgment of Blake as master in any essay
or letter. It is true that Lawrence's early friend Jessie Chambers
(Wood) gave him Blake's *Songs of Innocence* and *Songs of Experience* one Christmas, but we have a more specific and telling
statement about Whitman. In her account of their early literary in-
terests, and referring to Lawrence's Croydon period (1908–1912),
Jessie Chambers wrote that "*Leaves of Grass* was one of his great
books." [3] (The only books she had previously given such an important status were Thoreau's *Walden*, over which Lawrence had
become "wildly enthusiastic," and Palgrave's *Golden Treasury of
Songs and Lyrics*, which he carried in his pocket and from which

his favorites included Shelley, Wordsworth, Keats, and Burns.) In both obvious and subtle ways, the poems, letters, and essays (particularly his "Whitman" in *Studies in Classic American Literature*) have abundant allusions to Whitman. In fact, to paraphrase a line from "Song of Myself," Lawrence seems to be stuccoed with Whitmanese all over. "Whitman, the great poet, has meant so much to me," he said in his Whitman essay. Will it help to understand the poetry of D. H. Lawrence if we know what that relationship was? I think so, even as definition is the first principle of knowledge, and in definition we must place an object in relation to both a general and a particular circle.

I. PERSON AND PLACE

Reviewers of Lawrence's books of poetry early caught the Whitman inflection: the poems were often in free verse, often daring, often electric with the sense of life that Whitman communicated. Although the sensuousness of Lawrence's first book, *Love Poems and Others* (1913), may have been only "pre-raphaelitish slush" to Ezra Pound (as he wrote in *Poetry* for July 1913), the second volume, *Amores* (1916), was reviewed in the *Times Literary Supplement* (10 Aug. 1916) as having Whitman's kind of frankness—"almost as outspoken as Whitman's [poetry], and with the same robust sincerity." Both *Look! We Have Come Through!* (1917) and *New Poems* (1918), in whose Preface Lawrence described his style in both books as the Whitman type of free verse, were accused by the reviewers of unselectiveness, wordiness, unpoetic style, overintensity, and a strained manner. With *Birds, Beasts and Flowers* (1923), concern for Whitman-like excessiveness changed to admiration of Lawrence's skill. Mark Van Doren wrote in the *Nation* (5 Dec. 1923) that "like Whitman, too, he often is incoherent and merely strident; but when he hits he hits like thunder." On *Pansies* (1929), Richard Church said in the *Spectator* (3 Aug. 1929): "As for his technique, it is unmatched. No artist has carried free-verse so far. He has the sweep and grandeur of Whitman, but with an added grace, a susceptibility to the touch of single words, vowels, and consonants." In general, the early shock at Lawrence's frankness and fullness, and the later admiration for his technique, dissolved at the last to an awareness of what he was after all along—the "life quality"

72

in his poetry. By 1928, when *Collected Poems* appeared, his pre-occupation with physical vitality was called "sex mysticism"; he could enlarge our imaginative response to life. Conrad Aiken wrote in the New York *Evening Post* (20 July 1929) that Lawrence's poetry "has no beginning and no end; it is everywhere vividly and terrifyingly alive. Like life itself, it is a process rather than a fulfillment—" And just as Whitman gives a strong human shape to *Leaves of Grass,* so the vigor and magic of Lawrence's personality came through the lines of the posthumous *Last Poems* (1932). The review in *Books* (26 March 1933) is typical: "They [the poems] present the tremendous personality of Lawrence, the man, the prophet. Their vitality is his own vitality."

Critical studies of Lawrence after his death have attempted in many ways to "place" him. As early as 1931, Glenn Hughes, in his *Imagism and the Imagists,* had already held that by Lawrence's own admission the strongest influence in his work was Whitman.[4] Dallas Kenmare, in *Fire-Bird: A Study of D. H. Lawrence,* classed him with the "life-poets"—Browning, Shelley, and Whitman.[5] Harry T. Moore, in *The Intelligent Heart,* stressed the Pre-Raphaelites as an influence, with Hardy and Verlaine mixed in and "Whitman strongly intruding a bit later." [6] Some saw the relationship—and Lawrence's deficiencies. When Richard Aldington, as editor, wrote his introduction to *Last Poems,* he compared Lawrence (at least in *Pansies*) to both Blake and Whitman: "Sometimes they [*Pansies*] are like the utterances of a little Whitman, but without Walt's calm *sostenuto* quality; and sometimes they are like a little Blake raving, but without the fiery vision." (Of course the *sostenuto* quality which Aldington rightly missed in *Pansies* did come in some of the posthumous poems, like "Bavarian Gentians" and "The Ship of Death.") Witter Bynner thought that "there was seldom the rounding flow of the chords of Whitman, which he took for a model but could not match." [7] The two essays on Lawrence's poetry in the 1953 collection, *The Achievement of D. H. Lawrence,* note a fairly strong but qualified relationship. Richard Ellman thinks that "If Lawrence is closest to Blake, he is not far from Whitman," and he makes some perceptive comparisons. Horace Gregory mentions only *Last Poems,* in which the Whitman influence is "written large on every page." [8]

Lawrence would no doubt have been alarmed at any serious attempt to pigeonhole him. Perhaps more than most writers, he was catholic in his tastes, unsystematic in his reading, unexpected in his admirations. He liked Shelley, Thoreau, and the *Rubaiyat.* Browning was a "great favorite," according to Jessie Chambers. He liked Swinburne and Flaubert. He wanted to write about Burns, and he did begin a work on Hardy. As he read everything, so he used everything. Memoirs about Lawrence are full of accounts of misrepresentation, for Lawrence had a habit of *nearly* faithful transcription from life. Houses and fields and flowers, friends and enemies—all were shifted slightly in the Laurentian glass and poured onto the paper. And he sometimes used their lines as well as their lives. A curiosity not generally noted is that the first three lines of one of Lawrence's most admired poems, "Spring Morning"—

> Ah, through the open door
> Is there an almond-tree
> Aflame with blossom!

—are taken from "Adventure," a poem by Ernest Collings which was apparently sent to Lawrence for criticism. Lawrence's letter to Collings (14 Nov. 1912) says that the poem "is so nice, and I love

> 'Now—go thy way.
> Ah, through the open door
> Is there an almond tree
> Aflame with blossom!
> A little longer stay—
> Why do tears blind me?
> Nay, but go thy way.'

That's a little poem, sufficient in itself." Lawrence's poem is of course his own—he gives it the memorable refrain, "Look! We have come through"—but it is clear that whatever excited his imagination came into use.

In spite of his eclecticism, Lawrence shows a remarkable affinity for the ideas, images, forms, and phrases of Whitman. They creep in everywhere, familiarly, without special comment. The poetry is, actually, so full of Whitman that in this essay I can do no more than give a sampling of themes and some of the more obvious correspondences, beginning with some familiar lines in "Song of Myself." Lawrence's "The American Eagle" repeats Whitman's "barbaric yawp over the roofs of the world." In Lawrence's poem, the eagle

>   . . . was growing a startling big bird
> On the roof of the world;
> A bit awkward, and with a funny squawk in his voice,
> His mother Liberty trying always to teach him to coo
> And him always ending with a yawp
> *Coo! Coo! Coo! Coo-ark! Coo-ark! Quark!! Quark!!*
> YAWP!!!

Lawrence also paraphrased Whitman's "Do I contradict myself? /Very well then I contradict myself" in the lines from "Pomegranate,"

> You tell me I am wrong,
> Who are you, who is anybody to tell me I am wrong?
> I am not wrong.

On his determination to publish *Lady Chatterley*, he wrote to Aldous Huxley (2 April 1928): "Too late! I am embarked. . . . All overboard but John Thomas.—Oh, captain, my captain, our fearful trip's begun—" Whitman's rather unusual phrase of generation from "I Sing the Body Electric"—the bath of birth—slips into Lawrence's essay, "On Being a Man": "I came, in the bath of birth, out of a mother." Whitman's passage:

This the nucleus—after the child is born of woman, man is born of woman,
This the bath of birth, this the merge of small and large, and the outlet again.

Far beyond the casual phrase, it is indeed with the thematic "bath of birth" that we begin to see in Lawrence's poetry the varied images of Whitman: a physical mysticism; a sense of generation; the living present and the fluid movement of the open road; the prophet and the bard.

Some of these are natural correspondences in poets of similar temper and belief, but other relationships are plainly marked out in Lawrence's prose and demonstrated in the poetry. What Lawrence actually said and did about Whitman makes a document of more than usual interest in the study of poetic companionship. We may begin with his stated Yes and No.

II. LAWRENCE ON WHITMAN

1. Yes

Lawrence did attempt to write like Whitman. Jessie Chambers tells that when he was teaching at Croydon, "He would sometimes write, 'I'm sending you a Whitmanesque poem,' when he was enclosing one of his own." [9] By "Whitmanesque" Lawrence may have meant both style (superficially, free verse) and subject. His first specific analysis of Whitman, however, is on verse form and poetic theory: one of the "Whitmanesque" qualities he admired, as he describes in his Preface to *New Poems,* is the quickness and flow of the "poetry of the sheer present, poetry whose very permanency lies in its wind-like transit. Whitman's is the best poetry of this kind." Lawrence might have said, "I sing the poem electric." For this kind of poem, there must be a verse form which has motion, whose rhythms do not return upon themselves, which has no stated perfection or finality: free verse which is "direct utterance from the instant, whole man." If he uses Whitman's technique, the poet removes clichés of rhythm, phrase, sound, and sense; he breaks down artificiality for spontaneity. Free verse in its highest sense is the recognition of being: "The quick of all the universe, of all creation, is the incarnate carnal self. Poetry gave us the clue: free verse: Whitman." If this is the "Whitmanesque" style, it is obviously more than a curl of irregular lines floating careless on a page, or a tangle of broken feet. Of course, Whitman's verse was also extremely artful, giving the *impression* of spontaneity and direct utterance in a controlled form. R. P. Blackmur astutely points out (in his essay on Lawrence in *The Double Agent*) that the "expressive form" of direct, emotional utterance which Lawrence tried contained the seed of its own disaster,[10] but he does not make the distinction between fact and effect in this type of poetry. Perhaps Lawrence in his enthusiasm for Whitman also failed to separate the two. His ideal was simply *organic* verse—fresh, moving, alive—but he did attempt to define the term.

Organic poetry (like Whitman's) was alive because, first, it emphasized the *physical* quality of the verse—rhythm and sound; second, it had *unity* of rhythm and mood or emotion; third, it had *movement*. Physically, Lawrence felt that sound and rhythm were of first importance. When he was writing "Whitmanesque" verse for Jessie Chambers, he was also developing his first theories about the primary nature of poetry. His headmaster at Croydon, Philip F. T. Smith, recalls that Lawrence thought the first approach to poetry should be through the body and not the idea, "through rhythm and the ring of words rather than the evasive appeal of an unreal and abstract morality." [11] And the physical sense must inhabit the lines. A few years later Lawrence pointed out to Ernest Collings (14 Nov. 1912) that there wasn't much poetry "inside" his lines: "It's the rhythm and the sound that don't penetrate the blood—"

The physical body of the poem and its mood or emotion (both from the poet and to the reader) must be all of a piece throughout. This organic unity Lawrence particularly admired in Whitman. Moods often put rhythms out of joint, he wrote to Edward Marsh (18 Aug. 1913): "I have always tried to get an emotion out in its own course, without altering it. It needs the finest instinct imaginable, much finer than the skill of the craftsmen. That Japanese Yone Noguchi tried it. He doesn't quite bring it off. Often I don't—sometimes I do. Sometimes Whitman is perfect."

Movement in poetry, on a simple level, comes through free rather than formed verse; in form poetry could become rigid, "corseted in rhymed scansion." More deeply, movement is pulsation, the "insurgent naked throb of the instant moment." [12] The pulse is also the motion of being, the very invisible body of man in time. One can give the sense of movement by letting the lines leap freely into space, by turning in some unexpected direction, and—ironically—by repetition itself (one of Whitman's characteristic devices). Repetition must, of course, be incremental, phrased by Lawrence in his own organic terms as "this pulsing, frictional to-and-fro, which works up to culmination." [13]

Lawrence's record in his poetry is quite plainly a turn from form to free verse and a correspondingly rougher, rangier movement than in most of *Love Poems and Others* and *Amores*. As Lawrence said of his manifesto on Whitmanesque verse in the

Preface to *New Poems*, "All this should have come as a preface to 'Look! We have Come Through,' " his third book (1917), and it carried through especially to *Tortoises* (1921) and *Birds, Beasts and Flowers* (1923). Both books have the abundantly rich, flowing poems that are incantations of the deepest sense of life. They have a good many poems which use the characteristic line repetition and catalogue of Whitman—for instance, the striking "I remember" sequence in "Tortoise Shout." It is not so obvious, perhaps, that in *Pansies* (1929) and *Nettles* (1930), those slim volumes of rapier remarks on the great beast of society, Lawrence was also taking a leaf from Whitman. As Lawrence gathered together three or four small poems on the same theme—fighting, old age, sun-democracy, the machine—so Whitman grouped poems on like subjects together, deliberately shaping a point by repetition. Whitman has many of the short idea-poems that Lawrence called "Pansies" (for *pensées*), especially in the last sections of *Leaves of Grass*—"Sands at Seventy" and "Good-Bye My Fancy." One example from the early poems might be compared with the form and general tone of Lawrence's slightly argumentative "thoughts." Whitman wrote,

I hear it was charged against me that I sought to destroy institutions,
But really I am neither for nor against institutions,
(What indeed have I in common with them? or what with the destruction of them?).

Though Whitman never has quite the reckless acidity or the flailing anger of Lawrence, he also writes brevities of personal comment that are rather drier, more didactic than his poems of intricate form and sustained music. Of course Lawrence had the music, too. Even while he must have been jotting the last "Pansies," his notebooks contained the blue-cello "Bavarian Gentians." And the sexual cosmos of "Whales weep not!," where mating is like Whitman's "The Dalliance of the Eagles," is finally a range of mystery where

. . . enormous mother whales lie dreaming suckling their whale-tender
   young
and dreaming with strange whale eyes wide open in the waters of the
   beginning and the end.

This later Lawrence would not have said he was writing "Whitmanesque" verse—that was for the apprentice. But Lawrence had at least joined his early master on the same road.

Lawrence began his collection of essays, *Studies in Classic American Literature* (1923), with a general motif, "The Spirit of Place." He put at the end—perhaps climactically—his essay on Whitman. In the Preface to *New Poems*, Lawrence had said that we profoundly fear and respect Whitman, and in the essay he makes this dual attitude explicit. We shall see later what he feared. But first of all, he honored Whitman as the great poet, "the one man breaking a way ahead." What did he mean by "great poet," by "breaking a way"? He meant Whitman's sense of life: first, the new morality of a physical mysticism which put the soul in the body and God in generation; second, the personal power of Whitman as leader on the open road of freedom, movement, and comradeship.

Physical mysticism (called mystic materialism by Aldous Huxley and "inverted mysticism" by James E. Miller, Jr.[14]), assumes first that the soul and body are one; that a spiritual realization must come *through*, not in rejection of, the physical world. And "Whitman," says Lawrence in the essay, "was the first heroic seer to seize the soul by the scruff of her neck and plant her down among the potsherds." Stay there, he said; and Stay there, said Lawrence. What is the soul? Whitman answers by enumerating "the parts and poems of the body" (or soul) in thirty-four lines of "I Sing the Body Electric." He asks in "Starting from Paumanok":

Was somebody asking to see the soul?
See, your own shape and countenance, persons, substances, beasts,
   the trees, the running rivers, the rocks and sands.

But there is still the ambivalence. If soul is body, the real body may be the soul:

All hold spiritual joys and afterwards loosen them;
How can the real body ever die and be buried?

"Behold," he said, "the body includes and is the meaning, the main concern, and includes and is the soul." Whitman's most familiar

79

statement is the credo of "Song of Myself": "I am the poet of the Body and I am the poet of the Soul." The substance of poetry is double, and the same:

I believe in the flesh and the appetites,
Seeing, hearing, feeling, are miracles, and each part and tag of me is a
    miracle.

Therefore, he says in "Starting from Paumanok,"

I will make the poems of materials, for I think they are to be the
    most spiritual poems,
And I will make the poems of my body and of mortality,
For I think I shall then supply myself with the poems of my soul and
    of immortality.

Physical mysticism is central in Lawrence's poetry and thought; the connection with Whitman is direct. Although he may have minimized Whitman's full use of the principle, Maurice Lesemann, writing in the *Bookman* for March 1924, pointed out the relationship: ". . . although Whitman sketched the thought, Lawrence is the first modern to body forth love as one inseparable experience, not as both physical and mental, but as one—one thing; and in that one living substance of love he looks for his solution." The serious sexuality of both Whitman and Lawrence has sometimes been called eroticism. But "Which Eros?" Lawrence asked in his "Unpublished Foreword" to *Women in Love*. "Eros of the jaunty 'amours', or Eros of the sacred mysteries?" The theme of physical sex was indeed sacred and serious to Lawrence. He continued in the Foreword: "Let us hesitate no longer to announce that the sensual passions and mysteries are equally sacred with the spiritual mysteries and passions. . . . Let man only approach his own self with a deep respect, even reverence for all that the creative soul, the God-mystery within us, puts forth." Lawrence explains his own physical mysticism (characteristically in sexual terms) most fully in his prose (the novels, the essays, *Fantasia of the Unconscious*). He makes the point in a letter to Harriet Monroe (15 March 1928) that it is the more serious, mystical "phallic consciousness," not the "cerebral sex-consciousness," which is "the root of poetry, lived or sung." In the poetry itself Lawrence says directly far less than does Whitman, who occasionally seems like a counsel for the body in some cosmic debate. But Lawrence thoroughly exemplifies his theme in the poems, most significantly in *Look! We Have Come Through!*, a book which is the equivalent of Whitman's "Children of Adam" poems. Both celebrate the mystery of the life force—the body, physical love, and sex—all the Adamic wonder in life incarnate.

In *Look! We Have Come Through!* and "Children of Adam," there is first of all the incantation of the body. Its catalogue is, in Whitman's terms, divine, complete. Whitman's enumerations of the parts of the body in "I Sing the Body Electric" might be compared with Lawrence's antiromantic listing in " 'She said as well to me.' " Then there is the celebration of the sexual relationship. Whitman's "A Woman Waits for Me" might be compared with Lawrence's "Song of a Man Who Is Loved"; Whitman's passage in "I Sing the Body Electric" beginning "This is the female form,/A divine nimbus exhales from it" with the golden radiance of Lawrence's "Gloire de Dijon." *Look! We Have Come Through!* is more personal, less symbolically complex, than "Children of Adam," but in both the sense of mystic realization through the flesh is exquisitely clear. Lawrence's lines concluding his title poem give the universal argument and the possible triumph:

> What is the knocking?
> What is the knocking at the door in the night?
> It is somebody wants to do us harm.
>
> No, no, it is the three strange angels.
> Admit them, admit them.

When one admits angels, he may also find his own perfection.

In the poetry of Whitman and Lawrence, sex is presented not as man's fall but as the possibility of his return to innocence. One of the most significant resemblances in the two groups of Adamic poems (*Look! We Have Come Through!* and "Children of Adam") is the theme of Paradise regained, the return to Eden through the acceptance of complete sexual love. Lawrence's "Paradise Re-entered" is a rather remarkable recapitulation of Whitman's "To the Garden the World," which begins,

> To the garden the world anew ascending,
> Potent mates, daughters, sons. . . .

The sense of the symbolic Paradise comes to one

Amorous, mature, all beautiful to me, all wondrous,
My limbs and the quivering fire that ever plays through them. . . .

The figures in Lawrence's poem return, too,

> Through the strait gate of passion,
> Between the bickering fire
> Where flames of fierce love tremble
> On the body of fierce desire:

As Whitman's speaker said to "behold my resurrection after slumber," in Lawrence's poem,

> Now, at the day's renascence
> We approach the gate.

Lawrence's scene is more graphic than Whitman's, but both poems show Adam and Eve on their solitary but victorious way. In Lawrence:

> But we storm the angel-guarded
> Gates of the long-discarded
> Garden, which God has hoarded
> Against our pain.
>
> .   .   .   .   .
>
> . . . and as victors we travel
> To Eden home.

In Whitman,

> Existing I peer and penetrate still,
> Content with the present, content with the past,
> By my side or back of me Eve following,
> Or in front, and I following her just the same.

Lawrence's garden of the sexual world has innocence "beyond good and evil." Whitman goes farther, with the joyous identification of man and the earth-garden in "Spontaneous Me," in which he extends the idea of primitive good to "the great chastity" of paternity and maternity. The true morality in the "Adamic Songs" of both Whitman and Lawrence, however, is to recognize and receive the God-power of generation and revere its signs and visitations. Whitman's was "the song of procreation" and the phallus, the mystique of sex in all of nature. Though Lawrence (and Whitman, too, in a milder sense) hurled confusion at the world in terms of insistent sexual imagery, he believed in the power and glory of the universal procreative force. As he says in one of his "Pansies"—this one ("Don't look at me!") published only in Lawrence's own limited edition of 1929—

> My dears, if you want the skies to fall
> they are established on the many pillars of the phallus.

The physical is not only the emblem of the spiritual. It is itself the mystery, the life-force, the cosmos.

The second profound acknowledgment of Lawrence (in his essay on Whitman) was to Whitman's "essential message" of the Open Road: "The leaving of the soul free unto herself, the leaving of his fate to her and to the loom of the open road." The soul finds herself, says Lawrence, not by the exploration of an inward heaven, or by exaltation and ecstasy, but by the journey itself down the open road of physical life in which the wayfaring is all —not the goal, not the direction, but the movement itself. One meets other comrades with understanding, "the soul in her subtle sympathies accomplishing herself by the way." This is the true morality of life—the journey, and the soul fully realizing herself.

Lawrence refers particularly to the imagery of Whitman's "Song of the Open Road," which begins,

> Afoot and light-hearted I take to the open road,
> Healthy, free, the world before me,
> The long brown path before me leading wherever I choose.

"I myself am good-fortune," says Whitman, and gains his freedom being "loos'd of limits and imaginary lines," inheriting the earth and realizing himself. He knows the way of going but not the end:

We will sail pathless and wild seas,
We will go where winds blow, waves dash, and the Yankee clipper
  speeds by under full sail.

You arrive and depart, you will not be held; days will happen to you. And you are not alone: "Allons! after the great Companions, and to belong to them!" All ways are open. The traveler knows "the universe itself as a road" in which "all parts away for the progress of souls." What Lawrence says about the open road in his essay on Whitman is merely a general paraphrase of this poem. But Lawrence had long before accepted Whitman's invitation at the end of "Song of the Open Road"—"Camerado, I give you my hand! . . . /will you come travel with me?"—when he began writing Whitmanesque poetry, the poetry of the incarnate, moving Now, in which the progress of the poem is only emblematic of the progress of the soul.

Lawrence believed in Whitman's "comradeship," a fair and open recognition of like souls. But he came to emphasize the personal duty of individual fulfillment rather than the union with others. His rewritten version of "Discipline" (one of the "school" poems in *Amores*) for *Collected Poems* (1928) makes this point in some of the added lines:

> I must not win their souls, no never, I only must win
> The brief material control of the hour, leave them free of me.

Let each live, with no trespass:

> . . . the fight is not for existence, the fight is to burn
> At last into blossom of being, each one his own flower outflung.

In the Whitman-like "Manifesto" of *Look! We Have Come Through!*, the vision contains man's uniqueness and his free journey—

> . . . moving in freedom more than the angels,
> conditioned only by our own pure single being,
> having no laws but the laws of our own being.

The last lines are an incantation of being-in-movement on the open road:

> We shall not look before and after.
> We shall *be, now.*
> We shall know in full.
> We, the mystic NOW.

2. No

Whitman, the great poet, was the mystic of the open road. But Lawrence had a great deal to say about the Whitman who had lost part of himself around false corners. Although he believed in the ideal of comradeship, Lawrence was skeptical about Whitman's insistence on love, on merging, on containing all. This, he felt, was the loss of self. He doubted, too, the Whitman *"en masse,"* the divine average, democracy. And he talked back in poem after poem, as if in sheer exasperation with an ideal that could not be whole.

The first, and perhaps the most thorough, attack on Whitman's ideal of "love" comes in Lawrence's "Bibbles," the poem in *Birds, Beasts and Flowers* about the little black dog in New Mexico who loves everybody, loves them all:

> Believe in the One Identity, don't you,
> You little Walt-Whitmanesque bitch?

(For one of Whitman's uses of "One Identity," see "Our Old Feuillage," a song of "my lands . . . inevitably united and made ONE IDENTITY.") Lawrence then half-quotes Whitman, "To you, whoever you are, with endless embrace!"—Whitman has several uses of the phrase "you whoever you are." One poem is entitled "To You," begins "Whoever you are . . . ," and continues in the next section,

Whoever you are, now I place my hand upon you, that you be my
    poem . . .
I have loved many women and men, but I love none better than you.

Bibbles does in fact become Lawrence's poem, for in spite of the small dog's indiscriminate affection, he is completely and in loving detail made alive in the lines. One of the best "organic" passages is the description of the dog running after horse and rider, in which the lines rock along as rolling and breathless and immediate as the moment itself:

So absurd
Pelting behind on the dusty trail when the horse sets off home at a
    gallop:
Left in the dust behind like a dust-ball tearing along,
Coming up on fierce little legs, tearing fast to catch up, a real little
    dust-pig, ears almost blown away,
And black eyes bulging bright in a dust-mask
Chinese-dragon-wrinkled, with a pink mouth grinning, under jaw
    shoved out

And white teeth showing in your dragon-grin as you race, you split-
face,
Like a trundling projectile swiftly whirling up,
Cocking your eyes at me as you come alongside, to see if I'm I on
the horse,
And panting with that split grin,
All your game little body dust-smooth like a little pig, poor Pips.

But Bibbles is also a "stinker":

> *Reject nothing*, sings Walt Whitman.
> So you, you go out at last and eat the unmentionable,
> In your appetite for affection.

And when Bibbles, herself rejected and attacked, returns to her
master for particular love, he says,

> You learn loyalty rather than loving,
> And I'll protect you.

Lawrence saw Whitman's all-embracing love as the merging of
self into nothing, without honor and without identity.

Even in his argument with Whitman, Lawrence discriminates.
It is only love that is tasteless and unreal that he cannot abide.
The excellence of love (in "Touch Comes—") is the "Soft slow
sympathy/of the blood in me, of the blood in thee." Whitman
said in "Song of Myself," "And whoever walks a furlong without
sympathy walks to his own funeral drest in his shroud." One of
Lawrence's posthumous "Pansies" is called "Retort to Whitman":

> And whoever walks a mile full of false sympathy
> Walks to the funeral of the whole human race.

It is the mental, deliberate assertion of love that corrodes.
Lawrence shuddered at one of Whitman's opening phrases in
Leaves of Grass, "the word Democratic, the word En-Masse,"
ignoring for the sake of a larger principle that Whitman's line
was only one side of a paradox:

> One's-self I sing, a simple separate person,
> Yet utter the word Democratic, the word En-Masse.

But Whitman makes it clear that his *Leaves of Grass* is fibered
with the idea of democratic man, both individual and united; his

chants are for America and the States (which sometimes left
Lawrence fuming, " 'These States!' as Whitman said,/Whatever
he meant"—lines concluding a poem on America, "The Evening
Land"). In the varying moods of *Pansies* (and "More Pansies" in
Last Poems), Lawrence attacks what he considers a loose idea of
Democracy, substituting his own definitions and the superior ideal
of aristocracy. He picks up Whitman's terms and motifs, as in
"En Masse":

To-day, society has sanctified
the sin against the Holy Ghost,
and all are encouraged into the sin
so that all may be lost together, *en masse*, the great word of our
    civilisation.

And he comments on and reverses Whitman's primary symbols
in two poems at the close of *Nettles*. "Leaves of grass, what about
leaves of grass?" he asks. It is not *leaves* of grass that matter, he
answers, but *flowers* of grass (for grass blossoms in a form not
far from the lily); not the multitude but the single separate glory
of all the intentions of grass:

Only the best matters; even the cow knows it;
grass in blossom, blossoming grass, risen to its height and its natural
    pride
in its own splendour and its own feathery maleness
the grass, the grass.
Leaves of grass, what are leaves of grass, when at its best grass blossoms.

The poem which follows is "Magnificent Democracy," Lawrence's nettle for Whitman:

      Oh, when the grass flowers, the grass
      how aristocratic it is!
      Cock's-foot, fox-tail, fescue and tottering-grass
      see them wave, see them wave, plumes
      prouder than the Black Prince,
      flowers of grass, fine men.

      Oh, I am a democrat
      of the grass in blossom
      a blooming aristocrat all round.

One of the later "More Pansies" varies the image, in "Amo Sacrum Vulgus":

> And so I sing a democracy
> a democracy, a democracy
> that puts forth its own aristocracy
> like bearded wheat in ear.
>
> Oh golden fields of people
> of people, of people,
> oh golden field of people
> all moving into flowers.

Sometimes Lawrence identifies "aristocracy" with "real democracy"—a group of poems in *Pansies* contrasting the "real" in which all men become the servants of life (and some look into the eyes of the gods) with the robot-democracy in which nobody works willingly and hate is struck from the friction of the machine (see "Real Democracy," "Robot Feelings," "Robot-Democracy," "Democracy is Service," "False Democracy and Real"). Or, perhaps the real democracy is "a democracy of touch," or there may be a democracy of "the free sun in men" which is actually a kind of aristocracy (see "Future Relationships," "Democracy," "Aristocracy of the Sun"). No, Lawrence did not want democracy, *en masse*, one identity, the average, even leaves of grass. *En masse*, it was too easy to forget man in his possible godhead. It is no matter that Whitman wanted plumes and flowers out of the rank grass as much as Lawrence, and that Lawrence may have mistaken Whitman's terms. The poet that Lawrence feared and respected so tremendously had also the power to shake him into anger. Should there not be evil as well as good?

III. AFFINITIES

If Lawrence knowingly walked in the same road with Whitman, he also took some ways without sign or greeting. A reader of both poets will be struck by resemblances (not derivations), a way of poetry that comes logically from the primary assumptions common to both. A poem of the pulsing moment will be shaped out of the brown and many-leaved earth. One may lay his hand on feather and fur and know it alive. This I would call immediacy: first of all in the extraordinary sense of physical realization and involvement in the matter of the poem; second, in the equally close touch of the poet's hand and the sound of his voice. In both Whitman and Lawrence, we have the intense physical experience, and the feeling that the poet-speaker is at our side.

Whitman said he began his studies with the wonder of the physical world—"The mere fact consciousness, these forms, the power of motion. . . ." These he celebrated in songs like "Salut au Monde" and "We Two, How Long We Were Fool'd." So the poetry of Whitman became the eternal delight in the fact of life, even his enumerations, catalogues, and inclusions attesting the magic of the physical thing. For one example, recall "Spontaneous Me" with its deep-turning exultation, including

The hairy wild-bee that murmurs and hankers up and down, that gripes the full-grown lady-flower, curves upon her with amorous firm legs, take his will of her, and holds himself tremulous and tight till he is satisfied;
The wet of woods through the early hours,
Two sleepers at night lying close together as they sleep, one with an arm slanting down across and below the waist of the other,
The smell of apples, aromas from crush'd sage-plant, mint, birch-bark,
The boy's longings, the glow and pressure as he confides to me what he was dreaming,
The dead leaf whirling its spiral whirl and falling still and content to the ground,
The no-form'd stings that sights, people, objects, sting me with,
The hubb'd sting of myself . . .

or the closely detailed realizations of passages in "Song of Myself": the Negro drayman holding four horses, sun on his blue shirt and polished limbs; the leap in the hay barn,

I jump from the cross-beams and seize the clover and timothy,
And roll head over heels and tangle my hair full of wisps;

visions of the prospector "Scorch'd ankle-deep by the hot sand"; places where "the rattlesnake suns his flabby length on a rock," or "the alligator in his tough pimples sleeps by the bayou," or "the fin of the shark cuts like a black chip out of the water." Whitman has an extravagance of such precision-prints of the world's motley. Lawrence has not so many, but he is sometimes even more completely immediate and involved in his most physical poems, those for example in *Birds, Beasts and Flowers,* or in scenes of the simmering marsh of "River Roses," of the golden woman bathing by a morning window ("Gloire de Dijon"), of priests in gold and black, and the black-scarved faces of the women ("Giorno Dei Morti"). Lawrence has some of the richest physical poems anywhere. Even leafing at random, one finds the peach stone and pomegranate, fish with a whorled tail and "water wetly on fire in the grates of your gills"; bats "that hang themselves up like an old rag"; snake that "flickered his tongue like a forked night on the air, so black"; "monolithic water-buffaloes, like old, muddy stones with hair on them"; eagle that may "pick the red smoky heart from a rabbit"; and the crown of all, the tortoise poems that are a slow, close watch over determined mortality from the bony shell ("a tiny, fragile, half-animate bean") to the last

> Strange, faint coition yell
> Of the male tortoise at extremity. . . .

The lyrical landscapes of the novels are in the poems, too—as in "Autumn at Taos," looking at

> . . . the rounded sides of the squatting Rockies,
> Tigress brindled with aspen,
> Jaguar-splashed, puma-yellow, leopard-livid slopes of America.

—It is like Whitman gone West.

Perhaps the poetry of Lawrence is so physically complete because he had the gift of identification, though not in Whitman's larger, more allegorical sense. The poetry of Whitman creates a figure that includes all, becomes all, as in "Salut au Monde" or the dramatic "I am the man, I suffer'd, I was there." Identification was a part of Whitman's technique. With Lawrence it was a natural way of realization, and he made a point of such sympathy in *Fantasia of the Unconscious:*

. . . between an individual and any external object with which he has an affective connection, there exists a definite vital flow, as definite and concrete as the electric current whose polarized circuit sets our tram-cars running and our lamps shining. . . . there is still a circuit. My dog, my canary has a polarized connection with me. Nay, the very cells in the ash-tree I loved as a child had a dynamic vibratory connection with the nuclei in my own centers of primary consciousness. . . .

If Lawrence's poetry (like Whitman's) is, at its best, the means by which one may become alive in the body of the world recreated, it is because knowing is in the self, not the mind. "It's no good looking at a tree, to know it," wrote Lawrence. "The only thing is to sit among the roots and nestle against its strong trunk, and not bother."

Another form of immediacy is the quality of endearment that can fuse poet and reader. Whitman, of course, made a particular point of establishing a person, a human voice to speak to the reader and a presence to hover at his side, as in "Crossing Brooklyn Ferry":

Closer yet I approach you . . .
Who knows, for all the distance, but I am as good as looking at you
  now, for all you cannot see me?

Or, in "Full of Life Now," "Be it as if I were with you. (Be not too certain but I am now with you.)" Although each must "tramp a perpetual journey" for himself, Whitman (in "Song of Myself") stays close by as comrade, guide, the insistent voice:

> I teach straying from me, yet who can stray from me?
> I follow you whoever you are from the present hour,
> My words itch at your ears till you understand them.

And Whitman concludes the poem, "I stop somewhere waiting for you." The "I" and "you" are paired throughout *Leaves of Grass*, and through this direct voice comes the magnetic conviction of reality:

> (I and mine do not convince by arguments, similes, rhymes,
> We convince by our presence.)

Although Lawrence does not speak to the reader with such complete and lordly conviction, he does use the magnetic voice that cuts away the sense of intervening distance. Lawrence begins his use of the direct poet-reader conversation in the poems at the close of *Look! We Have Come Through!* While many of the earlier poems are dramatically spoken to another figure, the reader has a sense of being addressed in the soliloquies of "New Heaven and Earth," "Manifesto," and "Frost Flowers." "Pomegranate," the first poem in *Birds, Beasts and Flowers*, opens with the strikingly Whitmanesque lines,

> You tell me I am wrong,
> Who are you, who is anybody to tell me I am wrong?
> I am not wrong.

"Peach" begins, "Would you like to throw a stone at me?/Here, take all that's left of my peach." It ends, "Here, you can have my peach stone." The talk continues through the volume with dramatic dialogue, sometimes irregular and fragmentary as in speech but always evocative, saying Here we are now, you and I and what this moment is. The poems in *Pansies* are drier, more discursive, occasionally flat, but even more in the tone of a speaker telling us all the Yes and the No of things—sometimes an angry, acid voice, not the rich exaltation of *Birds, Beasts and Flowers*, but one that gives a sharp and lively sense of man in action. In all, Lawrence's tone is generally frank and open, with something of that "perfect personal candor" which Whitman, in the 1855 Preface, said he admired.

In much of his poetry (particularly *Birds, Beasts and Flowers* and *Pansies*) Lawrence was the poet as prophet; and here again he had an affinity with Whitman, whose intention was to "project the history of the future": "Solitary, singing in the West, I strike up for a New World." Lawrence, too, had the idea of a new world, both in the general sense of greater human life and in the particular plan of establishing colonies to achieve the new life. It is perhaps due to Lawrence's "indignant temperament" [15] that where, in the spell of Whitman's incantation, his new world seemed possible, Lawrence's ideal appeared to most as no more than visionary madness. On the other hand, Whitman's joyous hope may occasionally strike one as naive and childlike in contrast with Lawrence's weary bitterness in *Pansies*. Yet it is unfair to Whitman to ignore his poems of attack. In "Respondez," for instance, he ironically reverses good and evil and slantly criticizes a civilization still uncleansed:

(Stifled, O days! O lands! in every public and private corruption!
Smother'd in thievery, impotence, shamelessness, mountain-high;

Brazen effrontery, scheming, rolling like ocean's waves around and
   upon you, O my days! my lands!
For not even those thunderstorms, nor fiercest lightnings of the war,
   have purified the atmosphere;)
—Let the theory of America still be management, caste, comparison!

Or in "I Sit and Look Out," Whitman knows the inhumanity of
abuse, jealousy, ruthlessness, war—"all the meanness and agony
without end. . . ." What both poets wanted was a new world in
which the quick of life will come through. The difference in the
poetry is that Whitman seemed to know; Lawrence first to hope,
and finally to despair. Lawrence's poetry is that of the unfulfilled
prophetic search. As Rebecca West wrote, "Lawrence travelled,
it seemed, to get a certain Apocalyptic vision of mankind that he
registered again and again and again, always rising to a pitch of
ecstatic agony." [16] He inveighed against the machine, against war,
against the desolation of insensitive man. He was indeed writing
of the waste land, but crying out like any prophet to wing
the ashes if he could. As he said of Whitman in his essay, he
too was trying to be "a great changer of the blood in the veins of
men."

In his prophetic role, Whitman created in *Leaves of Grass* an
archetypal personality. In his 1872 and 1876 Prefaces, he described
the book, in its intentions, as "the song of a great composite
Democratic Individual." His general object was to make "a type-
portrait for living, active, worldly, healthy Personality, objective
as well as subjective, joyful and potent, and modern and free."
As the "Poem of Identity," *Leaves of Grass* thus creates a total
ideal, larger and more inclusive than any single man. Here, I
think, is where a recognition of Lawrence's knowledge of and
correspondence with Whitman can do considerable service to an
evaluation of Lawrence's own artistry, and make irrelevant most
of the biographical gossip that has sometimes passed for criticism.
Is not Lawrence in both novels and poems creating the same kind
of "type-portrait" that Whitman planned? Of course, the Laurentian man is larger than life. He has stronger emotions, greater
exaltations, more lavish expression than can be expected of the
ordinary human being. No doubt Lawrence himself knew very
well that he was actually writing in some ideal terms, although
he used both autobiography and biography for the kind of authen-

ticity that appealed to him. He let it slip, I think in a remark
recorded by Dorothy Brett: In New Mexico one day Lawrence,
his wife Frieda, and Brett were cantering along on their horses,
Frieda on the large gray Azule. She called out to Lawrence:

'Oh, it's wonderful; wonderful to feel his great thighs moving, to
feel his powerful legs!'
'Rubbish, Frieda!' you call back. 'Don't talk like that. You have
been reading my books: you don't feel anything of the sort!' [17]

Rubbish, he said. You don't really feel it. You got it from my
books—in which man is ideal and larger than life. Not many (or
any) of us can have our blood changed that much. . . . Lawrence, like Whitman, wrote in hyperbole. They *created* the figure
of man as the half-god, the better to see his possibilities. Even to
approach the gods is a destiny to be desired.

Lawrence says in his essay in *Studies in Classic American Literature* that Whitman is a very great poet of the end of life, life
which moves in a pattern of merge into woman ("Children of
Adam"), into comrades ("Calamus"), into death; and he quotes
from "Out of the Cradle Endlessly Rocking." In another curious
likeness, Lawrence, too, is a great poet of death, with the culmination of his poetry in the sheer magical richness of "Bavarian
Gentians" and "The Ship of Death" in *Last Poems*. Here is the
somber, musing, dark-bright incantation which Whitman also had
in "Out of the Cradle" and "When Lilacs Last in the Dooryard
Bloom'd." Lawrence repeats the message of Whitman's grey-
brown bird in "Lilacs" ("Come lovely and soothing death") with
his own "Song of Death":

> Sing the song of death, O sing it!
> for without the song of death, the song of life
> becomes pointless and silly.

Where still we sail, the ship of death must go darkly, "for we
cannot steer, and have no port." The prospect of Whitman's journey to "that inaccessible land" in "Darest Thou Now O Soul" is
in the same terms:

Walk out with me toward the unknown region,
Where neither ground is for the feet nor any path to follow?

No map there, nor guide,
Nor voice sounding, nor touch of human hand,
Nor face with blooming flesh, nor lips, nor eyes, are in that land.

"For we are bound where mariner has not yet dared to go," he says in "Passage to India," "And we will risk the ship, ourselves and all." Yet the soul arrives at last somewhere in time and space, as it does in Lawrence's poem. Whitman and Lawrence were great poets of death because they had a preternaturally strong sense of life. By the old contrarieties, they were thus given the most poignant sense of death—the melancholy seen of none, says Keats, save him who bursts joy's grape upon his palate fine. So death must be drawn in the life-images of fire and generation. Bavarian gentians are the "Torch-flowers of the blue-smoking darkness," at "the marriage of the living dark." [18]

D. H. Lawrence did not want the merging and the allness that he saw in Whitman's poetry. Yet he too had a sense of a cosmos to which all belong and whose shape may be seen in the heightened intensity of the poetic imagination. Whitman called it the great scheme of mystic evolution. Lawrence preferred to see it as unfolding, rather than evolving; death reverses,

for the cosmos even in death is like a dark whorled shell
whose whorls fold round to the core of soundless silence and pivotal
    oblivion. . . .

The sun itself is "pivoted/upon a core of pure oblivion." The unfolding and the refolding is the motion of one life:

All flows, and every flow is related to every other flow.
Flowers and sapphires and us, diversely streaming.

Space is alive and wandering, and the wild heart of space is the sun of suns, the mystery of all which may pulse in the life of man. To Lawrence, this life-force became synonymous with God. His revisions of "Corot" for the *Collected Poems* (1928) changed "God" to "life," but in his last poems the old words of Lord and God slipped easily from his pen. The meaning, though, was still the cosmic force of which all creation is the sign.

The earth leans its weight on the sun, and the sun on the sun of suns.
Back and forth goes the balance and the electric breath.

Life direct is

Contact with the sun of suns
that shines somewhere in the atom, somewhere pivots the curved
   space. . . .

Life is to receive the generative force of the cosmos, "the godhead of energy that cannot tell lies." Man's need to be contained
in the cosmic rhythms is in many ways the whole theme of
Lawrence—not merging, but connecting, "feeling oneself unin-
terrupted in the rooted connection/with the centre of things."
Therefore the lonely ones are those who

. . . must have lost something,
lost some living connection with the cosmos, out of themselves,
lost their life-flow
like a plant whose roots are cut.

It may be that death alone can then

. . . melt the detached life back
through the dark Hades at the roots of the tree
into the circulating sap, once more, of the tree of life.

D. H. Lawrence knew that the final mystery for man in the
cosmos meant the archetypal search, the journey of the soul on
the open road which Whitman had so humanly dramatized. The
key images in Whitman are the sea, the ship, the passage into the
new world of both America and the Soul. For Lawrence, too, this
eternal exploration was man's destiny and his only possible glory.
(It is at least curious, if not symbolic, that on the last day of his
life Lawrence was reading the life of Columbus.) [19] Both Whitman and Lawrence wrote of a mystery beyond the usual sense,
though they sometimes took characteristically different ways to
represent it. In "Song of Myself" and "Passage to India" Whitman goes by close involvement of the self with all things and
with the "other" and by a release is projected *outward* to the
mysteries: "I depart as air, I shake my white locks at the runaway
sun," he says in "Song of Myself." "I bequeath myself to the dirt
to grow from the grass I love." In his early "New Heaven and
Earth," Lawrence also has a vision which inverts the usual mystical experience. His release, he says, was *from* the enormity of

self, bound and constricted in its identification with the known world, to the glory of possibilities in the unknown, or the recognition of "otherness" through the meeting of man and woman. He is on the shore of a new world, a continent of green and illumined streams in which he is drowned with the strong current of life, down to the source where life is kindled again at the core of utter mystery. Lawrence generally sees the search as an *inward* movement, with the phoenix-release in fire at the heart of a mystic darkness. "Bavarian Gentians" has the same direction.

These are some of the relationships that may help to define Lawrence through Whitman. Those who read both poets closely will not be surprised to find more—Lawrence's dark sun in Whitman, or Whitman's sea images in Lawrence, or essays on manly love in both; for Whitman somewhere along the way had got into Lawrence's blood. Although Lawrence had read Whitman very early, we may safely say that between 1917 and 1923 he made a much more thorough study of the older poet; and that, corresponding with the writing of his Preface to *New Poems* and his work on the Whitman essay for *Studies in Classic American Literature*, he recognized and heightened the themes they had in common. The revisions Lawrence eventually made in his poems when he was preparing the collected edition of 1928 all sharpen and define the physical, sexual, and cosmic themes implicit in the earlier forms. Now of course by 1928 Lawrence was simply a better poet than he was in 1913, and he knew the effect of vivid exactness. Yet his revisions can be instructive. For example, in "Come Spring, Come Sorrow" he changed the vague "sky and earth and water and live things everywhere" of the original "Mating" (*Amores*) to "hidden bodies mating everywhere," and "begets the year in us" to "plants his new germ in us." The first version of a line in "Lilies in the Fire" (*Love Poems and Others*), "God stepping down to earth in one white stride," was changed to the more physically mystic "God stepping through our loins in one bright stride." Stanzas on cosmic creation—the womb of worlds—were added to "Red Moon-Rise" (*Love Poems and Others*), and to "Dreams Old and Nascent" (*Amores*): "And what is life, but the swelling and shaping the dream in the flesh!"

The *Leaves* of D. H. Lawrence were his own, yet they might lie with perfect naturalness in Whitman's grass. Here is the land where the poetry of Lawrence belongs. Like Whitman's, it is the poetry of the instant Now, man alive in the immediate earth and the cosmos; the poetry of inclusion (body and soul, good and evil); the poetry of prophecy and the initiation of mystery. Lawrence and Whitman were bardic poets who performed in the priesthood of physical mysticism. And there is a final likeness. Haunted by Whitman, angry with Whitman, loving Whitman— Lawrence called him the "great leader," yet "fearfully mistaken." Perhaps Lawrence would be amused (or did he already know?) that many people think *him* fearfully mistaken—but able to strike the fire that makes him, in spite of all, a very great leader.

BERNICE SLOTE

After this book had gone to the printer, the publication of A D. H. Lawrence Miscellany, *edited by Harry T. Moore (Carbondale: Southern Illinois University Press, 1959), added three more critical references to the Whitman influence on the Lawrence poems. See especially "Black Flowers: A New Light on the Poetics of D. H. Lawrence" by Christopher Hassall, as well as the essays by A. Alvarez and Harold Bloom.*

The Dance of Rapture

We ought to dance with rapture that we should be
alive and in the flesh.

D. H. LAWRENCE

MUCH has been written about Walt Whitman's influence on
modern poets as diverse as Carl Sandburg and Hart Crane, but
little attention has been given to his contribution to the novel.
The influence on Thomas Wolfe's style of frenzied abundance
seems plain enough, and E. M. Forster calls attention to thematic
parallels by titling his novel about British-Indian tensions *A Passage
to India*, after one of Whitman's great poems.

But Whitman's greatest imaginative descendant in the novel,
D. H. Lawrence, has not been recognized for the heir that he is
to the poet's central vision. Shortly after Lawrence's death in
1930, J. Middleton Murry wrote his personal, violently involved
exposé of Lawrence (*Son of Woman*), and saw, rightly, that in
Lawrence's treatment of Whitman in *Studies in Classic American Literature*, Lawrence identified himself with the poet in his
progression from the merge of man-woman love, to the merge
of man-man love, to, finally, the last great merge in death. Murry
perceptively comments, "For Lawrence was one of the great
mergers, who love to extremes; and in Whitman he finds a comrade and a forerunner." [1]

99

But Murry, probably because he was so taken with contrasting a sexually obsessed Lawrence of the novels with a sexually impotent Lawrence of real life, did not go beyond this intuitive insight into a Whitman-Lawrence comradeship. And in the more recent criticism, which has largely passed by now from the hands of those who were personally involved with Lawrence to those who know him only through his work, Whitman is generally ignored or, where recognized, curiously denied.

Probably the most distinguished of Lawrence critics, and certainly one who has been instrumental in promoting Lawrence's reputation as a novelist of major stature central to the tradition of English literature, is F. R. Leavis. In his book on Lawrence, Leavis dismisses Whitman with a judgment that seems also straining to demolish: "As for Whitman, with his expansive 'Camerado!,' his large democratic embraces, his 'ache' of 'amorous love,' and his enthusiasm for merging, it would be difficult to think of a writer more radically unlike Lawrence (whose treatment of him in *Studies in Classic American Literature* should alone have been enough to warn anyone off the assimilation)." [2] The language is energetic if not violent, and seems, when closely examined, a little uneasy in its exaggerated assurance. And furthermore, the comment is misleading: Lawrence's treatment of Whitman in his work on American literature is not, as Leavis implies, simple and obvious, but complex and ambivalent.

I. THE PULSATING, CARNAL SELF

Leavis' views are difficult to comprehend in the face of a number of Lawrence's comments on Whitman. As early as 1919, in describing the kind of poetry he was trying to write (in the Preface to *New Poems*), Lawrence ruled out past and future and labeled it the poetry of the "immediate present" or of the "incarnate Now." Whitman's poetry, he said, was the best poetry of this kind: "The clue to all his utterance lies in the sheer appreciation of the instant moment, life surging itself into utterance at its very well-head. . . . The quivering nimble hour of the present, this is the quick of Time. This is the immanence. The quick of the universe is the *pulsating, carnal self*, mysterious and palpable." And in this same year, Lawrence wrote in a letter to a friend: ". . . you are a great admirer of Whitman, R. said. So

am I. But I find in his Calamus & Comrades one of the clues to a
real solution—the new adjustment. I believe in what he calls
'manly love,' the real implicit reliance of one man on another:
as sacred a union as marriage: only it must be deeper, more ultimate than emotion and personality, cool separateness and yet the
ultimate reliance." [3]

These two early comments testify to the strength of the impact
of Whitman on Lawrence's imagination. Lawrence's allegiance
was not easily granted to any of his literary predecessors; indeed,
his constant impulse was to scorn and deny them. One of his
passionately wrought, spontaneously alive sentences—"The quick
of the universe is the *pulsating, carnal self,* mysterious and palpable"—seems not only to strike deep into Whitman, but also
into Lawrence—and not just into the poet Lawrence but also, and
primarily, into Lawrence the novelist. Moreover, Lawrence's insight into the real meaning of Whitman's "Calamus" and acceptance of its doctrine of "manly love" are highly relevant to a
major theme running through all of Lawrence's fiction.

Innumerable references by Lawrence to Whitman may be
cited, all of them suggesting the prophetic role which the novelist
always, if sometimes reluctantly, assigned the poet. In "Pan in
America" (*Phoenix*), Lawrence named Whitman's "Song of
Myself" as an American embodiment of the Great God Pan; in
"David," he cryptically connected the Michelangelo Florentine
sculpture with Whitman's "Calamus"; in "America, Listen to
Your Own," he listed Whitman as one of the authentic voices; in
"The Proper Study," he envisioned Whitman with Jesus and St.
Francis as walking the same "great road." In one strange essay,
"Democracy," which remained unpublished during his life,
Lawrence placed *Leaves of Grass*, with its simultaneous emphasis
on the Average and the Individual, at the center of his discussion.
The piece reads like a lovers' quarrel, full of both attraction and
repulsion. In a typical passage, Lawrence confessed: "In Whit-
man, at all times, the true and the false are so near, so interchange-
able, that we are almost inevitably left with divided feelings."
Lawrence's profoundest feelings were clearly divided, erratically
alternating between violent rejection and passionate acceptance.

But Lawrence's major comment on Whitman appears in *Studies
in Classic American Literature* (1923). Beginning with his theory

that "out of a pattern of lies art weaves the truth," Lawrence dashes and darts his way through the major American writers, recklessly undressing and exposing, concluding finally with Whitman. And clearly with Whitman Lawrence is an offspring wrestling to reject an embarrassing parent. The first half of the essay is a curious attack:

> Your mainspring is broken, Walt Whitman. The mainspring of your own individuality. And so you run down with a great whirr, merging with everything.
> You have killed your isolate Moby Dick. You have mentalized your deep sensual body, and that's the death of it.

But about midway through the essay, Lawrence shifts abruptly to the lyricism of a love poem:

> Whitman, the great poet, has meant so much to me. Whitman, the one man breaking a way ahead. Whitman, the one pioneer. And only Whitman. No English pioneers, no French. No European pioneer-poets. In Europe the would-be pioneers are mere innovators. The same in America. Ahead of Whitman, nothing. Ahead of all poets, pioneering into the wilderness of unopened life, Whitman. Beyond him, none.

In context this passage seems like an unpremeditated, spontaneous —even reluctant—confession.

And after it Lawrence attempts to explain his astonishing, wide-sweeping claims for the American poet:

> Whitman was the first to break the mental allegiance. He was the first to smash the old moral conception, that the soul of man is something "superior" and "above" the flesh. . . .
> His was a morality of the soul living her life, not saving herself. Accepting the contact with other souls along the open way, as they lived their lives. Never trying to save them. As leave try to arrest them and throw them in gaol. The soul living her life along the incarnate mystery of the open road.

In this essay, with its flippant tone of reproval alternating with its intimate tone of shy adulation, Lawrence appears determined to be one of those independent souls traveling Whitman's open road: he will be a comrade in the "incarnate mystery," but he will never merge and lose his identity. In carefully limiting his

102

love of Whitman, Lawrence seems to be struggling counter to a strong emotional magnetism.

II. THE FORM AND THE SUBJECT

Before noting in detail the intricate relationship of Whitman's poetry and Lawrence's novels, we might well glance at some broad parallels in emotional constitution, temperament, and fundamental outlook.

A good initial clue to these parallels, ironically, appears in T. S. Eliot's distaste for both writers. Eliot said that he had to conquer an aversion to both Whitman's form and his subject matter before being able to read him. And he said of Lawrence that he was an ignorant man who was frequently wrong ("drawing the wrong conclusions in his conscious mind from the insights which came to him from below consciousness") and who often wrote badly.[4]

No doubt Eliot felt in both Whitman and Lawrence the absence of the restraining and shaping hand of the artist. Both poet and novelist scorned the purely esthetic, the purely literary, and their work—Whitman's free, even wild, verse and Lawrence's misshapen, chaotic novels—give the impression of loss of control if not of frenzied abandon.

But this kind of "ignorance" was probably not so repugnant to Eliot as the "ignorance" involved in such intense celebration of the physical as found in Whitman and Lawrence. Whitman was in love with the body of the world. He confessed in an opening poem in *Leaves of Grass* that he was so awed by the "forms, the power of motion,/The least insect or animal, the senses, eyesight, love" that his sole desire was to "stop and loiter all the time to sing it in ecstatic songs." Born on rural Long Island, early an inhabitant of populous Brooklyn, Whitman embraced the sheer physicality of both country and city in his work, celebrating alternately, and with heady excitement, the quiet retreat of a still, hidden pond and the hum and blab of a busy city street.

Lawrence seemed also to yield this intensely sensitive response to things physical, which developed, in his writing, into an acute sense of place. Whether in the English countryside, Italy, Australia, or Mexico, Lawrence seemed to respond sensuously to the physical locale and to embody the response vividly in his work. One has but to see Lawrence's childhood home in the Midlands—the dismal, dreary little company row-house where he was born, the view of the nearby hills blighted by the great heaps of dead earth-bowels—to understand something of his restless search over the face of the earth for a land with a living spirit. And after seeing the gashed and wounded Midlands, one can feel with Lawrence his sympathetic vibration when he encounters the ancient and somehow unviolated earth of Italy or New Mexico, of Sicily or Taos.

This keen attunement to the physical manifested itself in the work of both writers in a similar response to people. Throughout *Leaves of Grass* Whitman conveys a sense of excitement in the simple scenes of individuals engaged in their natural activities:

The young fellow hoeing corn, the sleigh-driver driving his six horses
    through the crowd,
The wrestle of wrestlers, two apprentice-boys, quite grown, lusty,
    good-natured, native-born, out on the vacant lot at sundown
    after work. . . .

Lawrence writes with this same sense of excitement—sense of engagement—about people, especially in his travel books, but also in his novels. The narrator introduces George Saxton on the opening page of *The White Peacock:* "My Friend was a young farmer, stoutly built, brown eyed, with a naturally fair skin burned dark and freckled in patches" (3).* George's physical presence, like that of other Lawrence characters, is intensely felt and evoked throughout the novel; when the narrator sees George at work in the fields, he pauses: "The movement of active life held all my attention, and when I looked up, it was to see the motion of his limbs and his head, the rise and fall of his rhythmic body, and the rise and fall of the slow waving peewits" (335).

Though there is this overwhelming engagement with the physical world in both Whitman and Lawrence, there is at the same time the constant effort to discover through it or in it the lurking, elusive spiritual. Whitman wrote in the 1855 Preface, as though in warning to himself, that the poet must "indicate more than the beauty and dignity which always attach to dumb real

* See Notes and Bibliography.

objects": he must "indicate the path between reality and their souls." Lawrence, though he always began with the land and the people, recurringly discovered in his sense of place a presence out of the past that was more than merely physical. Both writers probed deeply into human relationships to question—or discover —what lay beneath the surface, or beyond the physical, or within the sexual.

Whitman and Lawrence seem endowed with fundamentally similar sensibilities. It is not irrelevant that both writers have been accused of abnormally strong attachments to their mothers or of sublimating in their art their sexual frustrations or of presenting a robust self-image of masculine potency which is largely wish-fulfillment rather than reality. Whatever the truth of these charges, they suggest a basic similarity in personalities as revealed both in their art and in their lives.

Moreover, Whitman and Lawrence seem to have encountered experience with identical strategy. One pre-Freudian and the other post-Freudian, the two are startlingly close in their concept of a purified personal unconscious. Although Whitman's language is romantic, his assertions appear psychologically at one with Lawrence's. After the sexual culmination dramatized in sections 28 and 29 of "Song of Myself," Whitman writes:

(What is less or more than a touch?)

Logic and sermons never convince,
The damp of the night drives deeper into my soul.

(Only what proves itself to every man and woman is so,
Only what nobody denies is so.)

Had he had the opportunity, Whitman would have quarreled with Freud for turning the unconscious into a kind of sewer designed to contain all of man's nastiness. Whitman's term— soul—suggests the reverence the poet held for the overwhelming impulses that became their own proof of truth as they arose from personal depths and burst forth in conscious feeling.

Lawrence did quarrel with Freud, in two passionately written volumes: *Psychoanalysis and the Unconscious* and *Fantasia of the Unconscious*. Like Whitman, Lawrence was intensely concerned with purifying that area of the self which he thought had been maligned, if not desecrated, by others. Lawrence conceived of a "pristine unconscious, in which all our genuine impulse arises" to replace "that sack of horrors which psychoanalysts would have us believe is source of motivity. The Freudian unconscious is the cellar in which the mind keeps its own bastard spawn. The true unconscious is the well-head, the fountain of real motivity." In elaborating his conception of the unconscious, Lawrence finally returned to that same old-fashioned word that Whitman had used—the soul: "But life is a general force, whereas the unconscious is essentially single and unique in each individual organism; it is the active, self-evolving soul bringing forth its own incarnation and self-manifestation. Which incarnation and self-manifestation seems to be the whole goal of the *unconscious* soul: the whole goal of life."

Whatever the differences of vocabulary, Lawrence and Whitman believed in the purity and the truth of the primal impulses, and they dramatized in their art the instinctual, spontaneous man of the senses as a being superior to the idealized, abstracted man of cerebration.

III. THE SELF, THE WOMAN, THE MAN

Central to the work of both Whitman and Lawrence is the search for the prototype new man. In this search both artists made extended redefinitions of the selfhood of the individual; and both reassessed the nature of the relationship of man with woman and of man with man. In the foundation poems and clusters of *Leaves of Grass*—"Song of Myself," "Children of Adam," and "Calamus"—Whitman set about systematically creating the prototype "New World" personality. Throughout his novels, Lawrence also seemed attempting to delineate a new personality—startlingly similar to Whitman's. On one occasion, in *Fantasia of the Unconscious*, Lawrence tried to formulate, in direct prose and without the complexities of fictional art, his version of such a man.

In an opening section of Whitman's great, long poem, "Song of Myself," the poet-narrator experiences a sensual fusion of body and soul as a prelude to his extended mystical journey. In this passage, the newly awakened consciousness of the poet seems to be given a physical location in the poet's body. The poet addresses his soul:

I mind how once we lay such a transparent summer morning,
How you settled your head athwart my hips and gently turn'd over
    upon me,
And parted the shirt from my bosom-bone, and plunged your tongue
    to my bare-stript heart,
And reach'd till you felt my beard, and reach'd till you held my feet.

This awakening consciousness is remote indeed from the poet's
mind. It seems to concentrate its intensity somewhere near his
middle.

Moreover, when it is realized that "Song of Myself" is, among
other things, a song of the achievement of selfhood through development of sexual identity, as in the autoerotic passages of sections 28–30, then it becomes clear that Whitman's location for
the central self cannot be far from Lawrence's in *Fantasia:* "Now,
your solar plexus . . . is where you are you. It is your first and
greatest and deepest center of consciousness. . . . At your solar
plexus you are primarily conscious: there, behind your stomach.
There you have the profound and pristine conscious awareness
that you are you. . . . There is your first and deepest seat of
awareness. There you are triumphantly aware of your own individual existence in the universe. Absolutely there is the keep and
central stronghold of your triumphantly-conscious self." Like
Whitman, Lawrence avoided the mind and the mental processes
in defining the essential self. His solar plexus, a complex of primarily instinctual responses, is located somewhere in man's middle—surely very near to that physical center of Whitman where
his soul settled athwart him to awaken his deepest being, causing
him to burst forth in the song of self.

Immediately after establishing the identity of self in *Leaves of
Grass,* Whitman turns to the man-woman relationship. "Children of Adam" dramatizes a return to the sexual innocence of
Adam and Eve before the Fall. In a program poem near the beginning of this cluster, Whitman announces his determination
to sing of this forbidden subject even though he must sing alone:

From pent-up aching rivers,
From that of myself without which I were nothing,
From what I am determin'd to make illustrious, even if I stand sole
    among men,

From my own voice resonant, singing the phallus,
Singing the song of procreation.

All of the poems of "Children of Adam" celebrate some aspect
of the sexual experience; and the poem which by sheer length
dominates the section, "I Sing the Body Electric," asserts the
divinity of the body aroused to new life through phallic or procreative consciousness.

As Whitman describes man's sexual initiation in woman as
a rebirth ("after the child is born of woman, man is born of
woman"), Lawrence analyzes the man-woman relationship in
a chapter of *Fantasia* entitled "The Birth of Sex"; and, in his
search for the terms in which to define precisely the nature of
the feelings during the sexual experience, Lawrence falls back on
a poetic vocabulary—close to Whitman's:

> But what is the experience? Untellable. Only, we know something.
> We know that in the act of coition the *blood* of the individual man,
> acutely surcharged with intense vital electricity,—we know no word,
> so say "electricity," by analogy—rises to a culmination, in a tre-
> mendous magnetic urge towards the magnetic blood of the female.
> The whole of the living blood in the two individuals forms a field
> of intense, polarized magnetic attraction. . . . A great flash of inter-
> change occurs, like an electric spark when two currents meet or
> like lightning out of the densely surcharged clouds.

In describing the strong, magnetic attraction, Lawrence is quite
close to Whitman's imagery of "I Sing the Body Electric," in
which the woman's body "attracts with fierce undeniable attraction": "Mad filaments, ungovernable shoots play out of it, the
response likewise ungovernable."

Both Whitman and Lawrence are acutely concerned with the
human relationship above and beyond the procreative man-
woman union. In the "Calamus" cluster, which immediately follows "Children of Adam" in *Leaves of Grass*, Whitman sings
the quiet, even shy, song of adhesiveness and comradeship. The
poems of "Calamus" dramatize the intensely passionate individual
attachment as well as the comradeship of the democratic land.
And, too, the poems suggest throughout a connection between
adhesiveness (the phrenological term for friendship) and creativity, as in "Sometimes with One I Love," which concludes:

"(I loved a certain person ardently and my love was not re-turn'd,/Yet out of that I have written these songs.)" In one poem Whitman distinguishes the "Calamus" relationship from the pro-creative relationship of "Children of Adam":

Fast-anchor'd eternal O love! O woman I love!
O bride! O wife! more resistless than I can tell, the thought of you!
Then separate, as disembodied or another born,
Ethereal, the last athletic reality, my consolation,
I ascend, I float in the regions of your love O man,
O sharer of my roving life.

From this and other poems, it is clear that Whitman views the "Calamus" relationship as the necessary complement to the man-woman relationship of "Children of Adam." The male relation-ship not only bestows a personal fulfillment, but becomes the essential component of a genuine, indissoluble, magnetic democ-racy. The "Calamus" plant, a rare kind of "grass" with "pink-tinged root" and "emblematic and capricious blades," emerges as a phallic symbol to serve as the token of this exalted relationship.

Like Whitman, Lawrence envisions a male relationship which serves to complement the relationship with woman, and he pre-sents it as necessary to the completion of the individual. After fulfillment with woman, says Lawrence in *Fantasia*, the man craves a "new collective activity. . . . a new polarized con-nection with other beings, other men. . . . A new, passionate polarity springs up between men who are bent on the same ac-tivity, the polarity between man and woman sinks to passivity." Lawrence, like Whitman, insists on a fundamental difference in these two basic relationships. Lawrence asks: "Is this new polar-ity, this new circuit of passion between comrades and co-workers, is this also sexual? It is a vivid circuit of polarized passion. Is it hence sex?" And Lawrence answers: "It is not." But Lawrence insists on this "grand consummation for men, this mingling of many with one great impassioned purpose." And he warns: "I am sure that the ultimate, greatest desire in men is this desire for great *purposive* activity. When man loses his deep sense of pur-posive, creative activity, he feels lost, and is lost. When he makes the sexual consummation the supreme consummation, even in his *secret* soul, he falls into the beginnings of despair." Like Whitman, Lawrence thus places the camerado attachment above and beyond the man-woman relationship.

As Lawrence hints by the insistence of his denial, this "Calamus" theme in his work (and in Whitman's) is easily open to sexual interpretation. And indeed, both writers, either directly or indirectly, have suggested some subterranean connection with the physical. But the sexual reading is too simple. Indeed, the scoffing reader may if he wishes reduce all the celebration of the self to autoeroticism; and he may reduce the song of procreation to a heterosexual obsession; and he may diminish the "Calamus" emotion to a homosexual impulse. But the reader who thus dismisses both Whitman and Lawrence has distorted life, as well as the two artists, in order to reduce it, and them, to an absurd simplicity.

IV. FROM FIRST TO LAST

To measure the full impact of Whitman on Lawrence's imagination, it is most illuminating to survey Lawrence's dozen or so novels with a glance at the major, as well as some of the minor, themes. Such a survey cannot be easily condensed without becoming almost meaninglessly general. We are confronted not only by the unwieldy bulk of the novel form but also by the almost staggering output of a writer who, though he died young, seems to have written through life without pause. In dealing with Lawrence, in diving deep for the themes that are of particular interest to a Whitman reader, it is sometimes necessary to risk becoming lost in the intricacies of plots and labyrinths of characters.

In order to maintain some semblance of direction in this journey through Lawrence's narratives, I have not departed from the chronological development, but within chronology I have grouped the novels in as meaningful a way as possible. The first three novels (*The White Peacock*, 1911; *The Trespasser*, 1912; *Sons and Lovers*, 1913) are variations on a single theme involving the experiences of Lawrence's youth. The next two novels (*The Rainbow*, 1915; *Women in Love*, 1920) explore the lives, both outward and inward, of members of a single family through several generations. After these first five novels, all set in England, Lawrence looked abroad for his settings. In two stories (*The Lost Girl*, 1920; *Aaron's Rod*, 1922) he relied heavily on Italy for both scene and theme. In still two more (*Kangaroo*, 1923; *The Boy in the Bush*, 1924), he turned to Australia for setting and meaning. The next two works (*St. Mawr*, 1925; *The Plumed Serpent*, 1926) were closely related in their exaltation of the primitive, in one case focusing on a stallion, in the other on the ancient Indian culture of Mexico—the two works a culmination of one important thematic development in Lawrence's work. After these two novels, there was a pause until the appearance of *Lady Chatterley's Lover* (1928), which must stand alone as Lawrence's final fictional treatment of an obsessive theme. Two briefer works (*The Man Who Died*, 1929; *Apocalypse*, 1931) comprise a kind of summing up as well as an impassioned epilogue.

By following Lawrence through the entire body of his work in the order in which he lived and wrote it, we shall not only catch glimpses of Whitman's presence, but we shall also see the broad outlines of a vital and dynamic twentieth-century vision.

V. "UTTERING JOYOUS LEAVES"

Lawrence's first three novels, *The White Peacock* (1911), *The Trespasser* (1912), and *Sons and Lovers* (1913), appear to form the first unit of his work, the last of these novels bringing to a climax Lawrence's exploitation of the autobiographical materials of his youth.

The White Peacock seems to lack focus, the title itself a semi-private symbol functioning only erratically in the novel. But the symbolic peacock is obscurely related to the recurrent failure in the man-woman relationships of the book. Though the setting is the idyllic farmlands of the English countryside, the human condition is far from ideal. Rich Leslie Tempest loves Lettie Beardsley, but Lettie is strongly attracted to farmer's son George Saxton. When Lettie marries Leslie, George marries his rather plain cousin, Meg. Although the narrator of the book, Cyril Beardsley, vaguely courts George's sister, Emily, she ends up marrying farmer Tom Renshaw, and Cyril ends up single. No one achieves the promise of happiness that life seemed to hold in childhood. Leslie becomes absorbed in public life and Lettie becomes hard and cold. And George, the main figure of tragedy in the novel, is last seen near death from the delirium tremens of his excessive drinking.

The many failures to find happiness in the novel are all traceable to the personal violations of the deepest, instinctual self and the capitulation to forces generally destructive of the self. In effect, the individuals fail because they refuse to be "Children of Adam." The narrator, Cyril Beardsley, does not, on one level, become intricately involved in the complicated life he observes and reports. But on a submerged level, he is passionately involved, specifically in his relationship with George Saxton. In a chapter entitled "A Poem of Friendship," the two boys, while rubbing each other down after a vigorous swim, achieve a sense of intimacy unparalleled elsewhere in the novel. Cyril confesses: "It satisfied in some measure the vague, indecipherable yearning of my soul; and it was the same with him. When he had rubbed me all warm, he let me go, and we looked at each other with eyes of still laughter, and our love was perfect for a moment, more perfect than any love I have known since, either for man or woman" (340–341). This moment is one of the few in the entire novel which suggests fulfillment. But though the striking relationship of Cyril and George appears vital, it is, except for this one instance, generally muted throughout the book.

At one casual moment of description in *The White Peacock*, Cyril relates that in the garden the "trees were 'uttering joyous leaves'" (260–261). This phrase is more than a mere echo of one of Whitman's "Calamus" poems (italics mine):

I saw in Louisiana a live-oak growing,
All alone stood it and the moss hung down from the branches,
Without any companion it grew there *uttering joyous leaves* of dark
  green,
And its look, rude, unbending, lusty, made me think of myself.

The casual quotation is important, not only because it connects with the obscure friendship theme of the novel, but also because it confirms Lawrence's early and deep reading into the "Calamus" cluster of *Leaves of Grass*.

Lawrence's next novel, *The Trespasser*, though it appears to be a gain in organization and coherence, seems to be a loss in massive power and life. The story is simple. Siegmund MacNair, in his late thirties, his attachment to his wife grown threadbare, rebels by taking a seaside vacation with his young girl friend, Helena Verden. Most of the novel is taken up with the simple yet strangely complex experiences of love at the seaside. Upon return from the vacation, Siegmund, his mind considerably muddled by a severe sunburn, decides that he can no longer face the hostility of his wife and children. He hangs himself in his bedroom.

But *The Trespasser* is no simple love tragedy. In the midst of the love-retreat by the ocean's side, Siegmund encounters briefly an old acquaintance, one Hampson, who seems to function solely and singularly as the book's chorus. Hampson explains: "These deep, interesting women don't want *us;* they want the flowers of the spirit they can gather of us. We, as natural men, are more or less degrading to them and to their love of us; therefore they destroy the natural man in us—that is, us altogether" (108). What Hampson says seems applicable not only to Siegmund and his wife. But Siegmund instinctively understands that somehow it applies also to him and Helena. Even were he free, he knows deep within, he would never achieve that complete fulfillment with Helena for which he yearns. The ease with which Helena turns to another man after Siegmund's suicide suggests the shallowness of her attachment. Siegmund yearns to be Adam's son, but he is unable to find Eve's daughter—not even in Helena.

In *Sons and Lovers* Lawrence combined the massiveness and complexity of *The White Peacock* with the coherence and concentration of *The Trespasser* to create what is generally considered his masterpiece. Paul Morel is so fully possessed by his mother that he finds it impossible to establish a satisfying relationship with any girl. With Miriam he finds a spiritual communion that ultimately endangers his very being—she seems trying to suck out and absorb his soul. The mother, sensing that her grip on Paul's spirit is being loosened by Miriam, encourages her son in his new relationship with the married Clara Dawes, temporarily separated from her husband.

With Clara, Paul finds the experience for which he is searching:

And after such an evening [of love] they both were very still, having known the immensity of passion. They felt small, half afraid, childish, and wondering, like Adam and Eve when they lost their innocence and realized the magnificence of the power which drove them out of Paradise and across the great night and the great day of humanity. It was for each of them an initiation and a satisfaction. . . . If so great a magnificent power could overwhelm them, identify them altogether with itself, so that they knew they were only grains in the tremendous heave that lifted every grass-blade its little height, and every tree, and living thing, then why fret about themselves? . . . It seemed almost as if he had known the baptism of fire in passion, and it left him at rest [415–416].

It is perhaps a coincidence that the dominant imagery—Adam and Eve, the grass-blade, baptism in passion—is comprised of some of Whitman's key symbols. Whatever the cause, there is a striking similarity in the functioning of these symbols in both Whitman and Lawrence.

But Paul finds the relationship with Clara ultimately unsatisfactory because, though a kind of fulfillment, it is impersonal. Clara loses her individuality in the embrace and becomes simply Woman. Thus Paul fails to find a whole or enduring love. But after the death of his mother near the end of the novel, Paul decides against suicide and turns from death to life. What the future holds may be uncertain, but Paul turns toward it with determination. No doubt he will seek for the complete woman, combining the spiritual identity of Miriam with the physical reality of Clara. Only such a woman, descendant of Eve, can respond properly to his own aroused Adamic consciousness.

VI. THE PAST AND THE PRESENT

In *The Rainbow* (1915) and *Women in Love* (1920) Lawrence dramatizes three generations of a single family as he probes more deeply into the frustrations and failures in human relationships. The setting is still the familiar English countryside of Lawrence's youth, but the events are considerably altered.

The Rainbow, devoted about equally to farmer Tom Brangwen, his stepchild Anna Lensky, and her daughter Ursula Brangwen, gives the peculiar effect of abolishing time in favor of mere cyclic recurrence. Tom Brangwen, in his courtship of Lydia Lensky and their subsequent marriage, suffers the same frustrations as the next generation—and the next. At one point in the middle of his life Tom Brangwen questions: "What was missing in his life, that, in his ravening soul, he was not satisfied? He had had that friend at school, his mother, his wife, and Anna? What had he done? He had failed with his friend, he had been a poor son; but he had known satisfaction with his wife, let it be enough" (118). In the same way Will Brangwen, married to Tom's stepdaughter Anna Lensky, acutely feels an unfulfilled longing—"A woman, he must have a woman. And having a woman, he must be free of her" (175). But Anna, like her mother before her, seems triumphant over her man (one chapter is appropriately entitled "Anna Victrix"), and Will, like Tom before him, must adjust to the deeply felt inadequacy of his relationships: "He was aware of some limit to himself, of something unformed in his very being, of some buds which were not ripe in him. . . . He was unready for fulfillment. Something undeveloped in him limited him, there was a darkness in him which he *could* not unfold, which would never unfold in him" (197).

Will's daughter Ursula steps to the fore next in the novel, but once again there is the frustrating deficiency in human relationships. Although strongly attracted to a young army officer, Anton Skrebensky, Ursula cannot bring herself to marriage—some strange longing which she herself cannot understand will not let her. But after Anton departs for India and she discovers that she is carrying his child, she writes to him accepting his proposal. But by this time he has married the daughter of one of his superiors. After she loses the child in a severe illness, Ursula attempts to remake her life: "In everything she saw she grasped and groped to find the creation of the living God, instead of the old, hard barren form of bygone living" (466). The novel closes on Ursula observing in a brilliant rainbow the faint but clear promise of the future: "She knew that the sordid people who crept hard-scaled and separate on the face of the world's corruption were living still, that the rainbow was arched in their blood and would quiver to life in their spirit, that they would cast off their horny covering of disintegration, that new, clean, naked bodies would issue to a new germination, to a new growth, rising to the light and the wind and the clean rain of heaven" (467). Ursula's bright vision is in fact a vision of a new Garden, essentially like that broadly sketched in Whitman's "Children of Adam."

Women in Love continues Ursula's story, but does not bring entire fulfillment of the rainbow's promise. Though Ursula plays a prominent role in the book, central attention shifts from her to her new lover, Rupert Birkin. Again Lawrence is concerned with probing deeply into man-woman relationships to discover their potentialities and their inadequacies. Paralleling the love story of Ursula and Rupert is the affair of Ursula's sister, Gudrun, and Rupert's rich friend, Gerald Crich. Ursula and Rupert, after many complications and hesitancies, make a mystic discovery as they reach the utmost limits of their intertwined beings: "She [Ursula] had thought there was no source deeper than the phallic source. And now, behold, from the smitten rock of the man's body, from the strange marvellous flanks and thighs, deeper, further in mystery than the phallic source, came the floods of ineffable darkness and ineffable riches" (306). It is clear that this mystery beyond the phallic provides Ursula that element in her relationship with a man which she had always desired, but had always missed.

And it is clear, too, that this source and this mystery are alien to the relationship of Gudrun and Gerald Crich, and the absence brings about the destruction of their affair. Indeed, Gerald's deficiency, which he comes subtly to recognize, becomes so acute as to transfigure itself into the death wish and to cause, in some obscure way, his suicide.

But, strangely enough, Gerald's chief mourner is Rupert Birkin. For, like Cyril and George in *The White Peacock*, Rupert and Gerald have felt a strong attraction to each other, and in one instance, in a chapter entitled "Gladiatorial," have reached a rare depth of intimacy in a curious wrestling match. After exhaustion in vigorous physical contact, Gerald speaks to Rupert of love: "I've never felt it myself—not what I should call love. I've gone after women—and been keen enough over some of them. But I've never felt *love*. I don't believe I've ever felt as much *love* for a woman, as I have for you—not *love*. You understand what I mean?" (267–268). Rupert does understand, for he detects the deficiency in Gerald that is to destroy him. But, unfortunately, it is a deficiency not only in his affairs with women, but also, ultimately, in his relations with men, and even in his friendship with Rupert.

At the close of the novel, as Ursula and Rupert sit brooding over the tragedy of Gerald's death, Rupert confesses his longing for something he has not yet found. When Ursula asks, "Aren't I enough for you?" he replies: "You are enough for me, as far as a woman is concerned. You are all women to me. But I wanted a man friend, as eternal as you and I are eternal. . . . Having you, I can live all my life without anybody else, any other sheer intimacy. But to make it complete, really happy, I wanted eternal union with a man too: another kind of love." Ursula answers: "I don't believe it. . . . It's an obstinacy, a theory, a perversity. . . . You can't have it, because it's false, impossible." And Rupert concludes, "I don't believe that" (472–473).

The sense of incompleteness which haunts Rupert is, fundamentally, a longing for the "Calamus" attachment. He has achieved his individuality of self, and he has found with Ursula a "Children of Adam" relationship that leaves little to be desired. But as both Whitman and Lawrence believed, there is a level of consciousness beyond these—the adhesive, creative communion. Rupert almost finds it with Gerald. But now Gerald is dead, and his death has created a void.

VII. THE ACT OF SELF-DISCOVERY

Lawrence's next two novels, *The Lost Girl* (1920) and *Aaron's Rod* (1922), have in common their Italian orientation. Italy was much more than merely another country or a home in exile for Lawrence. Italy seemed to haunt his imagination. Somewhere in it, he believed, lurked the elusive secret for which he searched. Lawrence wrote two books about his Italian sojourns, *Twilight in Italy* (1916) and *Sea and Sardinia* (1921); and a third book, *Etruscan Places*, posthumously published in 1932, about the modern remains in Italy of the ancient Etruscan civilization, a lost way of instinctual life that Lawrence imagined and admired. The first two volumes have been erroneously labeled travel books. In fact, they are imaginative books of personal experiences and encounters in Italy. Lawrence sought among the simple, primitive people and their ancient ways for those qualities which he felt had been lost by modern civilization. At one point in *Sea and Sardinia*, Lawrence says: "So that for us to go to Italy and to penetrate into Italy is like a most fascinating act of self-discovery—back, back down the old ways of time. Strange and wonderful chords awake in us, and vibrate again after many hundreds of years of complete forgetfulness" (179).

This search "back down the old ways of time" for the vibrant, forgotten chords of man's being is the theme of both *The Lost Girl* and *Aaron's Rod*. *The Lost Girl* is one of Lawrence's rare attempts at humor in the traditional Dickensian vein, and is surprisingly successful. Alvina Houghton, the "lost" girl of the title, is the daughter of one of those men whose grandiose dreams of success are always punctuated by abysmal failures. In the small English mining town of Woodhouse, the Houghton family seems bypassed, and in Manchester House, the Houghton's declining commercial establishment, Alvina seems destined to develop into a proper lady—or frigid old maid—like her father's two assistants, Miss Frost and Miss Pinnegar. But into the country comes the fantastic traveling Natcha-Kee-Tawara Troupe, with Madame Rochard and four young men. And into Alvina's lonely, lost life enters one of the young men, the Italian Ciccio.

Gradually the tone of the novel changes as Alvina becomes attached to Ciccio, ultimately giving up all—becoming truly lost—in her desire to follow him. Somehow his dark Italian masculinity is able to bring back to full blaze the flame of response in Alvina that had burned so low as to be virtually extinguished. After marriage, Alvina accompanies Ciccio home to Italy, to the ancient family farm where life is lived on the most primitive level. There is a presence in the rugged Italian landscape that makes itself keenly felt. "How unspeakably lovely it was, no one could ever tell, the grand, pagan twilight of the valleys, savage, cold, with a sense of ancient gods who knew the right for human sacrifice. It stole away the soul of Alvina. She felt transfigured in it, clairvoyant in another mystery of life. . . . Coming over the brow of a heathy, rocky hillock, and seeing Ciccio beyond leaning deep over the plough, in his white shirt-sleeves following the slow, waving, moth-pale oxen across a small track of land turned up in the heathen hollow, her soul would go all faint, she would almost swoon with realization of the world that had gone before" (351–352). Ciccio and Alvina, like Ursula and Rupert in

Women in Love, have somehow in their relationship approached the mystic communion that lies beyond the phallic. Although the novel ends with Ciccio's departure for the war, there is the hope of strong determination in Alvina's request, "You'll come back to me," and in his simple reply, "I'll come back" (378). They will come together again in the ancient Garden they have discovered deep within themselves.

Like *The Lost Girl*, *Aaron's Rod* begins in England but soon becomes deeply involved in Italy, a movement with much the same thematic implications in both novels. Aaron Sisson one day decides that he is superfluous—a defeated outcast—in his own home, and, with his flute (his "rod"), walks out on his wife and children in search of human relationships that can give him what his family cannot or will not. He has come to a crucial stage in his belief: "Love was a battle in which each party strove for the mastery of the other's soul. So far, man had yielded the mastery to women. Now he was fighting for it back again. And too late, for the woman would never yield. But whether woman yielded or not, he would keep the mastery of his own soul and conscience and actions. . . . To be alone, to be oneself, not to be driven or violated into something which is not oneself, surely it is better than anything." Already Aaron thinks of the future and defines the relationship of a perfect union: "Let there be clean and pure division first, perfected singleness. That is the only way to final, living unison: through sheer, finished singleness" (123).

As Aaron progresses on his travels and becomes alternately entangled in and extricated from a variety of societies and affairs and personal encounters, he periodically studies through the failure of his marriage and carefully outlines in his imagination the perfect communion for which he searches. In describing to himself the vital elements of such a communion, he turns to Whitman:

One toils, one spins, one strives: just as the lily does. But like her, taking one's own life-way amidst everything, and taking one's own life-way alone. Love too. But there also, taking one's way alone, happily alone in all the wonders of communion, swept up on the winds, but never swept away from one's very self. Two eagles in mid-air, maybe like Whitman's Dalliance of Eagles. Two eagles in mid-air grappling, whirling, coming to their intensification of love-oneness there in mid-air. In mid-air the love consummation. But all the time each lifted on its own wings: each bearing itself up on its own wings at every moment of the mid-air love consummation. That is the splendid love-way [163].

In Whitman's poem (in the "By the Roadside" cluster of *Leaves of Grass*), after the "rushing amorous contact high in space together,/The clinching interlocking claws, a living, fierce, gyrating wheel," the two eagles rise "upward again on slow-firm pinions slanting, their separate diverse flight,/She hers, he his, pursuing." The poem is a small vignette combining the spirits of both "Song of Myself" and "Children of Adam"—as does, indeed, the primary theme of *Aaron's Rod*.

But Aaron fails to find the union which he seeks. His affair with the Marchesa in Florence, though it is brought to a climax, is by no means the "love consummation" of his dreams ("In the dark sightlessness of passion, she seemed almost like a clinging child in his arms" [254]). But there is another relationship, more important as well as more complex than any other in the novel, to which Aaron at the last finally turns. It is with his friend, Rawdon Lilly. Like Cyril and George of *The White Peacock*, or Rupert and Gerald of *Women in Love*, Rawdon and Aaron develop an intimacy far beyond the common in man-man relationships. Rawdon nurses Aaron through a serious illness, giving him a vigorous rubdown (recalling the swimming and wrestling scenes of the previous novels), and thereby restoring, almost mystically, his vitality.

The climax of this "Calamus" relationship is reached at the end of the novel, as Aaron and Rawdon Lilly meet in Florence. In a chapter appropriately entitled "Words," Lilly assumes a Whitmanian, prophetic stance and lectures Aaron on the necessity of preserving one's individuality in all relationships: "You *are* yourself and so *be* yourself. Stick to it and abide by it. . . . If your soul's urge urges you to love, then love. But always know that what you are doing is the fulfilling of your own soul's impulse. . . . Remember this, my boy: you've never got to deny the Holy Ghost which is inside you, your own soul's self. . . . But remember, your soul inside you is your only Godhead" (285–287). In his long harangue, Lilly gradually, if somewhat ob-

scurely, works his way around to the ideal in all human relationships, realizable only in the future. The fundamental fact which
must be recognized is the "deep power-urge" in man: "And there
will be profound, profound obedience in place of this love-crying,
obedience to the incalculable power-urge. And men must submit
to the greater soul in a man, for their guidance: and women must
submit to the positive power-soul in man, for their being" (289).
Thus each man must dominate in the man-woman relationship,
but each man, too, must offer a "deep, fathomless submission to
the heroic soul in a greater man." This complex of relationships
will render a man whole and will satisfy all of his deepest yearn-
ings. But when Aaron asks to whom he should submit, Lilly replies (in the concluding sentence of the novel): "Your soul will
tell you" (290).

VIII. THE GREAT DARK GOD

If *Aaron's Rod* seems not much of an advance over *Women
in Love* in clarifying the male relationship which Lawrence is
proposing, the next novels seem to fill the promise of a deeper
exploration. *Kangaroo* (1923) and *The Boy in the Bush* (written
with M. L. Skinner, 1924) seem to probe the brand-new culture
in Australia much as the preceding works had sounded the mystic
presence of an ancient paganism in Italy.

In *Kangaroo*, poet Richard Somers and his wife Harriet, shortly
after their arrival in Australia, become involved in the country's
social and political entanglements. Somers' neighbor Jack Callcott
belongs to a new, vital, but somewhat obscure movement which
attracts Somers' imagination. Somers' interest is intensified after
he is introduced to the dynamic leader, Kangaroo. Gradually
Somers becomes aware of two powerful forces at odds in Australia, the one, nationalistic in character, composed of a large
organization of Diggers clubs led by Kangaroo; the other, motivated largely by economics, composed of the mass labor movement, led by Willie Struthers. In large measure *Kangaroo* represents an ideological—and ultimately physical—clash between
these opposed forces, with Somers making an intense intellectual
examination of each in turn, and rejecting both for his own compelling reasons.

Against the wishes of Kangaroo, who believes that he is winning

Somers over to his organization, Somers pays Willie Struthers a
visit to hear him out on his views. When Struthers begins to speak
of creating a "new bond between fellow-men" and a "real fellow-
feeling between fellow-men," Somers immediately translates the
idea into Whitmanian terms:

Now Richard [Somers] knew what Struthers wanted. He wanted
this love, this mate-trust called into consciousness and highest honour.
He wanted to set it where Whitman tried to set his Love of Comrades.
It was to be the new tie between men, in the new democracy. It was
to be the new passional bond in the new society. The trusting love
of a man for his mate.

Our society is based on the family, the love of a man for his wife
and his children, or for his mother and brothers. The family is our
social bedrock and limit. Whitman said the next, broader, more un-
selfish rock should be the Love of Comrades. The sacred relation of
a man to his mate, his fellow-man [230].

But by the end of his talk with Struthers, Somers is rejecting the
Struthers concept of brotherly love as too abstract and self-
defeating: "It all seemed so far from the dark God he wished to
serve, the God from whom the dark, sensual passion of love emanates, deeper than the spiritual love of Christ. He wanted men
once more to refer the sensual passion of love sacredly to the
great dark God, the Nameless, of the first dark religions" (235–
236). This obscure, dark element, absent in Struthers but so
precious to Somers, seems strongly akin to the submerged phallic
symbolism present throughout Whitman's "Calamus."

In the climax of the narrative of *Kangaroo*, a mass meeting of
the laborites degenerates into a violent brawl between Struthers'
followers and Kangaroo's Diggers. Kangaroo is fatally injured,
but before he dies, Somers pays him a final visit to discuss once
again his ideas of love. Ironically, Kangaroo's views are quite
close, superficially at least, to Struthers': "They have never
known the full beauty of love, the working classes. . . . Work,
bread has always stood first. But we can take away that obstacle.
Teach them the beauty of love between men, Richard, teach them
the highest—greater love than this hath no man—teach them how
to love their own mate, and you will solve the problem of work
for ever" (382). This concept is not only close to Struthers' but
also to Christ's. But again, and finally, Somers rejects such abstract

and unindividualized love: "Man's isolation was always a supreme truth and fact, not to be forsworn. And the mystery of apartness. And the greater mystery of the dark God beyond a man, the God that gives a man passion, and the dark, unexplained blood-tenderness that is deeper than love, but so much more obscure, impersonal, and the brave, silent blood-pride, knowing his own separateness, and the sword-strength of his derivation from the dark God" (384–385).

When Somers sails from Australia, he remains uncommitted to either of the movements which have so strongly attracted him in his search for an idea to which he can give his allegiance. But even the rejection may be considered an advance in his quest: in rejecting, Somers has had to formulate more precisely for himself the nature of that which he so earnestly desires to discover.

The Boy in the Bush, because it is a jointly written work, does not figure importantly in Lawrence's development, but it nevertheless bears the stamp of his genius. The boy of the title, Jack Grant, is sent to Australia at an early age because of some embarrassing affair in England. The story is his story of initiation, his development from a boy into a man. Lawrence's hand is most strongly felt in the accounts of Jack's relationship with men and women. For example, his vagabond friend Tom, turning up unexpectedly some time after their parting, says: "I sortta felt I couldn't stand even Len being mates with you, an' me not there. I was your first mate, Jack. I've never been myself since I parted with you" (327). When, near the end of the novel, Jack is contemplating simultaneous marriage with more than one woman (". . . if I felt I really wanted two wives . . . I would have them and keep them both. If I really wanted them, it would mean it was the God outside me bidding me, and it would be up to me to obey, world or no world" [336–337]), the reader strongly senses Lawrence's presence. Jack Grant, as Lawrence transfigures him, appears to be developing into the kind of spontaneous creature in communion with that obscure dark God that Somers yearned for in *Kangaroo*.

IX. THE STALLION AND THE SERPENT

In *St. Mawr* (1925) and *The Plumed Serpent* (1926), Lawrence seems to have reached an extreme in the main direction of his development. Both books seem totally committed to the primitive instinctual life, in the one case symbolized by the powerful stallion, in the other represented by the ancient Indian culture of Mexico. *The Plumed Serpent*, indeed, is the final working out of that social organization based on the male relationship toward which all Lawrence's previous novels, especially *Women in Love* and *Kangaroo,* seem obscurely directed.

St. Mawr, hardly greater in magnitude than a novelette, has all of the intensity of a lyric poem. The American Lou Witt and her Australian husband Rico, a handsome, dilettante painter, have settled in the English countryside into a sexually uneasy married life. In her vague restlessness, Lou acquires the magnificent stallion, St. Mawr, and insists on her husband riding it, until he one day is seriously injured in one of St. Mawr's moments of high spirits. As time passes, the center of Lou's emotional life gradually shifts to St. Mawr. She confesses to her mother: "I don't want intimacy, mother. I'm too tired of it all. I love St. Mawr because he isn't intimate. He stands where one can't get at him. And he burns with life. And where does his life come from, to him? That's the mystery. That great burning life in him, which never is dead. Most men have a deadness in them that frightens me so, because of my own deadness. Why can't men get their life straight, like St. Mawr, and then think?" (70–71). Lou's love for St. Mawr brings to a focus her vague discontent that is to cause her gradual withdrawal until, finally, she has found her way to a remote estate in New Mexico, pledging—"either my taking a man shall have a meaning and a mystery that penetrates my very soul, or I will keep to myself" (220).

Though the narrative seems to trail off inconclusively, *St. Mawr* remains one of Lawrence's most powerful tales. The reader will be reminded of Robinson Jeffers' *Roan Stallion*—or of Walt Whitman's "Song of Myself." In one of the climactic sections of Whitman's poem, beginning "I think I could turn and live with animals," a stallion which seems the prototype of St. Mawr is introduced:

A gigantic beauty of a stallion, fresh and responsive to my caresses,
Head high in the forehead, wide between the ears,
Limbs glossy and supple, tail dusting the ground,
Eyes full of sparkling wickedness, ears finely cut, flexibly moving.

His nostrils dilate as my heels embrace him,
His well-built limbs tremble with pleasure as we race around and
   return.

The poet sees in his stallion the same symbolic meaning that Lou
sees in St. Mawr: a great, burning, instinctual life that springs
from the deepest, mysterious sources of the blood. Lou seems to
be saying with Whitman, "I think I could turn and live with
animals."

The Plumed Serpent represents a search in an ancient pagan
civilization for the lost spirit that Lou discovers lurking in the
stallion, St. Mawr. In this novel Lawrence seems to be in quest
of that spirit of place which was the major driving force of the
Italian books. Kate Leslie, a middle-aged, unattached English-
woman in Mexico, finds herself drawn gradually into a complex
primitivistic movement which ultimately and radically changes
her life. The leader of the movement, Don Ramon, has predicted
the return of the ancient Aztec god, Quetzalcoatl (emblemized
by the feathered snake), whose spirit represents all that vital life
that has gone out of the modern white man and his pale Christian
religion. The movement comes into direct conflict with the
Catholic church, represented in Don Ramon's own home by his
wife Carlota; but gradually, through its power and violence, the
revived pagan religion becomes dominant.

The ingredients of the religion are familiar by now to the
reader of Lawrence. They affirm a new selfhood, a new mystery
in sex, and a new relation between men. Kate Leslie observes the
primitive natives who instinctively support and intuitively understand this ancient paganism:

The men were the obvious figures. They assert themselves on the
air. They are the dominant. Usually they are in loose groups, talking
quietly, or silent: always standing or sitting apart, rarely touching
one another. Often a single man would stand alone at a street corner
in his serape, motionless for hours, like some powerful spectre. Or
a man would lie on the beach as if he had been cast up dead from
the waters. Impassive, motionless, they would sit side by side on the
benches of the plaza, not exchanging a word. Each one isolated in
his own fate, his eyes black and quick like a snake's, and as blank.
   It seemed to Kate that the highest thing this country might produce would be some powerful relationship of man to man. Marriage

itself would always be a casual thing. Though the men seemed very gentle and protective to the little children. Then they forgot them.

But sex itself was a powerful, potent thing, not to be played with or paraded. The one mystery. And a mystery greater than the individual. The individual hardly counted [149].

The nature of self, the relation with men, and the relation with women—these are Lawrence's obsessive concerns. And in Mexico, more even than in Italy, he finds the remnants of an ancient culture which can be imaginatively invested with the revitalized life for which he is searching.

Much of *The Plumed Serpent* is devoted to working out, in full ritualistic detail, the new religion of Quetzalcoatl. Don Ramon himself becomes the author of hymns and prayers that are widely circulated to bring in new worshippers of the old Indian deities:

"And the dream of the phallos reaches the great I Know Not.
"And the dream of the body is the stillness of a flower in the dark.
"And the dream of the soul is gone in the perfume of Now.

.   .   .   .   .

"And what falls away is a dream, and what accrues is a dream. There is always and only Now, Now and I Am" [176].

These few lines from one of the long chants suggest something of the tone and direction of the new ritualism for the old gods. The mystic affirmation in the self and in the now, as well as the initial iteration and the long sweeping line, are strong reminders of Whitman.

Kate Leslie, fascinated by the ritualistic pageantry and mystic brotherhood of the religion of Quetzalcoatl, is drawn deeper and deeper into the movement until she is inextricably involved. The center of her interest is Don Ramon's dark, somber assistant, the Indian General Cipriano Viedma. Cipriano seems to represent a living embodiment of the ancient Aztec spirit of mystic phallic life; and indeed he takes on the name and character of the old Indian god of war and the knife, Huitzilopochtli. When Kate becomes his wife in a pagan ceremony that is also a consummation in the converted Catholic church, she becomes Malintzi, bride of Huitzilopochtli, finally and totally committed to the Quetzalcoatl religion. Although the violence and brutality are repulsive to her, particularly in one scene of human sacrifice (actually the execution of those who have attempted to murder Don Ramon), she decides at the end of the novel that she passionately prefers her pagan commitment to the pale, lifeless existence of modern civilization as she has known it in the past.

In a sense, *The Plumed Serpent* represents the end of Lawrence's long quest, for it concludes not in a restless desire for further search (as *Women in Love* and *Aaron's Rod*) nor in rejection (as *Kangaroo*) but with an acceptance, perhaps not entirely unqualified, but nevertheless finally affirmative.

X. LADIES AND LOVERS

With *The Plumed Serpent* Lawrence brought to a close his search for the organizational answer to the modern dilemma. His final full novel was a continuing exploration of the possible personal answer.

The merit of *Lady Chatterley's Lover* (1928) has been somewhat obscured by the notoriety of its language. Actually, the meaning of the novel is not essentially changed by the purging of the so-called offensive passages, but no doubt the sensational impact is somewhat lessened. With or without the words (which all recognize but few tolerate), *Lady Chatterley's Lover* is Lawrence's last great song of the phallus and procreation.

There are two strong themes running through *Lady Chatterley's Lover*, one negative and the other affirmative. In Lady Chatterley's sterile, empty, meaningless alliance with her impotent husband Clifford, Lawrence condemns modern industrial society and its draining of the vital life of all individuals entangled in it. Clifford's sexual impotence symbolizes the death of his individuality brought about by his commitment to the coal mines he presumably possesses—but which really possess him.

The affirmation of *Lady Chatterley's Lover* is vividly dramatized in the relationship established and developed between Lady Chatterley and the gamekeeper, Mellors. Never before in Lawrence has there been such complete and beautiful fulfillment in the man-woman relationship. It is as though Lawrence has finally discovered the Garden of sexual innocence for which he has searched throughout his work.

Connie and Mellors are true "Children of Adam" as Whitman

described them in *Leaves of Grass*. They achieve new, vibrant individualities through their awakened sexual consciousness. And through their innocent physical sharing and abandon, they achieve the baptism and renewal promised by true primitive sexuality.

Mellors has two basic qualities that enable him to discover and maintain the ideal relation with a woman. He is nonintellectual (as distinguished from anti-intellectual) and does not permit the mind to turn the concrete physical life into a series of empty abstractions. Mellors is a kind of savage or pagan. And moreover, he has not only said (with Whitman), "I think I could turn and live with animals," but he has actually done so. In his role as game-keeper, he has discovered that the animals can show a man how to live in all the innocence of his flesh.

Lawrence's *Lady Chatterley's Lover* and Whitman's "Children of Adam" are both works of sexual discovery and joyous affirmation. Many passages in the one recall lines from the other. Connie, in the intensity of her awakening, might well cry out in the "mystic deliria" of Whitman's lines:

We two, how long we were fool'd,
Now transmuted, we swiftly escape as Nature escapes,
We are Nature, long have we been absent, but now we return. . . .
We are seas mingling, we are two of those cheerful waves rolling
    over each other and interwetting each other.

When Connie is finally drawn away from her contemptuous scepticism into the magic of sex by Mellors' gentleness, she wonders at her previous reluctance: "And it seemed she was like the sea, nothing but dark waves rising and heaving, heaving with a great swell, so that slowly her whole darkness was in motion, and she was ocean rolling its dark, dumb mass. . . . the quick of all her plasm was touched, she knew herself touched, the consummation was upon her, and she was gone. She was gone, she was not, and she was born: a woman" (207–208). As Connie explores Mellors' body, she exclaims to herself: "What a mystery! What a strange heavy weight of mystery, that could lie soft and heavy in one's hand! The roots, root of all that is lovely, the primeval root of all full beauty" (209). Connie's wonder seems verging on pagan worship, close in tone and intensity to such Whitman poems as "I Sing the Body Electric."

Lady Chatterley's Lover closes with Mellors' letter to Connie, expressing his desire and hope to be with her (with the implication that all of the complications of divorce will eventually be worked out), and also expressing Lawrence's simple suggestion for curing the industrial sickness of society. Mellors writes of the mass of deadened people getting and spending money in the world: "If you could only tell them that living and spending isn't the same thing! But it's no good. If only they were educated to *live* instead of earn and spend, they could manage very happily on twenty-five shillings. If the men wore scarlet trousers as I said, they wouldn't think so much of money: if they could dance and hop and skip, and sing and swagger and be handsome, they could do with very little cash. . . . They should be alive and frisky, and acknowledge the great god Pan. He's the only god for the masses, forever. The few can go in for higher cults if they like. But let the mass be forever pagan." To "acknowledge the great god Pan" is a basic impulse in the literary dedication of both Lawrence and Whitman. And in their wholehearted dedication, both become a bit pagan.

XI. RESURRECTION REWRITTEN

Although *Lady Chatterley's Lover* closes Lawrence's career as a novelist, two later works seem necessary to the completion of his vision: *The Man Who Died* (first published as *The Escaped Cock*, 1929) and *Apocalypse* (1931).

In *The Man Who Died*, a short, brilliant novelette, Lawrence retells the Christ story as it might have happened had Lawrence been Christ. Instead of resurrecting an old religion, as in *The Plumed Serpent*, Lawrence attempts to revitalize a current one—Christianity itself.

As Christ comes to consciousness in the tomb, he realizes that he has miraculously regained actual, physical life, and a feeling of revulsion sweeps over him for all that he has stood for in the past. When he encounters Madeleine hovering about the tomb, he tells her, "The Teacher and the Saviour are dead in me; now I can go about my business, into my own single life" (32). Gradually the wounded figure disengages from all the entanglements of his previous existence and ventures out into the world. In his wandering flight, he acquires a cock from a peasant and meditates upon its significance: "How hot he is with life! Soon, in some place, I shall leave him among the hens. And perhaps one evening, I shall meet a woman who can lure my risen body, yet leave me my aloneness" (45).

Such precisely is what takes place. In a distant land this new Christ happens upon a Temple of Isis presided over by a young, beautiful priestess. As she anoints his wounds in a healing embrace, he suddenly begins to feel life flow tingling into his limbs: "A new sun was coming up in him, in the perfect inner darkness of himself. He waited for it breathless, quivering with a fearful hope" (89). His true resurrection takes place with the full return of sexuality:

He crouched to her, and he felt the blaze of his manhood and his power rise up in his loins, magnificent.
"I am risen!"
Magnificent, blazing indomitable in the depths of his loins, his own sun dawned, and sent its fire running along his limbs, so that his face shone unconsciously [90].

The renewed Christ stays with the priestess of Isis, fulfilling for her the role of the male god, Osiris, until she is with child. Entirely healed and restored, he departs to escape recapturing—and to live the life of physical fulfillment that seems now in store for him.

Although Whitman did not rewrite the Christ story, he did, in his poetry, identify himself with Christ and attributed to Him characteristics like those of Lawrence's Christ. In "Song of Myself" Whitman exclaims: "That I could look with a separate look on my own crucifixion and bloody crowning! . . . Corpses rise, gashes heal, fastenings roll from me./I troop forth replenish'd with supreme power, one of an average unending procession." This revitalized figure becomes the "friendly and flowing savage" who

Wherever he goes men and women accept and desire him,
They desire he should like them, touch them, speak to them, stay with them.

There is a vital, physical magnetism in both Whitman's and Lawrence's resurrected Christs that represents a radical departure from tradition. In violation of that tradition, both *The Man Who Died* and "Song of Myself" portray the exhilaration of sexual consciousness and the joy of life's physical involvement.

This sheer delight in life is a strong theme in Lawrence's work to the very end. Some of the last lines of his last work—*Apocalypse*—are expressions of such delight. Most of *Apocalypse* is devoted to an attack on Christianity as it has been dominated by the attitude of Revelations, an attitude which Lawrence traces to the pathological desire of the weak to pull down and rule the strong. The concluding paragraphs of this theological tract, however, are an impassioned plea for the mystic love of life:

But the magnificent here and now of life in the flesh is ours, and ours alone, and ours only for a time. We ought to dance with rapture that we should be alive and in the flesh, and part of the living, incarnate cosmos. I am part of the sun as my eye is part of me. That I am part of the earth my feet know perfectly, and my blood is part of the sea. My soul knows that I am part of the human race, my soul is an organic part of the great human soul, as my spirit is part of my nation. In my own very self, I am part of my family.

At the very end of *Apocalypse*, Lawrence exhorts his fellowman to "re-establish the living organic connections with the cosmos, the sun and earth, with mankind and nation and family. Start with the sun, and the rest will slowly, slowly happen." Whitman, as Lawrence well knew, had never broken those "organic connections," but had sung about them, in magnificent celebration, in "Song of Myself":

I am an acme of things accomplish'd, and I an encloser of things
    to be. . . .

Before I was born out of my mother generations guided me,
My embryo has never been torpid, nothing could overlay it.

For it the nebula cohered to an orb,
The long slow strata piled to rest it on,
Vast vegetables gave it sustenance,
Monstrous sauroids transported it in their mouths and deposited it
    with care.

All forces have been steadily employ'd to complete and delight me,
Now on this spot I stand with my robust soul!

Like Lawrence, Whitman spoke with the enraptured voice and the supreme self-confidence of one who had found his place in the sun, his kinship to the universe.

XII. CONNECT WITH THE COSMOS

Whitman was the great nineteenth-century poet of procreation, of friendship, of self. Lawrence was his spiritual heir, the twentieth-century novelist of Adam's children, of the Calamus relationship, of the revitalized selfhood of the individual. After seeing the vast panorama of Lawrence's novels, we become conscious of the persistent recurrence of the Whitmanian themes and the Whitmanian images.

Whitman's "Calamus" threads through Lawrence from beginning to end. The possibilities of the male relationship on a personal level are examined in the Cyril Beardsley–George Saxton friendship in *The White Peacock*, in the Rupert Birkin–Gerald Crich friendship in *Women in Love*, and in the Aaron Sisson–Rawdon Lilly association in *Aaron's Rod*. But already in *Aaron's Rod*, Lawrence is seeking (as Whitman sought in "Calamus") a significance broader than the personal in the male relationship. The search is conducted in the new society of Australia in *Kangaroo*, and in the ancient Indian culture of Mexico in *The Plumed Serpent*. The "great dark God" that seems absent in the Australian societies is finally and mystically apprehended in the Mexican. And *The Plumed Serpent* with its full portrait of a pagan, male-dominated society, draws to a close Lawrence's repeated treatment of the "Calamus" theme.

Perhaps even more persistent in Lawrence's novels than the "Calamus" theme is the quest for Whitman's garden of the "Children of Adam" poems. The search seems never to cease in any of the novels, but holds the foreground in *The Trespasser*, with Siegmund MacNair's fatal attempt to establish a liaison outside his marriage, and in *The Rainbow* and *Women in Love*, with a whole succession of marriages from generation to generation— marriages that somehow fail to live up to their brilliant, dazzling promise. In *The Lost Girl* Lawrence begins that search for the new Adamic man, the man who has not been drained of his procreative vitality or deprived of his dark phallic consciousness by the tempo and temper of a brittle and empty modern life. In *The*

Lost Girl, Alvina Houghton finds herself when she finds the Adamic Italian, Ciccio. In *The Plumed Serpent*, Kate Leslie similarly discovers her deepest being awakened by the Adamic Indian Cipriano Viedma. And in the last great dramatization of this theme, in *Lady Chatterley's Lover*, Lady Chatterley finds a new and vital awareness of self and life in her relationship with the gamekeeper Mellors. Lady Chatterley and Mellors are true "children of Adam," immediate offspring of Lawrence, but true lineal descendants of Whitman.

Fundamental to the conception of both "Calamus" and "Children of Adam" is "Song of Myself." Keystone of Whitman's vision, this poem dramatizes the fulfillment of a glorious selfhood. The self, said Whitman, must first establish its identity and independence with joy and vigor before it can gain or contribute in man-man or man-woman relationships. Throughout Lawrence, too, is the quest for a genuine and inviolate selfhood. In *Sons and Lovers*, Paul Morel must find his freedom, first from his mother, and then from both Miriam and Clara, before he exists in his own right, his soul his own possession. Aaron Sisson in *Aaron's Rod* must likewise cut himself off, not only from his family, but from successive relationships in order to preserve his identity, to maintain his independent self. The magnificent stallion in *St. Mawr* serves as reminder to all those who come to know his fierce spirit of the vitalized self which modern man has suffered to become degraded or desecrated. And Lawrence's last long tale, *The Man Who Died*, is a tale of a Christ who is resurrected not to a spiritualized essence but to a physical vitality and an awakened consciousness of the *whole* self, the selfhood which unites in an inseparable entity the spiritual and the physical, the soul and the body. The Christ of *The Man Who Died*, as he sets off to encounter life at the end of the story, is, like Whitman in "Song of Myself," launching the mystic voyage to a fulfilled selfhood.

Lawrence and Whitman were brothers of the blood, both calling for a joyous affirmation of life and a courageous confrontation of the here and now with a robust and singing soul. They both sketched remarkably similar embryos of a new kind of man and drew strikingly similar blueprints of a new social order. In short, they were Camerados of the spirit, strolling together, in

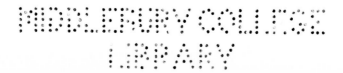

their lifelong quests, down the same open road, yet neither violating the sacred separateness of the other. Poet and novelist, their art was the dance of rapture, their connection the "living organic connection with the cosmos."

JAMES E. MILLER, JR.

Part III

WHITMAN *and* CRANE

Our Meistersinger, thou set breath in steel;
And it was thou who on the boldest heel
Stood up and flung the span on even wing
Of that great Bridge, our Myth, whereof I sing!

HART CRANE
The Bridge

Views of The Bridge

BECAUSE contemporary literature has offered few enough long poems, it is unfortunate that Hart Crane's *The Bridge* has been generally held unworthy as a whole, though poetically rich in texture. While many have believed in the poem, following the favorable tone of Malcolm Cowley's early review in the *New Republic* (23 April 1930), critical judgments have been cut more generally from the whole cloth of the Tate-Winters "archetypal" pattern.[1] Crane's long poem is ironically and somewhat sadly viewed as a shape without form, a bridge with uncertain connections, as chaos come again and lost Atlantis doubly lost. But there are signs that this both puzzling and brilliant poem is being reconsidered,[2] and in that spirit I should like to offer a skeleton design for a unified *Bridge,* a design on Crane's own terms.

From one position, and with one type of critical glass, *The Bridge* does certainly seem to be a series of unrelated poems in which disillusion makes a shambles of a hope brighter than its logic. But approaching the poem from another position with the glass in a somewhat different focus, adjusted to Crane's conceptions, the elements fall into place. First, Crane thought of *The Bridge* as a complex symphonic structure with intricate repetitions of form within the whole, rather than an epic with the usual narrative logic. Although complicated, it is "one poem" with an

137

"integrated unity and development" in which "motives and situations recur" throughout. Secondly, as Crane said, he was writing in an affirmative rather than a negative tradition: "The poem, as a whole, is, I think, an affirmation of experience, and to that extent is 'positive' rather than 'negative' in the sense that *The Waste Land* is negative." He saw in the poetry of *The Waste Land* "complete renunciation," and preferred to identify himself with others of a "new vitality" and vision.[3]

And finally, in this affirmative tradition Crane used the point of view, the poetic theory, and the specific patterns of Walt Whitman, with whom he repeatedly and explicitly aligned himself, and whom he knew in part through Waldo Frank. In a letter to Gorham Munson (2 March 1923), he said, "I begin to feel myself directly connected with Whitman. I feel myself in currents that are positively awesome in their extent and possibilities." This identification is made clearer in *The Bridge*, in which he takes Whitman as guide: "My hand/in yours,/Walt Whitman—/so—" Here, of course, is the key. Since Crane so clearly took the Whitman position, he will be misunderstood as long as that position is misunderstood. If Whitman is seen as a bubbling exploiter of American chauvinism, *The Bridge* will seem like a hapless panegyric of American history and science, with many of the individual poems obviously unconnected. If, however, Whitman is seen as a deeply spiritual thinker, a mystic of cosmic consciousness (as he was to Waldo Frank and to Crane), the pattern in *The Bridge* has a chance to come into focus.[4] And it is critical here to note that whatever anyone else may think of Whitman, Crane considered him a mystic of a particular oneness. The shape of *The Bridge* derives from that principle.

With these premises in mind, we may find a more unified poem if we look at *The Bridge* from three positions: first, through the materials and ideas in Whitman which Crane used; second, through its structural tracing of the symbolic curve or arch of mysticism; and third, through some evidences of Crane's organic technique in poetry.

I. BACKGROUNDS IN WHITMAN

Both Whitman and Crane were writing the Myth of America—Whitman forming the composite of democratic man in *Leaves of*

Grass, and Crane tracing the shape of America in the lines of *The Bridge*. Whitman's "Crossing Brooklyn Ferry" and his "Song of the Universal" are ready antecedents for Crane's images of connection and fusion in *The Bridge*. Whitman's "Passage to India" is an even more explicit prototype for Crane's poem. One recognizes the images of sea into land, of mariner and bridgemaker, of union and the visionary search. But in both poems the theme is not material conquest but spiritual exploration. "Passage to India," it is important to note, records the journey of the soul farther than the knowledgeable mind can record. The geographical terms are emblematic only. India is the image of mystic fulfillment, and the mariner is the soul itself. Crane, in the "Cape Hatteras" section of *The Bridge*, explicitly aligns himself with Whitman. And if "Passage to India" is not primarily a celebration of history, neither is *The Bridge* thematically drawn on any map of America. The deepest affinity which Crane found with Whitman was their mysticism.

That others thought of Whitman as only a blatant exploiter of the glories of America and the mass disturbed Crane, as he wrote despairingly to Allen Tate (13 July 1930):

as you, like so many others, never seem to have read his *Democratic Vistas* and other of his statements sharply decrying the materialism, industrialism, etc., of which you name him the guilty and hysterical spokesman, there isn't much use in my tabulating the qualified, yet persistent reasons I have for my admiration of him, and my allegiance to the positive and universal tendencies implicit in nearly all his best work.

These "positive and universal tendencies" are the currents of the larger tradition to which both poets belonged—the affirmation of a spiritualized cosmic union in which opposites are paradoxically identified: body and spirit, past and present, good and evil. The parabolas of mystic evolution, the encirclement of all experience as necessary to the generation of a spiritual force, the movement of consciousness which in its very kinetic poise also unites man and the cosmos—these central conceptions in Whitman's poetry help to explain the mystical curve of unity which informs the structure of Crane's Bridge.

The union, totality, and inclusion suggested by the curve or the circle are in Whitman, whose "vast similitude" spans and encloses life and death and time. Equating the spiritual and physical, Whitman saw the body as identity and selfhood, and the threshold for a complete consummation in the mystic vision. The wholeness of the cosmos is the true good; therefore, the "devilish and the dark" are also a part of "earth's orbic scheme," the "Rounded Catalogue Divine Complete." In the mystic evolution, Whitman wrote in "Song of the Universal," not only the right is justified, but "what we call evil" is "also justified." From "the huge festering trunk, from craft and guile and tears," health and joy emerge. In the affirmative acceptance of experience, all things have their place.

Whitman's "mystic evolution" is the upward, spiral lift of generation and fulfillment towards immortality, or spiritual essence. In Whitman's "Passage to India," the mystical center of the cosmos is seen as "Light of the light, shedding forth universes." The climax to *The Bridge* is a vision of "Thee, O Love," the "whitest Flower" whose "petals spend the suns about us." Movement to such an end is a journey of the soul. When Crane says of Whitman,

> O, something green,
> Beyond all sesames of science was thy choice
> Wherewith to bind us throbbing with one voice,

he could have been reading directly from Whitman's "Song of the Universal":

> Yet again, lo! the soul, above all science,
> For it has history gather'd like husks around the globe,

and "in spiral routes by long detours," the real to the ideal tends. There are ever the "Eidólons,"

> Ever the growth, the rounding of the circle,
> Ever the summit and the merge at last.

Man's green force impels him on the open road, on the passage to India: "Are thy wings plumed indeed for such far flights?" Crane's flight of the gull, the eagle, and "Easters of speeding light" repeat the upward and outward aspiring of the arch.

The paradox of balance and movement at one in the span of

Crane's bridge suggests Whitman's idea of the poet whose immediate eye becomes the ever-present moving consciousness which unites past and present with one look and sees in diversity a spiritual whole. Whitman speaks of the "full-grown poet" standing between the round globe of Nature and the Soul of man, holding each by the hand, blending and reconciling the two. And in "Passage to India" the poet is seen as an instrument of divine union:

All these separations and gaps shall be taken up and hook'd and link'd together,

. . . . .

Nature and Man shall be disjoin'd and diffused no more,
The true son of God shall absolutely fuse them.

This end—the union of separations and discordances—is part of the "more than India" to which Whitman's poetry set sail.

Crane saw in his own function as poet the same joining of diversity in the creation of a whole. "What I am really handling, you see," he wrote to Otto Kahn (12 Sept. 1927), "is the Myth of America. Thousands of strands have had to be searched for, sorted and interwoven." What implications, then, do Whitman's ideas of spiritual totality and force have for an understanding of Crane's "Myth of America," a myth which also belongs to the older poet? The relationship is clearly intended, as Crane writes in "Cape Hatteras":

Our Meistersinger, thou set breath in steel;
And it was thou who on the boldest heel
Stood up and flung the span on even wing
Of that great Bridge, our Myth, whereof I sing!

Both the life in the object (the breath in steel) and the shape of the idea make the span possible. This body-spirit of the myth of America Whitman emphatically articulated. It was most clearly *not* a celebration of the present glories, power, and scientific achievements of America, either in Whitman's day or very soon to come. As Crane observed, in *Democratic Vistas* Whitman agonized over the failures, the weakness, the slow maturing of America: "I say we had best look our times and lands searchingly in the face, like a physician diagnosing some deep disease. Never was there, perhaps, more hollowness at heart than at present, and here in the United States." He found the apparently successful New World democracy "an almost complete failure in its social aspects, and in really grand religious, moral, literary, and esthetic results." It was a society "canker'd, crude, superstitious and rotten." Crane was often disillusioned, as his letters show, but Whitman more than matched him in despair: "We sail a dangerous sea of seething currents, cross and under-currents, vortices— all so dark, untried—and whither shall we turn?" However, the dark moods are matched with more knowledgeable insights: "Thought you greatness was to ripen for you like a pear? If you would have greatness, know that you must conquer it through ages, centuries—must pay for it with a proportionate price." These are the hard views of America that Crane found in *Democratic Vistas*. If Whitman could feel in "Thou Mother with Thy Equal Brood" an "ominous greatness evil as well as good," his own mythic bridge must be of something other than chauvinistic steel.

For Whitman, the "Myth of America" was the possible spiritual fulfillment of its people (who are its individuals), a fulfillment hoped for, believed in, but not yet accomplished. It was the whole structure and act of a human society moving toward brotherhood and complete selfhood. The story of America's past could be only the statement of its birth pangs and its peculiar identity, but there was also the certainty that if ever a people might reach a state of spiritual force, it might well be America where there already existed a symbolic union and a kind of Adamic "new earth" whose strength might nourish the seed of perfection. Thus a celebration of America's present could be in truth the celebration of the life force and its potency.

It is clear in all of Whitman's writing that he believed the greatness possible for America must include spiritual unity and aspiration. Both individualism and brotherhood are to be

vitalized by religion . . . breathing into the proud, material tissues, the breath of life. For I say at the core of democracy, finally, is the religious element . . . . Nor may the scheme step forth, clothed in resplendent beauty and command, till these, bearing the best, the latest fruit, the spiritual, shall fully appear.

If there is no spiritualization, "we are on the road to a destiny . . . of the fabled damned." In the notes to his 1876 Preface, Whitman spoke of "the ultimate Democratic purports" as "the ethereal and spiritual ones." In the poems of "death, immortality, and a free entrance into the spiritual world" he wished "to set the keystone to my democracy's enduring arch." The central poem in this group is "Passage to India."

Crane said in his essay "Modern Poetry" that Whitman, "better than any other, was able to coördinate those forces in America which seem most intractable, fusing them into a universal vision which takes on additional significance as time goes on." In relation to Whitman's "universal vision," America is not great in herself, but she may *become* great through the fulfillment of the scheme, and the search of the soul through time and space is the most significant part of the myth of America. As Whitman wrote in "Song of the Universal,"

> And thou America,
> For the scheme's culmination, its thought and its reality,
> For these (not for thyself) thou hast arrived.

America is second; the "mystic ensemble," the "plan of Thee enclosed in Time and Space" is first. The end (India? Cathay?) is the spiritual end, and *it* will give the glory to America if the ship of the soul can sail far enough into the mystery of that ethered sea.

To conceive of the Whitman-Crane myth of America as even partially a glorification of science or the machine age is to miss the point again. If science is praised, it is as a means, not as a final glory, just as all that is physical is good because it is a way of becoming. In "Modern Poetry" Crane is clearly saying that science is to be used, not deified—to be blended, not isolated. This is only the most practical of poetic views, when a twentieth-century poet wishes to speak with some contemporaneity. He must of course use the mechanical manifestations of his own time. But when he also wishes to speak in the eternal, spiritual present, he turns more especially to that "something green," beyond all sesames of science. The "rebound seed" wielded by Whitman involves generation and the cyclic meaning of life: the circle which spans, encompasses, and identifies birth and death, space and time, past and present, flesh and spirit, good and evil. Because it is the core of Whitman's meaning, the principle of such a cosmic union cannot be ignored in determining the symbolic Bridge of Crane, whose allegiance was to "the positive and universal tendencies" in Whitman's work.

II. THE INFORMING IMAGE

Crane's invocation to the bridge concludes: "And of the curveship lend a myth to God." Here, I believe, he has given the essential symbol and the essential form of the poem. In statement, structure, and idea, the curve or the arch—with its implied completed circle and its mystical direction—is the image which informs and illuminates *The Bridge.* Moreover, the sections of the poem are composed in united curves of space, time, and spiritual movement so that the whole is rounded into one. Although Crane uses the thematic curve repeatedly, it will be possible here to describe only the very general framework of the poem, with something of the origin and meaning of that structure. Others have noted the appearance of curves in *The Bridge;* I wish to go further in suggesting that the basic design of body and meaning depends upon that form.

The Bridge is divided into two parts, the first half including the "Proem," "Ave Maria," "Powhatan's Daughter," and "Cutty Sark." The second section begins with "Cape Hatteras" as theme, and continues through "Three Songs," "Quaker Hill," "The Tunnel," and "Atlantis." This division is Crane's own, for in asking his publisher to place a photograph ("of the barges and tug") between the "Cutty Sark" section and "Cape Hatteras," he wrote: "That is the 'center' of the book, both physically and symbolically." [5] The first half explores the fused past and present of America and the meaning of self. It is the realization of identity, or position in time and space. The second half is the movement to spiritual vision, or the journey of the soul.

The structural curves of *The Bridge* are on three levels—space, time, and psychological action—and are accented by innumerable visual repetitions. In the first half, the space curve begins in mid-ocean ("Ave Maria"), moves to the bridge and city ("Harbor Dawn"), through subway and highway west ("Van Winkle"), across the land and down the river ("The River"), up the Appalachian River and to the far west ("The Dance"), back from the west and down the river again to the sea ("Indiana"), and returns in "Cutty Sark" to city, sea, and bridge. The time curve uses the present as a base, with a simultaneous historical movement from Columbus ("Ave Maria") to present consciousness ("Harbor Dawn"), exploration and settlement ("Van Winkle" and "The River"), the ancient Indian world ("The Dance"), and a return through pioneers ("Indiana") to the invocation of whaling ships at the close of "Cutty Sark." These passages also suggest the cyclic life movement from birth to maturity to old age, with life and land encircled by the farther reaches of being suggested by the sea.

In the second half, "Cape Hatteras" first ties the identity of the self-America to the dilemma of human failure after aspiration. Then begins a dramatization, in three inverted curves, of action which moves in a fall from illusion, through purgatorial punishment and evil, to the upward aspiring climb toward a mystic end. The first curve is a thematic statement in "Cape Hatteras" in which Whitman is chosen as the Virgil to lead the protagonist from death to soaring flight (and this is Whitman the mystic, not Whitman the so-called American optimist). The second curve is that of "Three Songs," in which the sexual or female principle is traced from death (or sterility) to life. And the final curve is the larger involvement of man dramatized through the failure of "Quaker Hill," the hell of "The Tunnel," and the final vision of "Atlantis." Around these sections is a space arc, from the sea of "Southern Cross," through the city's depths and heights, and back to bridge and sea at the close.

This general pattern of *The Bridge* can be verified by letting the imagination move rapidly through the course of the action. How those arcs of movement derive from the original image of Brooklyn Bridge, and how they function symbolically, will be considered further.

Brooklyn Bridge, the initial image, is a suspension bridge, its main line tracing across and through two stolid piers in a shallow curve to the land on either side. From the tops of the piers fall cables in three inverted arches, one half-moon in the center and two slighter curves at the ends. In the piers are openings arched like Gothic windows. It is this symmetry of substance and grace, beaded with lights by night, gull-circled by day, holding at once both stillness and movement, that aroused Crane's most mystical imagination.

One of the best descriptions of its quality he found in a painting and an essay by Joseph Stella, to whom Crane wrote (24 Jan. 1929) of the coincidence that "you . . . have had the same sentiments regarding Brooklyn Bridge which inspired the main theme and pattern of my poem." Stella's essay describes the bridge as

a weird metallic Apparition under a metallic sky, out of proportion with the winged lightness of its arch, traced for the conjunction of WORLDS, supported by the massive dark towers dominating the surrounding tumult of the surging skyscrapers with their gothic majesty sealed in the purity of their arches, the cables, like divine messages from above, transmitted to the vibrating coils, cutting and dividing into innumerable musical spaces the nude immensity of the sky; it impressed me as the shrine containing all the efforts of the new civilization of AMERICA—the eloquent meeting point of all the forces arising in a superb assertion of their powers, in APOTHEOSIS.[6]

In Stella's painting, reproduced in the article, two of the arched openings of a pier are at the forefront of a vista of cables in sweeping curves, and are crossed by circles of light and brighter arcs against the distant perpendicular lines of the steel city. It is important to note that Stella's response to the bridge emphasized not the steel power of the scientific bridge, but the mystical movement and music of its lines, its *curveship*.

In Crane's poem, the visual curveship of the bridge as theme is stated in the last line of the proem, "To Brooklyn Bridge." The culmination of the visual images is in the last section, "Atlantis," where the shape sustains "the arching path/Upward" which blends into "one arc synoptic of all tides below—" Here are the "arching strands of song" and its "lariat sweep" which imply the rainbow's arch of promise as "Deity's glittering Pledge."

But the immediate visual curves of the bridge are only thematic beginnings, even as the gods who take on mortal forms must then use the mythic word and act. The arch of the mind and emotions of the man who follows the curve of the bridge is the kinetic image that is also important to the effect of the poem. "All architecture is what you do to it when you look upon it," wrote Walt Whitman in "A Song for Occupations." The lines continue,

(Did you think it was in the white or gray stone? or the lines of the
arches and cornices?)

All music is what awakes from you when you are reminded by the
instruments . . . .

Whitman turned the arena of the poem from the page to the person, the variable poetic movements tracing their own designs in
the consciousness.

Crane, too, in a letter to Harriet Monroe, printed in *Poetry*
(Oct. 1926), said that he considered the *effect* of images in series
the only essential logic in his poetry and the source of its meaning.
That he deliberately tried to make the motion of the curve organic in *The Bridge* is indicated in a letter to Waldo Frank (18
Jan. 1926): "I have attempted to induce the same feelings of
elation, etc.—like being carried forward and upward simultaneously—both in imagery, rhythm and repetition, that one experiences in walking across my beloved Brooklyn Bridge." "Motion
forward and upward" is reinforced by the use of words like
"sweep," "flight of strings," "spiring cordage," "ascends," "leap
and converge." From the seagull's flight "with inviolate curve"
to the last ring of rainbows, the curveship of *The Bridge* projects
into parabolas of imaginative movement in time and space that fit
the action and the idea of the poem into a single comprehensible
pattern.

What, then, is involved in the curveship of Crane's bridge, the
shape which can "lend a myth to God"? A form that includes,
unites, and completes is performing a spiritual act; or, to paraphrase Crane's line further, spiritual action is the myth of God,
and it can be represented physically in the symbolic curve and
circle. Crane's bridge, both visual object and course of action,
means whatever its lines trace upon the consciousness. These
traceries are, first, the sense of wholeness; and, second, the sense
of lift and resolution, or its reverse in fall and recovery.

The curves and circles of Crane's bridge perform the ancient
ritual of eternity: what is whole, total, and perfect is circum-
scribed with unending motion; what is divided is made one. The
bridge is called "one arc synoptic of all tides below." Elements
that are unlike or separate can in this one structure be tied together and made one identity: the two shores of Here and There,

of Now and Then—Space in the enclosure of the arc, and Time in the going across. The piers of the bridge are heavy and rooted in earth, but its upward curves are of the air.

Both wholeness and resolution are represented in the peak of balance at the center of the arch, where the double thrust of two halves are fused into one. This is the highest moment of the curve, and the point of vision. Such a fusion blends into the symbolism of sexual union and fulfillment of the life force, much as D. H. Lawrence used the image of the male and female joined to make a spiritual whole. For example, the arch to Will Brangwen in *The Rainbow* "leapt up from the plain of earth," until with it he "leaped clear into the darkness above, to the fecundity and the unique mystery, to the touch, the clasp, the consummation, the climax of eternity, the apex of the arch" (190). At the same "climax of eternity" Whitman had placed his keystone of democracy's arch—the poems of spiritual vision— and here the "Eidólon" circle found its "summit and the merge at last." Such a "merge" or union of duality holds the paradox of "kinetic poise" in the structure of the bridge (both object and poem), where motion is caught in the moment of fulfillment. The creative force toward completion is also a part of spiritual experience.

Another important element in the curveship of the bridge is the kind of wholeness in which man meets the elemental world and rounds act and being to nature's creative force and mysterious darkness. Waldo Frank, Crane's friend and critic, gave in a 1925 essay called "Straight Streets" an analysis which could well be related to Crane's conception of the curve. "The curve is the way of acceptance: the angle is the way of resistance," said Frank. Nature is "the sinuous, rounded being," exterior and interior:

Man's mind moves in curves. His thoughts arch, vault, melt into reverie. Dream and sense swerve into each other. His heart, too, is full of arcuations. And the heart's desires are parabolas.

Frank saw in the highest Indian culture a kind of sophisticated primitivism which has learned to follow the curve of nature:

The Indian culture began when his innate spiritual and intellectual values formed a solution with the world about him: his culture was achieved when the responses between his soul and the world had rounded into a unified *life* which expressed both fully.[7]

The curve is here the tracery of a kind of ultimate cultural health, suggesting man's acceptance of his place in the wholeness of life. As in "Song of Myself" Whitman considered all living things and saw in them and himself "the same old law," each thing having a place in the scheme or ensemble, so man must join with nature in the curve of acceptance. The "identification of yourself with *all of life*" was to Crane happiness, related to "the true idea of God." [8]

The concept of the whole, of unified duality, is dramatized in another way by the act of the curve whose lines go in continuous upward and downward movements—or which fall from high, and out of descent create another rising force. These are patterns of the journey of the soul in its struggle with the unwieldy, unequal, and fragmentary forms of mortal experience that must be reconciled before the final vision is attained. Both the lines of Crane's physical bridge and the movement of imaginative action in the poetic bridge turn to the same thematic key: that the whole form can exist only *because* it has joined division, diversity, and motion; and that such an identity has a living dimension which can touch an infinite spiritual power.

Two elements of meaning and form in the curveship of *The Bridge* can be considered representative of the body of the poem: the union of duality, and spiritual realization through that duality. For whatever chaos Crane may personally represent, his poetic vision did seize upon this kind of wholeness, and he dramatized it in the curved union, the encircling lines of *The Bridge*.

To achieve an identity, man or America is shown in the first half of *The Bridge* to be contained in time and space, aware of what is incomplete and mortal, and envisioning the eternal. Thematic imagery in the "Proem" introduces the "inviolate curve" of the gull's flight, repeated later in the "unfractioned idiom" of the bridge. At the close of the "Proem," the descending sweep of the vaulting curve is invoked to link the man standing by the shadowy pier to the initial skyward flight. Here two elements of the bridge—its root in earth and its lift to air—are joined in the imagery of the poem. By shadow, the darkened city, and the snow that "submerges an iron year," the "Proem" further implies the duality of darkness and light, of death and generation, that the curveship of the bridge can include and unify.

In the mid-ocean of "Ave Maria," looking both forward and back to the hoped-for Cathay and the discovered continent, the ship of Columbus links past and present and moves into the "steep savannahs" of the double Word: "Eden and the enchained Sepulchre." These oppositions of life and death, or the corollary of time-eternity and body-spirit, are repeated throughout the poem. What Crane called the "sea swell crescendo" of "Ave Maria" culminates in a vision beyond the waves' green towers in night and chaos, but this spiritual vision comes down to rest in naked kingdoms of the trembling heart, the movement here paralleling the turn at the close of the "Proem," in which the downsweeping curve of the bridge is to touch the man who waits in its shadow.

The central figure of "Powhatan's Daughter" is Pocahontas, the natural body of America and a symbol of fertility and the life-force. In this section is performed the ritual of union with nature and the sexual-physical as a progress toward spiritual identity. This principle is the same as Whitman's identification of body and soul and Waldo Frank's curve of acceptance. This element of earth and the flesh is the physical half of duality, and its complete acceptance is necessary for any final mystic vision. When the drama of "Powhatan's Daughter" explores the body of America, the land symbolizes the physical and creative body of man as much as Pocahontas symbolizes the soil of natural America. In history, the complete realization of the body of America is through its exploration in space and time, and this narrative line is traced in the five sections of "Powhatan's Daughter," but with a fusion of present and past so that all of it happens in a simultaneous grasp of consciousness. Crane wanted to show "the continuous and living evidence of the past in the inmost vital substance of the present." [9]

Throughout the drama of movement over America, described in "Powhatan's Daughter," there is a consciousness of the natural world, "a body under the wide rain," but its meaning is evanes-

150

cent, and the "iron dealt cleavage" of an age that has nearly obliterated the natural union of physical and spiritual needs to be joined. As the time-river blends into sea and prefigures the eternal Atlantis, so in the Indian world of "The Dance" Maquokeeta is phoenix-like brought out of time, and the nature-figure of Pocahontas fulfills the cyclic body-life. On one level, the poem traces the seasonal change of the physical world— spring to winter. Symbolically, Crane uses the serpent-time and eagle-space duality. The separation of White and Indian cultures is a corollary of the cleavage which has denied the natural and primitive reality and thus a spiritual wholeness. But in a possible union of nature and man, best demonstrated in the cyclic, genera-tive, fertility principle, time and eternity may also be reconciled, as well as time and space: "The serpent with the eagle in the boughs." Thus the white mother of "Indiana" takes on the na-ture symbolism of Pocahontas, and the son continues to sea in man's perpetual search.

In "Cutty Sark" the fugue of time (the derelict sailor) and eternity (Atlantis out of the pianola song) prepares the protago-nist for a union of the real and present walk across the bridge and the phantasy of whalers and clipper ships, whose quest joins the dreams of India, Cathay, and Melville's elusive whale. But identity and selfhood are made of these very contradictions: the real and the visionary, time and mortality bound in the visible land surrounded by eternal seas where may lie the mystic rose of Atlantis.

The drama of spiritual vision, the journey of the soul, is demon-strated in the second half of *The Bridge* as a downward and up-ward curve: the fall from the attempted ideal, and the re-trial through chaos and the stark ugliness which is part of the human commitment to the flesh and mortality. But it is through this very death that the upward lift to mystical fulfillment is achieved, as light is known by darkness. This configuration can be seen most completely in the details of "Cape Hatteras," the ode to Whit-man which Crane said was a two years' effort at a synthesis of his themes,[10] and which draws on Whitman's "Passage to India" for its design.

The first scene of "Cape Hatteras" ("Imponderable the dinosaur/ sinks slow") suggests the turning of the earth (the sinking eastern Cape, the rising western range) and the simultaneous recession of the primitive creature into the past. At the center of this natural machine is the dynamo of flux and creative energy, and (known, too, by Whitman) the natural body of America in Pocahontas, which still lives under the surface structures. Whatever has been discovered in space and time is reduced finally to the contained view of the past-reversed self; but the circle of infinity, the crucible of endless or unconquered space, has eternal motion for the "free ways still ahead!" Here Whitman is taken for the Virgil to conduct the soul upon the search for infinity, spiritual knowledge to be gained through eyes that know the full acceptance of the great cyclic mystery —"Sea eyes and tidal, undenying, bright with myth!" Such a myth had been Whitman's theme in "Passage to India" in which he envisioned the voyage of the self, or the soul, to a mystical realization.

Turning again in "Cape Hatteras" to the pattern of the search, Crane introduces the dynamo of earth's creative force as the "nasal whine of power" in the air-conquering machine. Through a violent re-creation of the physical force of the airplane, the reader is careened upward to splinter the yet "unvanquished space." Lines move up, like hurtling javelins, above the lightning, yet the ascensions are aimed farther still: in the wrist (the blood-pulse) of the symbolic flyer is yet the charge "To conjugate infinity's dim marge—" In the images of the poem, the man-machine is forced downward before it reaches the heights of infinity, and with the "skull's deep, sure reprieve" all movement twists in spirals downward in the falling curve, crashing the brave attempt into debris. So Whitman had spoken of shores "strew'd with the wrecks of skeletons," the failures to achieve "more than India."

The last part of "Cape Hatteras" shows the way in which the ascending curve can rise out of the "beached heap of high bravery" by Hatteras. From Whitman and his prophetic voice, ascensions hover, and with belief in the "rebound seed," with "pure impulse inbred/ To answer deepest soundings! O, upward from the dead/ Thou bringest tally." Whitman's lines had indeed asserted life:

(Curious in time I stand, noting the efforts of heroes,
Is the deferment long? bitter the slander, poverty, death?
Lies the seed unreck'd for centuries in the ground? lo, to God's due
    occasion,
Uprising in the night, it sprouts, blooms,
And fills the earth with use and beauty.)

To find God is perhaps to find the freshness of "primal thought," the intuitive force of creation.

Whitman's song, says Crane, has known both heights and depths of experience, the whole arc. He has understood the true meaning of death and has been the interpreter of life's seasonal cycle, in which gold autumn (or death) "crowned the trembling hill!" Whitman is clearly used as a messianic, prophetic figure whose spiritual force and understanding could create the true bridge to infinity, "set breath in steel" and fling the span of the mythic bridge, or set the pattern for the ascending, encircling movement toward a spiritual fulfillment. Because Whitman has passed the barrier of death (both actually and in the poetic vision), he can lead out of the debris of mortal failure to the farthest space of consciousness. Movement ascends, "launched in abysmal cupolas of space,/ Toward endless terminals, Easters of speeding light—" The final "curveship" is the rainbow's arch that "shimmeringly stands/ Above the Cape's ghoul-mound." The theme in both Crane and his Meistersinger Whitman is life out of death, the daring passage on the open road for which one may well take the hand of the older poet who knows the way.

In Crane's poem, the tracing of a curve across symbolic skies has very little significance as a eulogy of air-power, or the conquering of physical space. Rather it is the image of the human situation diagrammed in the language of the modern world. It is the way a poet of the machine age would tell the story of Icarus. "Passage to India" had closed with the fused imagery of air and sea: "Are thy wings plumed indeed for such far flights?" Whitman asked of the soul—

> For we are bound where mariner has not yet dared to go,
> And we will risk the ship, ourselves and all.

The climb toward infinity in "Cape Hatteras" is the Icarian voyage of man on the sea of air, on the air-borne ship. The old trial toward "something beyond" and the mortal failure—perhaps in death—are again dramatized. In "Cape Hatteras" the physical terms of air-flight and destruction prepare for the spiritual ascensions. For it is only out of the total experience of both high and low that the final ascending "passage" is made possible. This is the journey of the soul to the mystic end, as it goes through the flesh, the evil, and the death which are the necessary parts of mortality. To think of the structure of "Cape Hatteras" as showing, first, the human condition; second, the human failure; and third, the rise to infinity through the way set down by Whitman, will give it a consistent form. As a miscellaneous praise of geology, or of science, or of Whitman, it will be a fumbling, sentimental effort. But Crane's two years of work on it as a synthesis are justified when it is seen as the diagram, the visualization, of a kind of modern *Commedia*. This pattern is to be retraced in other symbols in the remaining sections of *The Bridge*.

The falling-rising curve of "Three Songs" enacts the life-giving, spiritualizing force of the sexual principle, uniting the dualities of male and female, fertility and sterility, lust and idealized love. Recognizing defeat through Eve, who brought death into the world, life is reborn by the acceptance of the flesh and generation, begun at its lowest form in Magdalene and rising to the idealized reality of Mary. The visual curve drops from the heights of the Southern Cross, to the dark waters, and up through dance hall and streets to the nickel-dime tower. In a similar curve, "Atlantis" is attained by way of the fallen ideal of "Quaker Hill" and the darkness of "The Tunnel." The visual descent begins in the autumn leaves of "Quaker Hill," falling farther into the depths of the subway and rising up to the bridge, at last a symphony whose leap is the circle of "the lark's return," which holds "in single chrysalis the many twain," and from whose curveship springs a mystical rainbow-prophecy.

The last four lines of "Atlantis" epitomize the three directives in Crane with which this paper began: the symphonic form, a positive spiritual belief, and this affirmation in the design of Whitman's cosmic unity:

> —One Song, one Bridge of Fire! Is it Cathay,
> Now pity steeps the grass and rainbows ring

The serpent with the eagle in the leaves . . . ?
Whispers antiphonal in azure swing.

The Bridge is one being of music and fire. Themes of the serpent and the eagle, time and space, are bound by rings of rainbows while "pity steeps the grass," recalling Whitman's microcosm of the *Leaves* infused by love. But to the question, "Is it Cathay . . . ?" the answers are dual, antiphonal. The point of stillness out of movement is not yet gained, for whispers swing somewhere in the blue. Yet "swing" suggests the balanced poise of the present, whose moment of Here and Now is what we know of the bridge of consciousness.

In fact, both sections of *The Bridge* end in questions. "Is it Cathay?" is matched at the end of the first half (at the close of "Cutty Sark") with the elusive quest of the whaling ships, and of "you rivals two—/ . . . /*Taeping?*/*Ariel?*" Both Leviathan and Atlantis are legendary objects of search, strangely shrouded in the mysteries of the sea, and their ambiguity adds to the unanswered questions. But neither did Whitman arrive at India in his voyage. "Passage to India" ends with the "daring joy" of sailing farther and farther on the seas of God. This swing between mythic object and immediate action reinforces the ambivalence which enters into much of the symbolic bridge, as the present moment joins past and future and identity fuses the separations. Here is the center of the "oneness" or acceptance which Crane celebrates, and which the curveship of the bridge dramatizes.

III. TRANSMUTATION IN IMAGERY

The ideal of wholeness in Whitman and other poets of the cosmic tradition contains two kinds of movement: the flow of consciousness and the continuity of generation. These creative forces, operating within the poem, form a particular kind of organic unity. Another view of *The Bridge* as a whole structure may be gained by noting some evidences of Crane's attempt at poetic order through metaphorical relationships, or genesis within the poem.

One organic technique in Hart Crane's poetry is the recurrence of imagery in slightly changed patterns, or the repetition of patterns in somewhat different imagery. This device, which as a verbal convenience I shall call transmutation, occurs often enough in *The Bridge* to be considered a part of the poem's unity, and in one instance, at least, an emphasis on its theme. I refer to the much-maligned "Three Songs," which few readers can fit into the logic of the whole, but which as a section is a rather remarkable anticipation of the pattern of the last three: "Quaker Hill," "The Tunnel," and "Atlantis." This relationship can be considered after a look at some individual examples of transmutation in Crane's poem.

The recurrence of image and situation in *The Bridge* was partly deliberate, partly unconscious with Crane, as he wrote to Waldo Frank (23 Aug. 1926): "Are you noticing how throughout the poem motives and situations recur—under modifications of environment, etc.? The organic substances of the poem are holding a great many surprises for me." When one image or situation reappears, thus modified, the transmutation gains something of the tension of life—the new moment out of the past one. Moving through the bridge of present consciousness, the transmuted image has both continuity and change, familiarity and surprise, thus achieving a paradoxical kinetic poise. But this very quality is in the bridge itself, described in the "Proem" as "silver-paced" by the sun whose unmoving movement leaves still "Some motion ever unspent in thy stride,—" When the same fusion, suggestive of time and stillness beyond time, occurs in the progress of the imagery, the thematic Bridge is organically constructed.

Crane, in another letter to Waldo Frank (18 Jan. 1926), noted one of the central transmutations of the poem—that the Bridge becomes ship, world, woman, and harp. These are not arbitrary shifts of the image-symbol, however, for in the "Proem" the Bridge is seen as "vaulting the sea, the prairies' dreaming sod," its extension through water and land preparing for the joining of histories and the search by sea, and the generative force of Pocahontas as the natural world of America. Its function as harp for the harmony of the mystic vision is defined in the visual cabled shape—the "choiring strings" and the "unfractioned idiom"—as well as the union which the sweeping lines of the Bridge invoke.

Other evidences of transmutation are in the details of the poem. For example, the frost and fog surrounding the lovers in "Harbor Dawn" becomes the snow of "Van Winkle," as action turns from the harbored room to the space movement across America. As the frost is transmuted to the snow screen, through it flickers the

> Sabbatical, unconscious smile
> My mother almost brought me once from church. . . .

This nearly visionary, lost smile, like Cathay or Atlantis, becomes the evanescent truth searched for in farther distances through the poem and reappears in undercurrents of the River, glimpses of Atlantis through a screen of dust and steel, and the last antiphonal whispers of Cathay. The childhood garter snakes and the launched paper monoplanes in "Van Winkle" become the time-serpent and space-eagle of later sections, as well as the aircraft of "Cape Hatteras." As the snakes (symbol of time in the poem) are struck from the ash heap by the boy in "Van Winkle," they flash tongues "as clean as fire." These blend into the fire of "red fangs/And splay tongues" that burn the Indian Maquokeeta in "The Dance." He is specifically called "snake," and from "pure serpent, Time itself," changes in apotheosis to timeless freedom, like a meteor or star. The lovers of "Harbor Dawn" reappear as Pocahontas and Maquokeeta in "The Dance." As Pocahontas "is the torrent and the singing tree," so it was said of the awakening women, "a forest shudders in your hair!" The time-nature marriage (Maquokeeta and Pocahontas) in "The Dance" and man's union with nature on what Crane, writing to Otto H. Kahn (12 Sept. 1927), called "the pure mythical and smoky soil" of Indian culture has a wholeness, an acceptance of both physical and spiritual, whose primitive life-force is a transmutation of the more submerged nature-spirit of "The River." There both gods and Pocahontas (the body-life of the land) are held down by an iron age, under the stream of train passengers that blend into the flow of pioneers and all in the flow of the great river which is time. Yet the river holds a deeper force, a "jungle grace" ("O quarrying passion, under-towed sunlight!") that will reach its mystic end in the silent depths of the sea. As the Indian destiny ends in isolation and near extinction on the stones of mesa sands (recalling the backyard cinder pile in "Van Winkle"), the next blend is into the stony nuggets of gold which man searches for rather than the fulfillment of the natural world of Pocahontas. As nature symbol, Pocahontas is united with the mother of "Indiana," and the sea-going Larry with the derelict sailor of "Cutty Sark" ("I can't live on land"). In the bar, the mechanical jingle of "Stamboul Nights," with its line of "O Stamboul Rose," fuses in the drinker's mind with "coral Queen," and finally in the coral depths of the sea, with "Atlantis Rose," a theme which is the "transmuted voice," as Crane himself said, "of the nickel-slot pianola." The song is carried to the close of the poem into the symphonic music of the mystical harp-like Bridge and the flowering center of eternity.

The instance of transmutation most important to the total unity of *The Bridge*, however, is that of "Three Songs" and the last sections of the poem. Mr. John R. Willingham's article in *American Literature*, " 'Three Songs' of Hart Crane's *The Bridge*," [11] does present a summary of the unity of the songs. He sees these short poems as a development of the female principle in several kinds of love, and although different in a few details, my interpretation of the songs themselves is essentially the same. It is my purpose to extend this demonstration of their unity by showing their transmutation in the last sections of the poem: the failure and death of Eve in "Southern Cross" is transmuted to the society of "Quaker Hill"; the hell of human experience in the Magdalene of "National Winter Garden" becomes that of "The Tunnel"; and the rise to the spiritualized Mary of "Virginia" becomes the mystical vision of "Atlantis." The three songs and the three sections move in the same line from sterility and death through crude humanity and black night to the genesis of harmony and vision. "Three Songs" is the prelude of a single instrument to the full orchestration of the last poems. And Crane's comment to Caresse Crosby (26 Dec. 1929) that "Quaker Hill," the last section to be added to *The Bridge*, was not important in itself but as an "accent," indicates that he realized the possibility of intensifying the theme by completing the rounded pattern.

The "Three Songs" are about three women—Eve, Magdalene, and Mary—but all fuse into "woman," or the female principle whose body repeats the Pocahontas symbolism of earlier sections. The introductory quotation simply names the two cities, Sestos and Abydos, in which lived the lovers Hero and Leander, divided by the Hellespont. The problem is to join them. The first song, "Southern Cross," is the yearning for the woman (Eve, Magdalene, or Mary?), and the defeat of yearning. The first hope is for a cool, unphysical ideal, as the Southern Cross takes night separate from the violent "vaporous scars," the "slowly smoldering fire," of the lower heavens. But that yearning is defeated in the presence of Eve, fallen from Eden and the symbol of plain mortality, death that is the unrelieved burden of the flesh. As mortality, Eve becomes Medusa, turning seed and spawn to stony death ("lithic trillions"); and the Southern Cross, a phantom height, drops below the dawn. There is nothing physical in this woman-figure. She is homeless, grieving, serpent-ridden—a phantom like the Cross and a denial of life.

To compare with the sterility and death of "Southern Cross," the transmuted form begins with the disillusioned, suburban Quaker Hill, a society conceived in idealistic hope but sunk to mediocrity. The introductory quotations, Isadora Duncan's "no ideals have ever been fully successful" and Emily Dickinson's lines on autumn, are motifs for the falling-off of perfection and life. As the wash of water in "Southern Cross" gave only the wraith of Eve, out of all the dreams of the Promised Land, here in Quaker Hill are only empty windows (of both hotel and people), "cancelled reservations," resignation to cheapness and vulgarity. The human desolation is for the poet-speaker "the curse of sundered parentage" (the separation of White and Indian cultures and the attendant loss of primitive serenity that Crane developed in "The Dance"), a falling-off of perfection, like the gardenless, death-giving Eve. The news of "birthright by blackmail" implies that the darkness and tragedy of mortal existence, the commitment to the flesh, must be fulfilled. Here "Quaker Hill" goes farther than "Southern Cross" and suggests a transition to the next stage. To gain any new destiny, we must drop from the high hawk's view (the ideal) to see and love the earth more humbly with a "worm's eye" (the actual destiny). Close to the earth, to the flesh, to mortality, accepting mortal defeat and singing even with the mortal "sheaf of dust" upon the tongue, we take it to the Gate of entry to other realizations, which in the epigraph to "The Tunnel" becomes Blake's "Gates of Wrath." In the paradox of life which rejoices even in loss, despair, and death, a song "transmuting silence" with a note of pain, the heart is broken and saved at the same time, love shielded from despair by patience even while the end is foreseen. The falling away of ideals and perfection is imaged again in the autumn leaves that "break off,/descend—/descend—" Both "Southern Cross" and "Quaker Hill" close with a realization of emptiness.

"National Winter Garden" and "The Tunnel" show human life at its crudest, its most starkly physical and degraded. As Crane said of "The Tunnel," "It's rather ghastly, almost surgery." [12] But the sterile sheaf of dust which symbolized the death of the previous section must be changed to life which is realized only through submission to physical reality, as even the force of generation through man's sexual nature is begun in Magdalene, the woman of "National Winter Garden." She is crudely, violently physical and all lust. The tom-toms and turquoise snake rings recall Pocahontas, but this is a caricature of the nature goddess, and all but the flesh escapes her. In the empty trapeze of her flesh alone there may be no possibility of soaring life. But even in this woman there is something of the whole, and in the very fact of the creative force implicit in her being, she impels toward life. Even in her burlesque of nature, there is an involvement in the totality of life. Through the recognition of the whole can come recreation, "bone by infant bone," through the human commitment to the flesh. As Crane wrote to Waldo Frank (7 Feb. 1923) about "Faustus and Helen" (a poem anticipating many of the themes of *The Bridge*), "the creator and the eternal destroyer dance arm in arm." Here is isolated the lowest common denominator of life. The mortality or death that Eve brought into the world is a mark of the human dilemma, but it is to be conquered by the life that is impelled by the continual forces of generation. In this light, the title of the song has dual connotations: the death of winter, but winter as a garden where life is enclosed though not yet flowering.

In the mechanical, material world of "The Tunnel," the protagonist again goes through hell in order to reach paradise. The theme is stated in the quotation from Blake:

> To Find the Western path
> Right thro' the Gates of Wrath.

From Times Square and Columbus Circle, movement of the "hiving swarms" goes by night to the subway where, underground,

> The phonographs of hades in the brain
> Are tunnels that re-wind themselves,

with nightmare grind of scenes chaotic, and humanity bleared with death. But even as the elemental creative force in Magdalene could "lug us back lifeward—bone by infant bone," the protagonist of the Tunnel's grave rises to the harbor and the bridge out of the subway

> like Lazarus, to feel the slope,
> The sod and billow breaking,—lifting ground. . . .

Here, too, the lines anticipate the following movement. The leap of faith and imagination is prepared for in

> —A sound of waters bending astride the sky
> Unceasing with some Word that will not die . . . !

The last poems to be related are "Virginia" and "Atlantis." In both, the imagination rises through love to a mystical theme. In "Virginia"—girl, Pocahontas, the Virgin Mary—the action moves upward, even as Crane called the poem, "virgin in process of 'being built.' " [13] From the crude dance-hall girl in "National Winter Garden," the action has turned to Mary, the girl that someone waits for after work on a rainy Saturday noon. Wish, separation, and doubt also correspond to the motif of yearning in "Southern Cross." But here the girl is glorified with reality in the second stanza, "blue-eyed Mary with the claret scarf," and higher images of bells and pigeons lift the eyes. Gayety and assurance sparkle in this stanza, and doubtless the figs and oysters have garden and sexual references. Finally, out of reality and over the spring flowers in the street scene, she is shown leaning out of the tower, like a medieval painting or an image of the golden-haired Blessed Damozel at the gold bar of heaven. Described through love and beauty, she is given a clear spirituality: "Cathedral Mary,/shine!" In "Three Songs," woman rises from Eve in the dark waters, to Magdalene in the dance hall, to Mary shining high in the flowers. But Mary is real, not a wraith like the figure of Eve.

In "Atlantis" the final mystic vision of *The Bridge* is invoked, the light and harmony more brilliantly embodied because of the Tunnel's demonic night (as the sun at the close of "Virginia" is brighter because of the smoky dance and the morning rain). In the first six stanzas of "Atlantis," the physical bridge is most immediate in the imagery; in the last six stanzas the imaged form is transmuted into the meaning of the symbol, so that the suggestive arc, union, and harmony of the Bridge are more nearly in view than the physical form. Love as harmony, or music, is the principle of the system. In its musical pattern the Bridge forms "one arc synoptic of all tides below." But even in the realization of the mystic beauty, memories of the way that led through the dance hall and the subway are contained in the "cypher-script of time" in which the traveler,

> through smoking pyres of love and death,
> Searches the timeless laugh of mythic spears . . . .

or the eternal rejoicing out of death through the pyres and spears which recall the mythic destruction of Maquokeeta and the eternity gained thereby. The human paradox of search that contains defeat, life that contains destruction, is recalled through Tyre and Troy, Jason and Aeolus. But from the ominous capes the Bridge rises, "lifting night to cycloramic crest/Of deepest day—" and translating time into the union of many in one, the psalm of Cathay.

The symbolic Bridge rises out of the physical image as we move back across the continent to surmount and include both space and time, where eyes must "stammer through the pangs of dust and steel." Vision is regained and made whole by the physical sky (like the Bridge),

> the circular, indubitable frieze
> Of heaven's meditation, yoking wave
> To kneeling wave. . . .

The "steeled Cognizance" of the Bridge—its meaning and its form—holds "in single chrysalis the many twain." Generation and union are suggested in the image of the chrysalis and in the bridge as "the stitch and stallion glow" of stars. Again, as a ship it moves on the voyage, and its "intrinsic Myth"—spiritual vision through total life—is time-borne and body-borne "through the bright drench and fabric of our veins." In all the land oppositions are joined, as tears "sustain" and life revolving through birth and harvest is a "sweet torment." The Bridge is river-throated (in time and the physical world), but out of it is the ascent of the eternal winged Deity. The culmination of the mystic vision is the ineffable white flower, here called Anemone but corresponding to Dante's great white rose, heaven's still center. The flower petals of light "spend the suns about us," as Mary in the May flowers let down her golden hair, shining in the "way-up" tower.

The last sections of *The Bridge* develop from the single movement of "Three Songs," but they are more than a simple recapitulation of the theme in other language. The "Songs" trace only the sexual motif, while the following poems embody that element in its larger context: the whole effort of man as he struggles through time to find some eternal order. That such a spiritual vision might be best accomplished through the whole reality of life, centering in its complete body and its creative force, is suggested by these poems.

Many have justly criticized *The Bridge* as a "Myth of America" for its chaotic historical and chronological sense and for the apparent lack of continuity between several of its sections. Yet it is fair to look again at the poem with a little more of Crane's eye. In the first place, he considered his poem symphonic, a "mystical synthesis" of America in which history, fact, and location "all have to be transfigured into abstract form." It was not to be a narrative epic which would proceed in historical sequence but an evolution in which idea and motif would in recurrence construct the imaginative body of the poem as an "organic panorama." [14] Thus one might dare to say that *The Bridge* is not the Myth of America in an historical sense at all, but a construction and ritual celebration of the spiritual consciousness and creative force possible to America. Because present and past are often simultaneous and chronology distorted (as in a Faulkner novel), *The Bridge* must rely on a psychological order that is more intuitive, emotional, and mystical than rational.

A further consideration, then, is that Crane's poetic technique used not the ordinary historical or dialectic logic, but an organic principle which he called "the logic of metaphor," or "the dynamics of metaphor."[15] Crane's use of words like *organic* and *dynamic* in his discussions of his poetic intentions suggests that form is to be found most naturally in growth and movement. One crucial thing here is that the sensibility of the reader is required to fuse the relationships of the metaphor as it evolves. The poem is not given *to* the reader, but the reader helps to create it. Thus the technique demands something of the generative quality of life itself. In a larger sense than the individual metaphor, this organic principle is exactly illustrated by transmutations in imagery. As one form blends into another, a kind of generation goes on within the poem, a cycle of life that repeats but is never exactly the same. The reader participates in its psychological movement, its ritual creation. Some of the urgency we feel in Crane's poetry is perhaps the sense we have of growth in the poem itself, and the logic we can recognize is an imaginative progression through pattern and image.

Transmutation of imagery is one organic technique in *The Bridge*. The few examples which have been shown here may indicate that Crane did attempt some unity out of chaos, and through the very form of life itself. The test is that individual elements like "Three Songs" are complete when placed in their setting, no longer erratic and incidental to the poem. They are actually liberated in meaning when, paradoxically, they are confined to the cycles of transmutation which help to make up the whole symphony of *The Bridge*.

The structural unity of Crane's *The Bridge* is more logically fulfilled in the poem than most criticism has been willing to allow. But the glass must, of course, be turned to more than the function of the visual object. As an identity of idea, movement, and form, the "bridge" operates in a kind of psychological logic. Crane's poem begins with Whitman's ideal of physical and spiritual connections; it develops through a circling, generative form. In the logic of metaphor, curves and arches are traced in a multitude of visual ways, but the reader must also feel himself lifted, poised, or ascending physically and emotionally; and he must see both action and concept rounded to each other. Because Crane assumed that the imagination of the reader would follow the "emotional dynamics" of the metaphor, the shape of the bridge has its own logic in the context of the poem, and comes alive in the sensibility of the reader. One of Whitman's statements on poetry (in his 1876 Preface) will have a particular significance here:

Poetic style, when address'd to the Soul, is less definite form, outline, sculpture, and becomes vista, music, half-tints, and even less than half-tints. True it may be architecture, but again it may be the forest wild-wood, or the best effects thereof, at twilight, the waving oaks and cedars in the wind, and the impalpable odor.

The architecture of *The Bridge* is the curve of union. But in the farther vistas opened by that curve blend circles upon circles, parabolas like petals that compose at last the impalpable flower of eternity.

BERNICE SLOTE

Part IV

WHITMAN *and* THOMAS

Time held me green and dying
Though I sang in my chains like the sea.
DYLAN THOMAS
Fern Hill

Of Monkeys, Nudes, and
the Good Gray Poet

ON the walls of his workroom at Laugharne, Dylan Thomas had tacked pin-ups of monkeys and nudes—and a large photograph of Walt Whitman. This story comes by letter from Derek Stanford, who got it from a lady who said it in a Welsh paper.[1] But John Malcolm Brinnin, writing in the *Atlantic Monthly* for October 1955, also mentions the Whitman portrait, which hung directly above Thomas's desk. The pictures were there all right—bent into the Welsh and singing elemental caul of words that Thomas grew. But what especially of the good gray poet? What was Walt Whitman doing in Laugharne?

One answer is by Thomas himself in a letter and a poem recently published in *Letters to Vernon Watkins*. Commenting on "The Countryman's Return," Thomas (19 March 1940) calls himself a "middle-class, beardless Walt"; and the satire in the poem (a "half comic attack on myself") is for a *little* Walt—identified but not identical with Whitman ("A singing Walt from the mower . . . / Beardlessly wagging in Dean Street").[2] But the link was certainly there, and it may be time to examine more closely the almost uncanny ways in which Whitman and Thomas participate in the same poetic tradition. In this tradition, the nudes and the monkeys are not irrelevant.

I. A COMMON ROOT

Both repelled and attracted by Whitman, Ezra Pound finally admitted that they were of "one sap and one root." [3] Others have found, too, that the poetic tradition in which they wrote, and in which Whitman was the most vivid and potent singer, had a common root; that in spite of individual differences, the common elements were essential in defining their poetic position. Such were D. H. Lawrence and Hart Crane, who once remarked, "I begin to feel myself directly connected with Whitman." [4] Thomas, too, may be defined best when he is placed in his organic tradition.

The tradition to which Whitman and Thomas belong is affirmative, physical, intuitive, incantatory. It is the poetry of the strong Yes; the poetry of the body made equal with the soul, and the world viewed as one; the poetry which springs from the elemental blood-roots of man's self and experience; the poetry which has the bardic invocation of chant and song. It is primarily the embracing of all of experience as one positive force in creation, with all that is physical and sexual desired rather than denied. But even in the duality of man is a oneness, and often the spirit is found through the body. In the body of the world, genesis becomes the greatest spiritual force. In this, the tradition of Whitman and Thomas may be more pagan than Christian, but it is also one of love and the brotherhood of man, of the enormous significance of the least part of the universe, of mystical truth which interprets even death.

The poetry of Thomas and Whitman contains elements singularly alike: the world as "scheme" and generation; the poet's selfhood as microcosm, as singer, and as priest; imagery both sensuous and sexual. Molding these elements into their own forms, Thomas and Whitman have further resemblances in their language and manner, which give the impression of richness and abundance, seemingly natural, at times inchoate, but actually forming poetry of the strictest order.

II. IDEA AND THEME

On many points of emphasis and manner, Dylan Thomas and Walt Whitman are quite different. Where Whitman sings expansively of man moving at ease in the world, Thomas works more intensely and hypnotically *inside* the physical cosmos. Whitman is generally sanguine; Thomas is more somber, more conscious of the effort to reconcile the forces of life and death. So each had his own particular day. Yet the same sun warmed them both, and in their poetry they move in the same direction. They are clearly related in matters of subject, ideas, and general attitude; and when one reads both alternately he is struck innumerable times with the startling similarity of individual lines and passages. It is impossible to repeat them all, but we can look briefly at some of the most significant.

The most apparent likeness in Whitman and Thomas is their attention to physical things, the body of man and the sensuous world in which he moves. Each drew images out of familiar soil: Thomas blending the herons, the owls, the woods, and the lovers on the "loud hill of Wales"; Whitman using the grass and cedars of America, the "voluptuous cool-breath'd earth," the "populous pavements" of "million-footed" Manhattan. Both heard and sang with the tides that swung perpetually out of the Atlantic. But most significantly, both Thomas and Whitman found imagery and subject matter in physical man (to Whitman "hankering, gross, mystical, nude"), writing more frankly and surely of the body and its meaning than have other poets. Whitman, in the "Children of Adam" poems, writes of the "meaning and being" of the life of the body and sings "the body electric" to celebrate the human form. But the body is important not so much in itself but in the miracle of creation. In "Song of Myself" he says,

I believe in the flesh and the appetites,
Seeing, hearing, feeling, are miracles, and each part and tag of me is a
    miracle.

To Thomas, it was "my holy lucky body," and eyes, hair, heart, womb, and blood became the first necessities of his language as he traced the "wizard shape" of his "animal." In physical life, in the metaphor of man, there is for both poets a close, earthy, electric excitement.

In both Thomas and Whitman, "body poetry" becomes always the poetry of birth and procreation. Moreover, the sexual nature of man is identified with his life force and is, in actuality, one aspect of the spiritual force of the world: that eternity is created and recreated in the paradox of man's dissolving flesh. Whitman's poetry is "the song of procreation"; in "Song of Myself" he speaks of

Urge and urge and urge,
Always the procreant urge of the world.
Out of the dimness opposite equals advance, always substance and
    increase, always sex,
Always a knit of identity, always distinction, always a breed of life.

Thomas's early poetry, especially, contains constant sexual images and references, and in the later poems like "In the White Giant's Thigh," sex is an urge even in the dead women in the hill. But like Whitman's, his theme is not primarily erotic sex but genesis, procreation, the seed and the "planted womb," conception and birth.

Thomas, notably, has a number of poems in which he extends the creative force back in time. "From Love's First Fever to Her Plague" begins with "love's first fever" through the "hollow minute of the womb" to the "first print of the unshodden foot" and the prospering of the body. In other poems too, such as "Before I Knocked" and "I Dreamed My Genesis," Thomas insistently assumes a state not confined to the "declension of the flesh." Man in the force of creation exists before birth. In this kind of spiritual extension the body is made mysterious, hallowed, doubly alive. The same sense of distance—life before birth—appears in "Song of Myself":

Before I was born out of my mother generations guided me,
My embryo has never been torpid, nothing could overlay it.

The continuity found in generation is also shown in Thomas's habitual blending of speaker, father, and child.

Whitman and Thomas thus have in common a body of poetry which is physical and sexual; but more important, it is the metaphor of eternal creation, the life force that is bound by neither time nor place. Genesis unites man with all other parts of creation. In fact, Thomas views the world as continuous movement,

growth, and generation with elements in man and nature inter-
fused:

> The force that through the green fuse drives the flower
> Drives my green age . . .

The theme of unity is repetitive in Whitman, who found in
animals and himself "the same old law" and saw "a vast similitude" interlocking all distances, spheres, identities; "the threads
that connect the stars, and of wombs and of the father-stuff."
This cosmic identity appears in Thomas's sexual account of creation, "In the Beginning," when

> Life rose and spouted from the rolling seas,
> Burst in the roots, pumped from the earth and rock
> The secret oils that drive the grass

and there was "the ribbed original of love." In "All All and All
the Dry Worlds Lever" the elements are made one:

> Out of the sea, the drive of oil,
> Socket and grave, the brassy blood,
> Flower, flower, all all and all.

Whitman's unity of "grass that grows wherever the land is"
and "the common air that bathes the globe" is perhaps a surface
tie, but his sense of the oneness of nature extends, as in Thomas,
to identifying man with all elemental forces—tides and the seasons, wind and fire. Man is integral with the sea, the sea of
"ground-swells" and "broad convulsive breaths," and he feels
the ocean within him "fathomless, stirring, preparing unprece-
dented waves and storms." The ocean poems in the "Sea-Drift"
section of *Leaves of Grass* and "With Husky-Haughty Lips, O
Sea!" are concentrations of Whitman's sense of the mutual life
of man and sea:

> The tale of cosmic elemental passion,
> Thou tellest to a kindred soul.

Another identification with nature is in "We Two, How Long
We Were Fool'd": "We are snow, rain, cold, darkness, we are
each product and influence of the globe. . . ." Whitman's ex-

pansiveness, strength, and somewhat primitive exuberance come partly from this sense of cosmic union. In Thomas, also, there is the pulse of excitement that seems related to an elemental strength. He imagines, for example, in "Before I Knocked," that even in the womb "I knew the message of the winter . . ./ Wind in me leaped." The turn of seasons and the tides are constant images in his poetry. In "Light Breaks Where No Sun Shines," the "waters of the heart/Push in their tides;" and

> Dawn breaks behind the eyes;
> From poles of skull and toe the windy blood
> Slides like a sea. . . .

Night and day, winter and spring, are in the sockets, bone, and lids.

Such rhythms in nature and man become prototypes of the larger cycles and movements which give pattern to time and the universe. This is Whitman's sense of "scheme," that "the universe is duly in order." Even though the cycle swings from birth to dissolution, there is in "Eidólons"

> Ever the dim beginning,
> Ever the growth, the rounding of the circle,
> Ever the summit and the merge at last, (to surely start again) . . . .

To Whitman all is "Form, union, plan." Thomas describes the circling order in "A Process in the Weather of the Heart," a process which turns damp to dry and, in the eye, forewarns the bones of blindness. Whitman's "scheme" is to Thomas the paradox of continuous birth out of continuous death; of "one sun, one manna" for what was "many sounding minded"; of all life implicit in the seed (conversely, the "sandgrain day" and the "mustardseed sun"). This sense of the cosmos in the microcosm is, of course, familiar in Whitman's "I believe a leaf of grass is no less than the journey-work of the stars." In cycles of time and elemental motion, in identities that compose and expand into simultaneous perfection, Whitman and Thomas agree on the fundamental, affirmative point of order out of apparent chaos.

Such order in the universe depends significantly on the fact that unity is seen in apparent contradiction—the union of opposites. One opposition is that of the soul and the body. Here the tradition of which Whitman and Thomas are a part differs sharply from the view that holds the duality of man a separation of body and soul, that denies the physical in order to achieve the spiritual. A line is drawn through being, and the believer turns to the one half as truth and cancels the other as illusion. Another view—and this is found in the poetry of Whitman and Thomas —recognizes that the halves exist but believes that to see one thing alone, without its implied opposite, is to be half-man, one-eyed in a flat-dimensioned world. The only unity is *through* duality. One recognizes that the mystery of the body is the same as that of the soul, for both exist in completion because of the other. Whitman went further than Thomas, sometimes suggesting that the body *is* the soul, but both poets reiterate the necessity of accepting and knowing both. To Thomas, the final spiritual glory comes out of the play of these contradictions.

On the theme of duality, Whitman asserts, "I am the poet of the Body and I am the poet of the Soul." Thomas says, "I, in my intricate image, stride on two levels," being both cadaver and ghost, the "pinned-around-the-spirit/Cut-to-measure flesh." The two are combined in "Before I Knocked":

> I, born of flesh and ghost, was neither
> A ghost nor man, but mortal ghost.

Flesh and triumphant spirit take on one form, even as other paradoxes fulfill themselves. "I find one side a balance and the antipodal side a balance," says Whitman. In the mystic evolution there is "not the right only justified, what we call evil also justified." In Thomas,

> Light and dark are no enemies
> But one companion. . . .

Opposites blend: "Beginning with doom in the bulb, the spring unravels," and

> Time held me green and dying
> Though I sang in my chains like the sea.

Even if one accepts the two halves as one, he is not exempt from the darker sense of decay in the flesh. Though Thomas shows this horror more than does Whitman, both are struck with

the bitterness of transient life. "You bitter hug of mortality,"
Whitman called it. He speaks of "the moaning gibberish of dry
limbs," and knows the downcast hours, "Weights of lead, how
ye clog and cling at my ankles." Then all ask, "Shall I not escape?" In Thomas the worm is in the flesh and time is a running
grave. Snow, dust, night, and the encompassing sea imperil the
mortal ghost. Death is implicit in birth, and in many of the poems,
the entire drama is man's journey to certain death. But the paradox continues, for it is to "That one dark I owe my light," even
as in the Saviour there was "calm to be done in his safe unrest."
Thomas finds light *through* darkness: In "Poem on His Birthday,"
he says

> That the closer I move
> To death, one man through his sundered hulks,
> The louder the sun blooms . . .

even as Whitman speaks of death: "The sun burst through in
unlooked-for directions."

The spiritual intensity found in both Whitman and Thomas
derives in no small sense from their capture of both dark and
light and the tension gained by the pull of the halves against each
other. The final glory becomes more ecstatic because it is made
of the whole, and mysticism thus grows out of the physical and
its signal force of generation. Beginning with their vision of the
pre-womb existence, both poets suggest the eternality of man: life
is a period of identity which has a *before* and *after*. The imaginative mixture of sexual and evolutionary imagery, of life emerging
from the total embryonic sea, conveys a compelling sense of the
immortality of man existent in his sexuality, in the procreative
force contained in the "limpid pool" within him. Immortality of
the "after" is seen as the victory of light over darkness, a progression to clarity and order. Thomas's "Poem on His Birthday"
shows man, of four elements and five senses, as

> a spirit in love
> Tangling through this spun slime
> To his nimbus bell cool kingdom come. . . .

If the country of death is the heart's size, and the earth a known
dark, "Vision and Prayer" ends with the lightning of God:

<pre>
          Now I am lost in the blinding
      One. The sun roars at the prayer's end.
</pre>

For the dead man aged a hundred, birth comes out of death:

<pre>
      The morning is flying on the wings of his age
      And a hundred storks perch on the sun's right hand.
</pre>

There is, much like Whitman's calm walk with the two figures of death in "When Lilacs Last in the Dooryard Bloom'd," Thomas's walk with love in the mortal garden of "Unluckily for a Death," "With immortality at my side like Christ the sky." And as Whitman refuses to linger in sorrow at death, accepting its natural universality in the song of the thrush, so Thomas refuses to mourn the death of a child by saying that once death is taken as a part of the whole, a universal thing which needs recognition only once, "After the first death, there is no other." The smallest sprout, says Whitman, shows there is really no death . . . "And to die is different from what any one supposed, and luckier." Thomas's most vivid evocation of immortality appears in "And Death Shall Have No Dominion":

<pre>
      Though they be mad and dead as nails,
      Heads of the characters hammer through daisies. . . .
</pre>

Whitman and Thomas both assert the mystical continuity of life. These perceptions relate to the intuitive knowledge of the glory of the universe, what Thomas calls "my heart's truth." In the country of the heart, man becomes partly instinctive, partly emotional, partly spiritual. Thomas, in "Light Breaks Where No Sun Shines," speaks of this subterranean winding of forces, concluding,

<pre>
      Light breaks on secret lots,
      On tips of thoughts where thoughts smell in the rain;
      When logics die,
      The secret of the soil grows through the eye,
      And blood jumps in the sun. . . .
</pre>

Whitman has a similar passage in "Song of Myself,"

<pre>
      Logic and sermons never convince,
      The damp of the night drives deeper into my soul.
</pre>

Intuition and feeling are thus in man's elemental nature, the blood-roots which signify his union with all other parts of the world. One might therefore say that not logic but love is the grace of mortal man. Much of Whitman's poetry, especially "Calamus," celebrates love and brotherhood. As Thomas says that he wrote "for the love of Man and in praise of God," for the lovers with "their arms/Round the griefs of the ages," so Whitman calls himself "the poet of comrades":

> These I singing in spring collect for lovers,
> (For who but I should understand lovers and all
> their sorrow and joy?)

Whitman's affectionate catalogue of the varied people of America is matched by Thomas's sympathetic sketches of men and women in "Under Milk Wood." For both, love is one of the universal ties, a spiritual affirmation. "In the White Giant's Thigh" implies for Thomas a union of physical love and eternal love: "Teach me the love that is evergreen after the fall leaved/Grave. . . ." In other poems, love gives "the first vision that set fire to the stars"; through it is "the globe of genesis spun." And Whitman in "Song of Myself" describes in terms of a physical act of love the mystical experience which revealed eternal and universal love as the framework of Creation.

Whitman and Thomas are also alike in their feeling for personal identity, man as the microcosm of the world in which the elements re-enact their tides of war and peace, and of which the poet tries to make a momentary order. "Walt Whitman, a kosmos," he called himself. To him "the converging objects of the universe perpetually flow;" he is an "acme of things accomplish'd" and an "encloser of things to be." As each leaf of grass has its significance in the universe, each man is individually important. With somewhat the same intensity, Thomas writes in a number of poems of his body, his birth, his origins—but like Whitman he sees himself in "Do You Not Father Me" as the symbolic encloser of all things:

> Am I not father, too, and the ascending boy,
>
> .   .   .   .   .
>
> Am I not all of you by the directed sea
> Where bird and shell are babbling in my tower?

"One's-self I sing," says Whitman, but as part of "The simple, compact, well-join'd scheme, myself disintegrated, every one disintegrated yet part of the scheme."

The poet of the tradition of Whitman and Thomas is also the singer and priest, the intermediary who invokes by incantation the response of love and mystical feeling. Praise is the affirmative note constant in both poets. Whitman "sings" and "chants" the sensual world; and the music of Thomas's "Fern Hill," "Poem in October," and "Over Sir John's Hill" gives what he called in *Quite Early One Morning* "affirmation of the beautiful and terrible worth of the earth." In his "Prologue" to the *Collected Poems* he calls himself "a spinning man" to

> Glory also this star, bird
> Roared, sea born, man torn, blood blest,
> Hark: I trumpet the place,
> From fish to jumping hill!

Finally, his "ark sings in the sun" against the flowering flood. And Whitman in his own symbolic flood tide of "Crossing Brooklyn Ferry" invokes and praises all things above it—appearances mysterious, loved, containing perfection—because they are parts of eternity and of the soul.

So the poetry of Whitman and Thomas expresses the same central theme. To delight in the world, to love, and to value all living—these are sacramental acts, for physical being is understood as the ritual of godhead made mortally plain.

III. WORD AND IMAGE

Thomas is clearly at home in the movement of modern English poetry toward syntactical disintegration. Not unlike other modern poets—Ezra Pound, Hart Crane, and T. S. Eliot—Thomas relies primarily on the connotative or suggestive quality of words and little on the denotative meanings derived from proper placement in the order of the sentence. But Thomas, like Walt Whitman before him, achieves unique effects by violating the laws and bursting the bonds of language. Thomas and Whitman, through their seemingly "careless" or "frenzied" eruption in words, achieve that quality of *bardic chant* which is peculiar to both and which constitutes a significant element in the tradition of which they are a part.

This poetic technique which results frequently in a strong impression of ecstatic abandon, an impression of the poet as primitive or pagan performing rites of magic as he chants his mystic song, has caused both Whitman and Thomas to be accused of lack of control and the heresy of "expressive" form. Such accusations have resulted from a confusion of cause and effect in poetry: too frequently it is assumed that the *effect* of abandon may be achieved only by the poet who has *abandoned* all form. Whitman understood that cause and effect had a much more complex relationship. He once said of one of his own works that "though to the ordinary reader let loose with wildest abandon, the true artist can see it is yet under control." And although when one listens to the records of Thomas reading his poems aloud there is the unmistakable "wild" tone of the bardic chant, when one sees the poems on the page he realizes the genuine complexity of form they represent. There is disruption of syntax in Whitman and Thomas, not because they are ignorant of language or careless of its use, but because through a "controlled abandon" they achieve precisely the "primitive" effects they desire.

The relationship of a disintegrated syntax to the primitive bardic quality is elusive and difficult to define. The most obvious connection is transgression or neglect of inherited and accepted conventions. The sentence which violates a normal word order, which ignores the normal relationships of words, which omits the usual connectives, or which submerges some important element such as the verb, suggests a voice of wild ecstasy bursting the bonds of propriety. Any badly garbled sentence would not have such an effect of abandon: only the sentence deliberately and premeditatedly constructed could convey an impression of the primitive. For although the successful sentence might ignore on the surface some of the usual relationships of words, nevertheless the sentence would exhibit a genuine sensitivity to subtle connotative relationships far beyond the ability of the ordinary writer of bad prose.

Both Whitman and Thomas remind us that poetry needs to be heard to be fully appreciated. Their poems are at their worst lying awkward and voiceless on the page. When read aloud, their poetry forces the ecstatic note into the reader's voice. Who can prevent his being swept into the joyful primitive abandon of a stanza from Thomas's "Poem in October":

> A springful of larks in a rolling
> Cloud and the roadside bushes brimming with whistling
>   Blackbirds and the sun of October
>   Summery
>   On the hill's shoulder,
> Here were fond climates and sweet singers suddenly
> Come in the morning where I wandered and listened
>   To the rain wringing
>   Wind blow cold
>   In the wood faraway under me.

The larks, the bushes, the blackbirds, and the October sun—all seem to press in on the poet, forcing him merely to *name* them in succession. The press of image on image in syntactically incomplete units (these substantives are never given finite verbs) creates a world of vivid abundance to which the poet surrenders in ecstatic joy. And it is an eternal world, for the verbs that do appear are infinite: *rolling, brimming, whistling.* This world on "the hill's shoulder" exists forever in the memory of the poet.

Whitman seems filled with an even more intense compulsion to *name*, resulting in the famous lengthy "catalogues." And some of Whitman's finest poetic effects are achieved through repetitive use of the "-ing" form. In the following passage, which appears immediately after the bird's sad lament of lonesome love in "Out of the Cradle Endlessly Rocking," an ecstasy more poignant than joyful is voiced:

The aria sinking,
All else continuing, the stars shining,
The winds blowing, the notes of the birds continuous echoing,
With angry moans the fierce old mother incessantly moaning,
On the sands of Paumanok's shore gray and rustling,
The yellow half-moon enlarged, sagging down, drooping, the face of
    the sea almost touching,
The boy ecstatic, with his bare feet the waves, with his hair the atmos-
    phere dallying . . . .

Like the stanza from Thomas's "Poem in October," this passage creates a "timeless" scene: all of these acts have their continuous existence in the poet's acute and sensitive memory—from which, indeed, they have been recreated. In both the Thomas and Whitman passages, the shattering of conventional syntax is a poetic device deliberately designed to achieve a calculated effect of abandon and heightened emotionality.

Whitman and Thomas show some similarity in their use of words, and particularly in the practice they both have in mixing levels of usage. Whitman once said that he sometimes thought that *Leaves of Grass* was a "language experiment." The Good Gray Poet was particularly fond of bastard foreign words, and some of his potentially finest effects are marred by weird concoctions which disturb the eye and jar the ear (as in "Our Old Feuillage"). Paradoxically, though, this apparent affectation is balanced by the frequent appearance of words and phrases of common, even "low," speech usually considered "unpoetic." Thomas shares with Whitman this habit of juxtaposing several levels of language-usage, the low with the high, the common with the uncommon, to achieve startling effects. Whitman said, "Apart from the pulling and hauling stands what I am." Or

> Come Muse migrate from Greece and Ionia,
> Cross out please those immensely overpaid accounts . . . .

Thomas said in "If I Were Tickled by the Rub of Love,"

> And that's the rub, the only rub that tickles.
> The knobbly ape that swings along his sex
> From damp love-darkness and the nurse's twist
> Can never raise the midnight of a chuckle . . . .

And, in "Fern Hill,"

> Now as I was young and easy under the apple boughs
> About the lilting house and happy as the grass was green,
> The night above the dingle starry,
> Time let me hail and climb
> Golden in the heydays of his eyes . . . .

Rub, tickles, knobbly, damp love-darkness, chuckle, dingle, heydays—Whitman would have delighted in this colorful and varied vocabulary. Thomas and Whitman not only share the enthusiastic delight in mixing words of all levels but even refer to their verbal gifts in similar "undignified" phrasing. Whitman boasted, "The spotted hawk swoops by and accuses me, he complains of my gab and my loitering. . . . / I sound my barbaric yawp over the roofs of the world." Thomas asserted, "The lovely gift of the gab bangs back on a blind shaft."

Frequently both poets focus primarily, sometimes solely, on the connotative meanings of words. The resulting surface illogicality is balanced by the underlying poetic coherence. In "Song of the Broad-Axe," among the shapes the axe gives rise to are:

> The shape of the shamed and angry stairs trod by sneaking footsteps,
> The shape of the sly settee . . . .

Shamed, angry, and *sly* are all precisely and finely misplaced. Such misplacement makes for a poetry that seems to be constantly straining against the bonds of convention and occasionally bursting fully and magnificently free. Sometimes in Thomas's poetry such straining seems to exist in line after line, conveying a feeling of a stretched tautness constantly on the verge of snapping. The opening lines of one poem read—

> When, like a running grave, time tracks you down,
> Your calm and cuddled is a scythe of hairs,
> Love in her gear is slowly through the house,
> Up naked stairs, a turtle in a hearse,
> Hauled to the dome . . . .

The words seem to merge, to run together; the more the reader sees, the deeper he is plunged, finally sucked down in the currents and crosscurrents of connotative meanings, dismayed at the impossibility of paraphrase. Although Whitman was working in this direction, never did he reach this complexity and compactness. Whitman could envision stairs as *shamed and angry* and a settee as *sly;* Thomas, in the space of a very few lines, could envision a grave as *running,* hairs as a *scythe,* stairs as *naked*—and much more (*calm* and *cuddled* seem at first to be used as nouns, but the singular *is* suggests that they are adjectives modifying an understood subject).

If Whitman and Thomas alike practice language-distortion and syntax-evasion, they are, in addition, fond of some similar images. One might be startled to find in Thomas's "Especially When the October Wind," the line: "The signal grass that tells me all I know." The "leaf" of grass is the title image of Whitman's book, and one that dominates the whole of *Leaves of Grass*. Thomas uses the grass in this single line, much as Whitman uses it, to suggest the miraculous that exists in the commonplace, to indicate the great and transcendent knowledge that lies close at hand. Moreover, in a poetry as dense and rich as Thomas's, it would not be farfetched to infer from his "signal grass" an oblique acknowledgment of Whitman's influence.

A dominant image common to both poets is the sea. When one reads the last line of "Especially When the October Wind"— "By the sea's side hear the dark-vowelled birds"—he perhaps recalls Whitman's seaside reminiscence, "Out of the Cradle Endlessly Rocking" and the "myriad thence-arous'd words" which are like "a flock, twittering, rising, or overhead passing." In both poets, the sight of the sea gives rise to thoughts of death which are, in turn, associated with flights of birds. Throughout Thomas's poetry and Whitman's *Leaves*, the sea is linked with death. Many of Whitman's so-called sea poems are poems in which the locale is the seashore, where land and ocean meet. There is the suggestion always that these "liquid rims and wet sands" symbolize the joining of material and spiritual, the act of death itself in which the one is transformed into the other. Many of the same suggestions are implicit in Thomas's "We Lying by Seasand." There is surely conscious punning in such lines as "For in this yellow grave of sand and sea" and "Of the grave, gay, seaside land." The "lunar silences, the silent tide" and the "heavenly music over the sand" —all suggest the spiritual insight bestowed by the sea as symbol of the life after death. In both Thomas and Whitman the setting forth on the voyage is the symbolic act of death, with the implicit suggestion of spiritual rebirth. In the final section (excluding the annexes) of *Leaves of Grass*—"Songs of Parting"—the poet's death is envisioned as a setting out to sea—"Our life is closed, our life begins,/The long, long anchorage we leave." In Thomas's "Poem on His Birthday," the sea is designated the final human destination: as man moves to death, the louder "the tusked, ramshackling sea exults." The sea in its exultation represents a triumphant spirituality—triumphant in its anticipation of reclaiming its wandering child. Thomas's poem ends—"As I sail out to die." In both poets the use of the sea as symbol of death suggests the quality of descent and resurrection, the close of the material and the launching of the spiritual existence.

Both Whitman and Thomas are fond of bird imagery. Whitman's two greatest poems, "Out of the Cradle Endlessly Rocking" and "When Lilacs Last in the Dooryard Bloom'd," feature birds in primary roles. At the opening of *Leaves of Grass* in "Starting from Paumanok," a poem designed to introduce the book's major recurring images, Whitman suggests the importance of birds to his poetic program as he systematically catalogues "the mockingbird's tones," "the flight of the mountain-hawk," and "the hermit thrush from the swamp-cedars." These vitally contribute as the poet, "solitary, singing in the West," strikes up "for a New World." The three birds become major images and symbols in *Leaves of Grass:* the mountain hawk symbolizing, in turn, freedom and sexuality; the mockingbird symbolizing unrestricted joy in both fulfilled life and, paradoxically, a "fulfilled" death; the hermit thrush symbolizing the world of spirituality, the triumphant perfection and order which exist in the midst of evil and chaos.

Thomas's "Over Sir John's Hill" consists almost exclusively of bird imagery. The poet, who thinks of himself as "young Aesop fabling," creates a life and death drama of birds in the sky. Implicit throughout, as the reference to Aesop suggests, is a symbolic meaning. The hawk, the sparrows, and the heron are, respectively, the attacker, the attacked, and the grieved. At the end of the poem, the poet asserts:

> I who hear the tune of the slow,
> Wear-willow river, grave,
> Before the lunge of the night, the notes on this time-shaken
> Stone for the sake of the souls of the slain birds sailing.

This tune of the "wear-willow river" is suggestive of Whitman's world of eidólons—"The infinite oceans where the rivers empty." As the poet hears the river "before the lunge of the night," so there is the strong suggestion that *night,* or pure oblivion, is not the bird's (or man's) sole fate. In presenting this bird-drama of rapacity, victimization, and grief, Thomas seems to be asserting an acceptance, like Whitman's, of all life—good and evil, joy and pain. The hawk is killer, but the poet sings, "All praise of the hawk on fire in hawk-eyed dusk be sung." In this vivid image the setting sun reflects brightly from the soaring, triumphant hawk, much as it reflects from the "slow-wheeling" sea gulls of Whitman's "Crossing Brooklyn Ferry." The poet-traveler "saw how the glistening yellow lit up parts of their bodies and left the rest in strong shadow." In both Thomas's hawk and Whitman's gulls there is, in their reflected sunlight, a hint of the divinity pervading and informing the universe.

But the imagery which draws Whitman and Thomas most closely together into a common tradition is sexual. Note the ambivalence in this stanza from Thomas's "My Hero Bares His Nerve":

> My hero bares my side and sees his heart
> Tread, like a naked Venus,
> The beach of flesh, and wind her bloodred plait;
> Stripping my loin of promise,
> He promises a secret heat.

Compare the connotations of these ambiguous lines with the famous passage in section 5 of "Song of Myself":

I mind how once we lay such a transparent summer morning,
How you settled your head athwart my hips and gently turn'd over
    upon me,
And parted the shirt from my bosom-bone, and plunged your tongue
    to my bare-stript heart,
And reach'd till you felt my beard, and reach'd till you held my feet.

In both of these passages, sexual connotations predominate, but the ultimate intent, in the "secret heat" of Thomas as in the "bare-stript heart" of Whitman, is not erotic: the suggestion is clear that a spiritual insight is achieved not through mortification and degradation of the senses but through their acceptance and transfiguration.

Thomas as well as Whitman is able to reconstruct through vivid imagery the "unknowable" existence of the individual before birth. Perhaps up from the dark depths of the unconscious flash images which succeed remarkably in evoking "pre-birth" feelings, sensations of the embryo in the dawn of time. Thomas's poem beginning "I dreamed my genesis in sweat of sleep," concludes:

> I dreamed my genesis in sweat of death, fallen
> Twice in the feeding sea, grown
> Stale of Adam's brine until, vision
> Of new man strength, I seek the sun.

"Adam's brine" connects Christian myth with Darwinian evolution: man's descent from Adam with man's derivation from the sea. Here, as in his "Before I Knocked," Thomas reverses prophecy and looks backward in time, discovering not only his existence but an unconscious feeling of being. "Before I knocked and flesh let enter," he says, he "Felt thud beneath my flesh's armour": "Ungotten I knew night and day." Though the being is shapeless as water, "in a molten form," it exists in a symbolic universe:

> The leaden stars, the rainy hammer
> Swung by my father from his dome.

In one of the most impressive passages in "Song of Myself," Whitman, in startlingly similar imagery, reveals the same acute sense of existence before birth: he "slept through the lethargic mist," and received "no hurt from the fetid carbon": "Monstrous sauroids transported [his embryo] in their mouths and deposited it with care."

Specifically and graphically sexual images abound in both Whitman and Thomas. In the "Children of Adam" poems Whitman sets out directly to celebrate the phallus and sing the song of procreation. And throughout *Leaves of Grass* this intent, though perhaps at times muted, is never absent. It seems, even, to burst forth in the midst of the poet's concentration on other themes. For Whitman, "Landscapes projected masculine, full-sized and golden." In one scene in "Song of Myself," in which the earth and sea are "half-held by the night," the great, rhythmic forces of nature are envisioned by the poet as joined in amorous embrace. The sexual life-force is thus invested with a fundamental and compelling inevitability. In Thomas, too, the sexual image seems obsessive, and recurs so frequently as to become symbolic of the identification of man with the life *sap* which constitutes the force "driving" all life. The most frequently recurring phallic symbol in Thomas is the worm ("the fathering worm"; "the worm beneath my nail") which ingeniously combines qualities of fertility and decay, life and death.

Both Whitman and Thomas utilize the imagery of birth in vivid and unusual ways. Whitman envisions death as the "accoucheur" who, "pressing, receiving," presides at the spiritual *birth* as the poet reclines "by the sills of the exquisite flexible doors." Or he contemplates the broadaxe—"Head from the mother's bowels drawn." Thomas, in " 'If My Head Hurt a Hair's Foot,' " demands that he be "unborn"—returned to the womb—if his birth has resulted in pain: "If my bunched, monkey coming is cruel/ Rage me back to the making house." In "Twenty-Four Years," Thomas vividly recreates the scene of his birth: "In the groin of the natural doorway I crouched like a tailor/Sewing a shroud for a journey."

Perhaps the poem in Whitman which most directly foreshadows Thomas's technique in the dramatization of imagery is "The Sleepers." In this poem, an early example of the stream-of-consciousness technique, the flood of images that pours forth seems to well up from subterranean depths—the dark abysses of the uncharted unconscious. Wandering all night in his "vision," Whitman witnesses the fantastic, experiences strange and unrecognized sensations, *becomes* many "things" other than self: "I am a dance—play up there! the fit is whirling me fast!/I am the ever-laughing—it is new moon and twilight." In a remarkable passage, unfortunately deleted by Whitman in his final published version of the poem, the flowing dream imagery becomes vividly and sexually charged:

The cloth laps a first sweet eating and drinking,
Laps life-swelling yolks—laps ear of rose-corn milky and just ripened;
The white teeth stay, and the boss-tooth advances in darkness,
And liquor is spilled on lips and bosoms by touching glasses, and the
    best liquor afterward.

The descent into the world of dreams seems to Whitman a liberating experience as he identifies himself with the night:

I descend my western course, my sinews are flaccid,
Perfume and youth course through me and I am their wake.

In many poems Thomas is specifically concerned with portraying the drama of dreams. In "I Fellowed Sleep," he asserts that sleep "kissed" him "in the brain" and then he "dropped on dreaming and the upward sky": "I fled the earth and, naked, climbed the weather,/Reaching a second ground far from the stars." In "I Dreamed My Genesis," the poet, in a "sweat of sleep," reconstructs from his "pre-natal" memories his own conception—

> breaking
> Through the rotating shell, strong
> As motor muscle on the drill, driving
> Through vision and the girdered nerve.

In many poems—among them "Our Eunuch Dreams," "Lie Still, Sleep Becalmed," "In Country Sleep"—Thomas utilizes the device of the dream as the basis for an array of rich and varied images associated primarily in their connotations. The technique of the phantasmagoria of dream seems also to be carried over to the poems not concerned with sleep. In Thomas, as in Whitman, passages or poems need frequently to be placed in the context of a "waking dream," an emotional "frenzy" or "soaring" which in its "release" of the poet and in its uncapping of the unconscious resembles the dream-state. When viewed in this way, images which at first appear as a disorderly and unrelated miscellany emerge as complexly ordered experience rich in depth and implication.

In several ways, the poetry of both Thomas and Whitman becomes itself a part of the creative body of the world, image creating image, word bursting into word, in a spiral plunge out of the dark seed to the larger, encompassing light, this same process to be repeated in each comprehension of a poem. Thomas's statement of his own process is revealing:

I let, perhaps, an image be 'made' emotionally in me and then apply to it what intellectual and critical forces I possess—let it breed another, let that image contradict the first, make, of the third image bred out of the other two together, a fourth contradictory image, and let them all, within my imposed formal limits, conflict. Each image holds within it the seed of its own destruction, and my dialectal method, as I understand it, is a constant building up and breaking down of the images that come out of the central seed, which is itself destructive and constructive at the same time.[5]

This creative force is shown first of all in the verve with which Whitman and Thomas use words and phrases that are daring, fresh, new in combination and implication. The somewhat arrogant "yawp," the "gift of the gab," sparks and thunders to the most irreverent, most exciting kind of language. And the rhythmic pulse, the beat or throb which is so easily recognizable in the lines of both Thomas and Whitman, is itself a repetition of the hypnotic, primitive dance which makes man a participant in the elemental rites. The whole sequence of eternal birth, growth, and death is not only recapitulated in the kind of creative "logic" of the poem: it is inevitably *felt* as a power moving through the interplay of images. And if, as Thomas admitted, some of his "earlier poems might appear to constitute a section from one long poem," so Whitman's poems become parts of one complex body through the successive, growing versions of *Leaves of Grass.*

We do not know how thoroughly Thomas read Whitman. It is possible that he may have been somewhat repelled by Whitman's expansiveness, looseness, and impulse for direct statement, elements which contrast severely with Thomas's own oblique compactness. But surely Thomas would quickly have penetrated, as did Ezra Pound, beneath these superficial elements and would have discovered a "blood" brother, of "one sap and one root" with himself. Whitman and Thomas discovered that techniques of distinctive kinds and images containing "elemental" qualities served them best in portraying the world they knew and the universe they imagined. The world and universe of Thomas's poetry are astonishingly similar to the world and universe of Whitman's. It is as though in Thomas, Whitman had found his ideal camerado-reader for "Crossing Brooklyn Ferry," one who responds fully and literally to the poem's central conceit which reaches a climax of direct identification:

What is more subtle than this which ties me to the woman or man that
　　looks in my face?
Which fuses me into you now, and pours my meaning into you?

BERNICE SLOTE and JAMES E. MILLER, JR.

Part V

EXTENSIONS

Leaving it to you to prove and define it,
Expecting the main things from you.
WALT WHITMAN
Poets to Come

The Greatest Living Patagonian

I WILL introduce Henry Miller with a quotation from *Tropic of Cancer:* "I sometimes ask myself how it happens that I attract nothing but crackbrained individuals, neurasthenics, neurotics, psychopaths—and Jews especially. There must be something in a healthy Gentile that excites the Jewish mind, like when he sees sour black bread." [1] The "healthy Gentile" is a good sobriquet for Miller, who usually refers to himself as the Happy Rock, Caliban, "just a Brooklyn boy," "someone who has gone off the gold standard of Literature," or—the name I like best—the Patagonian. What is a Patagonian? I don't know, but it is certainly something rare and *sui generis.* We can call Miller the greatest living Patagonian.

How is one to talk about Miller? There are authors one cannot write a book or even a good essay about. Arthur Rimbaud is one (and Miller's book on Rimbaud is one of the best books on Rimbaud ever written, although it is mostly about Henry Miller). D. H. Lawrence is another author one cannot encompass in a book "about" (Miller abandoned his book on Lawrence). And Miller himself is one of those Patagonian authors who just won't fit into a book. Every word he has ever written is autobiographical, but only in the way *Leaves of Grass* is autobiographical. There is not a word of "confession" in Miller. His amorous ex-

193

ploits are sometimes read as a kind of Brooklyn Casanova or male *Fanny Hill* but there is probably not a word of exaggeration or boasting to speak of—or only as much as the occasion would call for. The reader can and cannot reconstruct the Life of Henry Miller from his books, for Miller never sticks to the subject any more than Lawrence does. The fact is that there isn't any subject and Miller is its poet. But a little information about him might help present him to those who need an introduction. For myself, I do not read him consecutively; I choose one of his books blindly and open it at random. I have just done this; for an example I find: "Man is not at home in the universe, despite all the efforts of philosophers and metaphysicians to provide a soothing syrup. Thought is still a narcotic. The deepest question is *why*. And it is a forbidden one. The very asking is in the nature of cosmic sabotage. And the penalty is—the afflictions of Job." [2] Not the greatest prose probably, but Miller is not a writer; Henry James is a writer. Miller is a talker, a street-corner gabbler, a prophet, and a Patagonian.

What are the facts about Miller? I'm not sure how important they are. He was born in Brooklyn about 1890, of German ancestry, and in certain ways he is quite German. I have often thought that the Germans make the best Americans, though they certainly make the worst Germans. Miller understands the German in himself and in America. He compares Whitman and Goethe:

In Whitman the whole American scene comes to life, her past and her future, her birth and her death. Whatever there is of value in America Whitman has expressed, and there is nothing more to be said. The future belongs to the machine, to the robots. He was the Poet of the Body and Soul, Whitman. The first and the last poet. He is almost undecipherable today, a monument covered with rude hieroglyphics, for which there is no key . . . . There is no equivalent in the languages of Europe for the spirit which he immortalized. Europe is saturated with art and her soil is full of dead bones and her museums are bursting with plundered treasures, but what Europe has never had is a free, healthy spirit, what you might call a MAN. Goethe was the nearest approach, but Goethe was a stuffed shirt, by comparison. Goethe was a respectable citizen, a pedant, a bore, a universal spirit, but stamped with the German trade-mark, with the double eagle. The serenity of

Goethe, the calm, Olympian attitude, is nothing more than the drowsy stupor of a German bourgeois deity. Goethe is an end of something, Whitman is a beginning.[3]

If anybody can decipher the Whitman key it is Miller. Miller is the twentieth-century reincarnation of Whitman.

But to return to the "facts." The Brooklyn Boy went to a Brooklyn high school in a day when most high schools kept higher standards than most American universities today. He started at City College of New York but quit almost immediately and went to work for Atlas Portland Cement ("Everlasting Cement"), then for Western Union, where he became the personnel manager in the biggest city in the world. The Western Union is called the Cosmodemonic Telegraph Company in Miller's books, or in moments of gaiety the Cosmococcic Telegraph Company. One day while the vice-president was bawling him out, he mentioned to Miller that he would like to see someone write a sort of Horatio Alger book about the messengers.

I thought to myself [said Miller]—you poor old futzer, you, just wait until I get it off my chest . . . I'll give you an Horatio Alger book . . . . My head was in a whirl leaving his office. I saw the army of men, women and children that had passed through my hands, saw them weeping, begging, beseeching, imploring, cursing, spitting, fuming, threatening. I saw the tracks they left on the highways, lying on the floor of freight trains, the parents in rags, the coal box empty, the sink running over, the walls sweating and between the cold beads of sweat the cockroaches running like mad; I saw them hobbling along like twisted gnomes or falling backwards in the epileptic frenzy . . . ; I saw the walls giving way and the pest pouring out like a winged fluid, and the men higher up with their ironclad logic, waiting for it to blow over, waiting for everything to be patched up, waiting, waiting contentedly . . . saying that things were temporarily out of order. I saw the Horatio Alger hero, the dream of a sick America, mounting higher and higher, first messenger, then operator, then manager, then chief, then superintendent, then vice-president, then president, then trust magnate, then beer baron, then Lord of all the Americas, the money god, the god of gods, the clay of clay, nullity on high, zero with ninety-seven thousand decimals fore and aft. . . . I will give you Horatio Alger as he looks the day after the Apocalypse, when all the stink has cleared away.[4]

Start with the Sun

And he did. Miller's first book, *Tropic of Cancer*, was published in Paris in 1934 and was immediately famous and immediately banned in all the English-speaking countries, and still is. It is the Horatio Alger story with a vengeance. Miller had walked out of the Cosmodemonic Telegraph Company one day without a word; ever after he lived on his wits. He had managed to get to Paris on ten dollars, where he lived more than a decade, not during the gay prosperous Twenties but during the Great Depression. He starved, made friends by the score, mastered the French language and his own. It was not until the Second World War broke out that he returned to America to live at Big Sur, California. Among his best books several are banned: the two *Tropics*—*Tropic of Cancer* (1934) and *Tropic of Capricorn* (1939); *Black Spring* (1936); and part of the present trilogy *The Rosy Crucifixion* (including *Sexus*, *Plexus*, and *Nexus*).

Unfortunately for Miller he is a man without honor in his own country and in his own language. When *Tropic of Cancer* was published he was even denied entrance into England, held over in custody by the port authorities, and returned to France by the next boat. He made friends with his jailer and wrote a charming essay about him. But Miller has no sense of despair. At the beginning of *Tropic of Cancer* he writes: "I have no money, no resources, no hopes. I am the happiest man alive."

George Orwell was one of the few English critics who saw his worth, though (*mirabile dictu*) T. S. Eliot complimented him and even Ezra Pound. Pound in his usually ungracious manner gave *Tropic of Cancer* to a friend who later became Miller's publisher, and said: "Here is a dirty book worth reading." Pound even went so far as to try to enlist Miller in his economic system to save the world. Miller retaliated by writing a satire called *Money and How It Gets That Way*, dedicated to Ezra Pound. The acquaintanceship halted there, Miller's view of money being something like this (from *Tropic of Capricorn*):

To walk in money through the night crowd, protected by money, lulled by money, dulled by money, the crowd itself a money, the breath money, no least single object anywhere that is not money, money, money everywhere and still not enough, and then no money or a little money or less money or more money, but money, always money, and if you have money or you don't have money it is the money that counts and money makes money, *but what makes money make money?* (p. 123).

Pound didn't care for that brand of economics.

But all the writers jostled each other to welcome Miller among the elect, for the moment at least: Eliot, Herbert Read, Aldous Huxley, John Dos Passos, and among them some who really knew how good Miller was: William Carlos Williams, who called him the Dean, Lawrence Durrell, Paul Rosenfeld, Wallace Fowlie, Osbert Sitwell, Kenneth Patchen, many painters (Miller is a fanatical water colorist); but mostly he was beset by his neurasthenics and psychopaths, as any cosmodemonic poet must be. People of all sexes frequently turn up at Big Sur (where Miller lives) and announce that they want to join the Sex Cult. Miller gives them bus fare and a good dinner and sends them on their way.

Orwell has written one of the best essays on Miller ("Inside the Whale"), although he takes a sociological approach and tries to place Miller as a Depression writer or something of the sort. What astonished Orwell about Miller was the difference between his view and the existential bitterness of a novelist like Céline. Céline's *Voyage au bout de la Nuit* describes the meaninglessness of modern life and is thus a prototype of twentieth-century fiction. Orwell calls Céline's book a cry of unbearable disgust, a voice from the cesspool. And Orwell adds that *Tropic of Cancer* is almost exactly the opposite! Such a thing as Miller's book "has become so unusual as to seem almost anomalous, [for] it is the book of a man who is happy." Miller also had reached the bottom of the pit, as many writers do; but how, Orwell asks, could he have emerged unembittered, whole, laughing with joy? "Exactly the aspects of life that fill Céline with horror are the ones that appeal to him. So far from protesting, he is *accepting*. And the very word 'acceptance' calls up his real affinity, another American, Walt Whitman."

This is, indeed, the crux of the matter, and it is unfortunate that Orwell cannot see past the socio-economic situation with Whitman and Miller. Nevertheless, this English critic recognizes Miller's mastery of his material, and places him among the greatest writers of our age; more than that, he predicts that Miller will set the pace and attitude for the good novelist of the future. This has not happened yet, but I agree with Orwell that it must. Miller's influence today is primarily among poets; those poets who follow Whitman must necessarily follow Miller, even to the extent of giving up poetry in its formal sense and writing that personal apocalyptic prose which Miller does. It is the prose of the Bible of Hell that Blake talked about and Arthur Rimbaud wrote a chapter of.

What is this "acceptance" Orwell mentions in regard to Whitman and Henry Miller? On one level it is the poetry of cosmic consciousness, and on the most obvious level it is the poetry of the Romantic nineteenth century. Miller is unknown in this country because he represents the continental rather than the English influence. He breaks with the English literary tradition just as many of the twentieth-century Americans do, because his ancestry is not British, and not American colonial. He does not read the favored British writers, Milton, Marlowe, Pope, Donne. He reads what his grandparents knew was in the air when Victorianism was the genius of British poetry. He grew up with books by Dostoyevsky, Knut Hamsun, Strindberg, Nietzsche (especially Nietzsche), Elie Faure, Spengler. Like a true poet he found his way to Rimbaud, Ramakrishna, Blavatsky, Huysmans, Count Keyserling, Prince Kropotkin, Lao-Tse, Nostradamus, Petronius, Rabelais, Suzuki, Zen philosophy, Van Gogh. And in English he let himself be influenced not by the solid classics but by *Alice in Wonderland*, Chesterton's *St. Francis*, Conrad, Cooper, Emerson, Rider Haggard, G. A. Henty (the boy's historian—I remember being told when I was a boy that Henty had the facts all wrong), Joyce, Arthur Machen, Mencken, John Cowper Powys, Herbert Spencer's *Autobiography*, Thoreau on "Civil Disobedience," Emma Goldman, the great anarchist (whom he met), Whitman, of course, and perhaps above all, that companion piece to *Leaves of Grass* called *Huckleberry Finn*. Hardly a Great Books list from the shores of Lake Michigan—almost a period list. Miller will introduce his readers to strange masterpieces like Doughty's *Arabia Deserta* or to the journal of Anaïs Nin, which has never been published but which he (and other writers) swear is one of the masterpieces of the twentieth century. I imagine that Miller has read as much as any man living, but he does not have that religious solemnity about books which we are brought up in. Books, after all, are only mnemonic devices; and poets are always celebrating the burning of libraries. And as with libraries, so with monuments, and as with monuments, so with civilizations. But in Miller's case (*chez* Miller) there is no vindictiveness, no bitterness. Orwell was bothered when he met Miller because Miller didn't want to go to the Spanish Civil War and do battle on one side or the other. Miller is an anarchist of sorts, and he doesn't especially care which dog eats which dog. As it happens, the righteous Loyalists were eaten by the Communists and the righteous Falangists were eaten by the Nazis over the most decadent hole in Europe, so Miller was right.

Lawrence Durrell has said that the *Tropic* books were healthy where Céline and D. H. Lawrence were sick. Lawrence never escaped his puritanism and it is his heroic try that makes us honor him. Céline is the typical European man of despair—why should he not despair, this Frenchman of the trenches of World War One? We are raising up a generation of young American Célines, I'm afraid, but Miller's generation still had Whitman before their eyes and were not running back to the potholes and ash heaps of Europe. Miller is as good an antiquarian as anybody; in the medieval towns of France he goes wild with happiness; and he has written one of the best travel books on Greece ever done (the critics are unanimous about *The Colossus of Maroussi*); but to worship the "tradition" is to him the sheerest absurdity. Like most Americans, he shares the view of the first Henry Ford that history is bunk. He cannot forgive his "Nordic" ancestors for the doctrines of righteousness and cleanliness. His people, he says, were painfully clean:

Never once had they opened the door which leads to the soul; never once did they dream of taking a blind leap into the dark. After dinner the dishes were promptly washed and put in the closet; after the paper was read it was neatly folded and laid away on a shelf; after the clothes were washed they were ironed and folded and then tucked away in the drawers. Everything was for tomorrow, but tomorrow never came. The present was only a bridge and on this bridge they are still groaning, as the world groans, and not one idiot ever thinks of blowing up the bridge.[5]

Start with the Sun

As everyone knows, Cleanliness is the chief American industry. Miller is the most formidable anti-cleanliness poet since Walt Whitman, and his hatred of righteousness is also American, with the Americanism of Thoreau, Whitman, and Emma Goldman. Miller writes a good deal about cooking and wine-drinking. Americans are the worst cooks in the world, outside of the British; and Americans are also great drunkards who know nothing about wine. The Germanic-American Miller reintroduces good food and decent wine into our literature. One of his funniest essays is about the American loaf of bread, the poisonous loaf of cleanliness wrapped in cellophane, the manufacture of which is a heavy industry like steel.

Orwell and other critics tend to regard Miller as a kind of hedonist and professional do-nothing. And morally, they tend to regard him as one of that illustrious line of Americans who undermine the foundations of traditional morals. Miller quotes Thoreau's statement, which might almost be the motto of the cosmic writer: "Most of what my neighbors call good, I am profoundly convinced is evil, and if I repent anything, it is my good conduct that I repent." One could hardly call Thoreau a criminal, yet he had his run-ins with the law, just as Miller has, and for the same reasons. The strain of anarchism and amorality is growing stronger in American literature, or that branch of it that I am talking about, and Miller is one of its chief carriers. It is not only Emma Goldman, Thoreau, Mark Twain, Whitman, and Salinger but that whole literature of detachment from political hysteria and over-organization. America is still the only country where social idealism and experimentation have elbowroom; there are still communities that practice primitive Christianity, such as the Catholic anarchists; and just plain little homemade gardens of Eden such as Miller's cliff at Big Sur. The life he describes in *Big Sur and the Oranges of Hieronymus Bosch* is a far cry from the little fascist dreams of the New Classicists. And it is a far cry from the bitter isolationism of Robinson Jeffers or even of Lawrence. Morally I regard Miller as a holy man, as most of his adherents do.

Miller says in a little essay on Immorality and Morality: "What is moral and what is immoral? Nobody can ever answer this question satisfactorily. Not because morals ceaselessly evolve, but because the principle on which they depend is factitious. Morality is for slaves, for beings without spirit. And when I say spirit I mean the Holy Spirit." And he ends this little piece with a quotation from ancient Hindu scripture: *Evil does not exist.*

Whitman, Lawrence, Miller, and even Blake all have the reputation of being sex-obsessed, Miller especially. Where Whitman writes "copulation is no more rank to me than death is," Miller writes hundreds of pages describing in the minutest and clearest detail his exploits in bed. Every serious reader of erotica has remarked about Miller that he is probably the only author in history who writes about such things with complete ease and naturalness. Lawrence never quite rid himself of his puritanical salaciousness, nor Joyce; both had too much religion in their veins. It is funny to recollect that Lawrence thought *Ulysses* a smutty book and Joyce thought *Lady Chatterley* a smutty book. Both were right. But at least they *tried* to free themselves from literary morality. Miller's achievement is miraculous: he is screamingly funny without making fun of sex, the way Rabelais does. (Rabelais is, of course, magnificent; so is Boccaccio; but both write against the background of religion, like Joyce and Lawrence.) Miller is accurate and poetic in the highest degree; there is not a smirk anywhere in his writings. Miller undoubtedly profited from the mistakes of his predecessors; his aim was not to write about the erotic but to write the whole truth about the life he knew. This goal demanded the full vocabulary and iconography of sex, and it is possible that he is the first writer outside the Orient who has succeeded in writing as naturally about sex on a large scale as novelists ordinarily write about the dinner table or the battlefield. I think only an American could have performed this feat.

I believe that Miller has furthered literature for all writers by ignoring the art forms, the novel, the poem, the drama, and by sticking to the autobiographical novel. He says in *The Books in My Life* (one of the available works),

The autobiographical novel, which Emerson predicted would grow in importance with time, has replaced the great confessions. It is not a mixture of truth and fiction, this genre of literature, but an expansion and deepening of truth. It is more authentic, more veridical, than the diary. It is not the flimsy truth of facts which the authors of these autobiographical novels offer but the truth of emotion, reflection and understanding, truth digested and assimilated. The being revealing himself does so on all levels simultaneously.[6]

Everything Miller has written is part of this great amorphous autobiographical novel and it must be read not entirely but in large chunks to make sense. Many of the individual works are whole in themselves, one dealing with his life in Paris, one with his life as a New Yorker, and there is, in fact, a definite span of years encompassed in the works. But the volumes of essays are also part of the story and there is no way to make a whole out of the parts. Miller is easy to quote if one quotes carefully; the danger is that one can find massive contradictions, unless there is some awareness of the underlying world and the cosmic attitudes of the author. These views are by no means unique, as they are the same as those of all those poets and mystics I referred to in a previous essay. What makes Miller unique is his time and place; he is the only American of our time who has given us a full-scale interpretation of modern America other than the kind of thing we find in the cultural journals. Incidentally, we do not find Miller in these journals, which, presuming an interest in letters and art, are really organs of social and political opinion.

Readers of Whitman recall that Whitman was blistering about the materialism of this country a century ago, and its departure from the ideals of the founding fathers. Miller is scorching. Now it is a commonplace of modern poetry that the poet dissociates himself from life as it is lived by the average American today. But there is a vital difference between Eliot's condemnation of his country, which is an ideological thing decrying the whole philosophy of democracy, or Pound's hatred of the economic system, or Cummings' peevishness at the vulgarity of modern city life, and Miller's blast at the national blindness to life. Whitman and Miller heap abuse on the failure of the country to live up to its promise; Pound and Eliot condemn the country for coming into being in the first place. Miller writes as a poet about the demonic hideousness of New York City, Chicago, the South, or in raptures when there is anything to be rapturous about. But it is not Art that he cares about; it is man, man's treatment of man in America, and man's treatment of Nature. What we get in Miller is not a sense of superiority but fury, even the fury of the prophet of doom. And there is one further difference between Miller and the other poets I have mentioned. Miller knows America from the bottom up and from coast to coast. In the same way he knows Paris as few Frenchmen do. But when Miller describes slums it is usually with the joyous eye of the artist, not with the self-righteous sneer of the social reformer. Here, too, one might describe his psychology as "oriental" rather than modern. The cultural situation is a matter of complete indifference to him. Miller frequently immerses himself in such modern Indian mystics as Krishnamurti and Ramakrishna, but without any of the flap-doodle of the cultist. He is himself one of the foremost of the contemporary men of detachment. His influence (like that of Lawrence) comes as much from his life as from his writings.

As far as combating the "system" goes, that is nonsense. There is only one aim in life and that is to live it. In America it has become impossible, except for a few lucky or wise ones, for people to live their own lives; consequently, the poets and artists tend to move to the fringes of society. Wherever there are individuals, says Miller (like Thoreau), there are new frontiers. The American way of life has become illusory; we lead the lives of prisoners while we boast about free speech, free press, and free religion, none of which we actually do enjoy in full. The price for security has become too great; abundance has become a travesty. The only thing for non-enslaved man to do is to move out to the edge, lose contact with the machines of organization which are as ubiquitous in this country as in Russia. "Instead of bucking your head against a stone wall, sit quietly with hands folded and wait for the walls to crumble . . . . Don't sit and *pray* that it will happen! Just sit and *watch* it happen!" [7] These sayings the culture litterateur condemns as irresponsible. Miller follows through with the complete program of nonparticipation in our machine society, organized from the cradle to the grave. "Just as Gandhi successfully exploited the doctrine of nonresistance, so these 'aberrants' [faith healers] practiced nonrecognition—nonrecognition of sin, guilt, fear and disease . . . even death." Whitman also believed in nonrecognition of death. His view of death as part of life is one of the many reasons for his unpopularity in America, where death is considered a crime against society. "Why try to solve a problem? *Dissolve* it! [says Miller]. Fear not to be a coward, a traitor, a renegade. In this universe of ours there is room for all, perhaps even *need* for all. The sun does not inquire about rank and status before shedding its warmth; the cyclone levels the godly and the ungodly; the government takes your tax money even though it be tainted. Nor is the atom bomb a respector of persons. Perhaps that is why the righteous are squirming so!"

To place the individual before the state, whether Russian or American, is considered the first crime of modern man. To interpolate Miller, man is like the common soldier on the battle-field; he can know nothing of the battle at large or of its causes; he can know only the fifty feet or so in his immediate vicinity; within that radius he is a man responsible for himself and his fellows; beyond that he is powerless. Modern life, having made everyone state-conscious, has destroyed the individual. America has as few individuals today as Russia and as many taboos to keep the individual from coming to life as the USSR. First, we have contaminated the idea of society; second, we have contaminated the idea of community. Miller, writing about his little community at Big Sur, frowns on the idea of community itself.

To create community—and what is a nation, or a people, without a sense of community—there must be a common purpose. Even here in Big Sur, where the oranges are ready to blossom forth, there is no common purpose, no common effort. There is a remarkable neighbor-liness, but no community spirit. We have a Grange, as do other rural communities, but what is a "Grange" in the life of man? The real workers are outside the Grange. Just as the "real men of God" are out-side the Church. And the real leaders outside the world of politics.[8]

"We create our fate," says Miller. And better still: "Forget, forgive, renounce, abdicate." And "scrap the past instantly." Live the good life instantly; it's now or never and always has been.

Miller is "irresponsible" as far as official and popular politics go, or as far as common church morality goes, and as far as lit-erary manners go. But he is not a poseur, he has no program, but he has a deep and pure sense of morality. I would call him a total revolutionary, the man who will settle for nothing less than "Christmas on earth." His message is precisely that of Whitman, of Gandhi, of Rimbaud: "Everything we are taught is false"; and "Change your life." As a writer Miller may be second or third rate or of no rating at all; as a spiritual example he stands among the great men of our age. Will this ever be recognized? Not in our time probably.

Miller leads us away from the charnel house of nineteenth-century poetry; he does not even recognize the existence of twentieth-century poetry. For poetry has lost its significance, its relevance, and even its meaning in our time. To begin again it must repair to the wilderness, outside society, outside the city gates, a million miles from books and their keepers. Almost alone of the writers of our time Henry Miller has done this; I would guess that his following is enormous and that it is just beginning to grow. Like Nietzsche, like Lawrence, his word somehow spreads abroad and somehow cleanses the atmosphere of the mind of its age-old detritus of tradition, its habits of despair.

One word more: at the close of his beautiful clown story *The Smile at the Foot of the Ladder,* Miller talks about the clown, the hero of so much of the best contemporary literature.

Joy is like a river [says Miller]: it flows ceaselessly. It seems to me that this is the message which the clown is trying to convey to us, that we should participate through ceaseless flow and movement, that we should not stop to reflect, compare, analyze, possess, but flow on and through, endlessly, like music. This is the gift of surrender, and the clown makes it symbolically. It is for us to make it real.

At no time in the history of man has the world been so full of pain and anguish. Here and there, however, we meet with individuals who are untouched, unsullied, by the common grief. They are not heartless individuals, far from it! They are emancipated beings. For them the world is not what it seems to us. They see with other eyes. We say of them that they have died to the world. They live in the moment, fully, and the radiance which emanates from them is a perpetual song of joy.[9]

And Miller is certainly one of these who have died to the world, like the clown. The ponderous absurdities of modern literature and the world it perpetuates dissolve in the hilarities of this almost unknown American author; this poet who dissociates himself from the so-called modern age and whose one aim is to give literature back to life. There are not many of these emancipated beings left in our world, these clowns and clairvoyants, celebrants of the soul and of the flesh and of the still-remaining promise of America. But of these few great souls the greatest is the Patagonian.

KARL SHAPIRO

205

The True Contemporary

WHEN I was twenty years old I published a little book of poems privately. It was a confused book, a mixture of Elizabethan and Modern. This volume I sent to several famous poets, only one of whom took the trouble to reply. He was William Carlos Williams. Williams did not praise my book, but his letter, the first I had ever received from a real writer, was full of sympathy and kindliness for a young man who wanted to be a poet. While he had nothing encouraging to say about my poems, he had a good deal to say about the month of March and his anger at T. S. Eliot. The month of March figures a great deal in Williams' poetry, a violent and beautiful season in Williams' New Jersey, as it was in Maryland, where I lived. The diatribe against Eliot disturbed me deeply. I was a worshipper of Eliot then and a devout reader of the *Partisan Review*, which, although a highbrow left-wing magazine, took Eliot to be the sovereign poet and critic of the twentieth century. I could not understand how any modern poet, especially Williams, who seemed of an extraordinary freshness and originality, could say unkind things about Eliot.

In his autobiography, Williams refers to the publication of *The Waste Land* as "the great catastrophe." Looked at from Williams' point of view and from that of all the avant-garde of his time, it was indeed the great catastrophe. "It wiped out our world," says

Williams, "as if an atom bomb had been dropped upon it . . . I felt at once that it had set me back twenty years . . . . Critically Eliot returned us to the classroom just at the moment when I felt that we were on the point of an escape. . . . I knew at once that in certain ways I was most defeated." [1] Williams' recognition of the true nature of *The Waste Land* marks him as first-rate prophet in criticism. And the effects of Eliot's poem were even more far-reaching than Williams said; not only was it the poem the academy needed as a pseudo-modern example; it was a poem that made poetry and criticism one and the same thing, and that provided a justification for a new critical philosophy. Williams was also right in seeing that he was more damaged by this poem than anyone else. He was left high and dry: Pound, who was the co-author of Eliot's poem, and Marianne Moore were now polarized to Eliot. Williams felt all this and would feel it for another twenty years. His own poetry would have to progress against the growing orthodoxy of Eliot criticism.

The radical difference between Williams and, say, Eliot is that Williams divorces poetry from "culture," or tries to. Williams is fighting for the existence of poetry (where Eliot and Pound have fought for the "uses" of poetry). Williams' entire literary career has been dedicated to the struggle to preserve spontaneity and immediacy of experience. His explanations of these aims are certainly not as impressive as Eliot's and in fact lead to such confusing theories as Objectivism. In defence of Williams one can say that his theorizing is innocent, while in the case of the Pounds and Eliots it is calculated and tricky. In any case, Williams does not stand or fall on theory; he is willing to void it at a moment's notice. But it is unfortunate for him that he must engage in theory at all. At bottom Williams is not an intellectual, and he is too human, too sympathetic, too natural to become an anti-intellectual. Besides, as he says in his published letters, he is illogical. He would never be able to impress the *Partisan Review* or the highbrows who consider him a kind of intellectual slob (which he may be). The literary quarterly follows a party line of Culture, any Culture, but Culture is a *sine qua non* for the poet, according to them.

Williams is a guinea pig of modern poetry. He lends himself to the literature of the laboratory and a thousand trials and errors of criticism. He even writes a "mythic epic" like Pound and Eliot which all the culture critics seize on as proof that Williams is not a literary imbecile but one you can practically write books about. Williams has somehow maintained the respect of the official literati. Simultaneously, he has maintained the loyalty of the literary "underground." (It was Williams who introduced Allen Ginsberg's *Howl!* and dozens of related works which only poets have ever heard of.) He is the only modern poet who searches everywhere for new poetry.

The new schools of criticism have always tried to give Williams the benefit of the doubt as a poet of their persuasion. Especially the poem *Paterson* appeals to them as a work comparable to *The Waste Land* and the *Cantos* or the *Anabase* of St. John Perse. *Paterson* to these critics seems an epic in modern style, a "mythic" poem. Controversy over *Paterson* has been considerable; but at least it is recognized by these critics that Williams is as ambitious as his contemporaries in such an undertaking.

Paterson is a typical culture poem, the toughest thing Williams ever wrote but, according to the critics, the most important, a kind of New Jersey *Waste Land*. Williams is so innocent that he would even do that; and so honest that he is the first man to say it is a flop. In writing his large bad poem Williams was perhaps trying to test the validity of works like the *Cantos* and *The Waste Land*, even to compete with them. While he carried on a lifelong fight against Eliotism—a one-sided fight, for Eliot never deigned to notice this gadfly—he maintained a lifelong relationship with Pound. Williams' relationship to Pound is very much like Yeats's: an antimagnetic relationship. Pound leaned on Williams in the same way that Eliot and Pound leaned on each other. And Williams remained loyal to Pound because Pound seems to remain American rather than English. Williams is faithful to Pound through thick and thin, always annoyed with him, and always attempting to understand his position. Williams, if he lived a thousand years, would never admit that Pound's attraction is that of the demagogue. He can see the demagoguery of Eliot but not of Pound. Somehow he identifies himself with Pound. Williams himself was unseated from the poetry consultantship of the Library of Congress, with no organized protest from writers and scarcely any mention of it in the press. Pound was awarded a prize from the Library of Congress which was backed up by all the self-styled Great Poets of the English-speaking countries. Pound got his prize, was feted in the editorials of the national magazines, and was eventually freed without a trial. Williams went home and had a series of strokes. My point is that because Williams abhors fixed positions in politics as in poetics, he cannot impress officialdom.

Williams is the American poet who tries to fight off Europeanism. He fights it off, singlehanded, but he cannot impress the European with his cause. Neither can he impress the American. Williams creates his own Limbo, bait for all comers. Lacking the arrogance of an Eliot or a Pound, lacking philosophy or religion or logic, he is battered back and forth by the literati, who are always armed to the teeth with Positions and who can make anything out of him they want, except a bad poet. Eliot tried to polish him off by remarking that he had a kind of "local interest." To Eliot anything that is not of world cultural interest is "local."

Williams belongs to the generation of Modern Poetry, those poets who suddenly organized literature in 1920 or thereabouts. He was not a high-powered Modern because he lacked the political instinct, but he was aggressive and fought the distortions of Modernism throughout his life. His letters and essays and even his poems are all "local" in the sense that they are contemporary. He wanted poetry to belong to the present, not the past. This is the clue to his involvements with Ezra Pound and his hatred of Eliot. He is uncharitable about Wallace Stevens; yet he adores Marianne Moore (the female T. S. Eliot of Brooklyn and Eliot's only American disciple).

Williams has written a good deal of literary criticism himself, but he is not a critic in any accepted sense of that word. He is a poet even in his criticism; he refuses to use terminology and everything terminology stands for. He builds up no system; he abjures "style" in his prose, except when he is not sure of his ground. In such cases he writes a jaunty, affected lingo reminiscent of Pound or Hemingway. A good many of his judgments seem to be affected by personal loyalty mixed with an overpowering desire to be fair. One time, because of a letter from Robert Lowell, he seemed about to revise his opinion of Eliot. In Williams' world there are no hard and fast rules; the entire literary process is fluid; the governing principle is contemporaneity—immediacy.

There are basic contradictions of judgment in Williams' appraisals. For instance, he praises Marianne Moore excessively while he sees nothing of importance in Eliot. Williams also places Gertrude Stein with Pound as an important innovator. Pound he is inclined to favor from the start, even to a slight imitation of Pound's ideas of American history and banking. But the treatment of Pound is always anguished. One is inclined to feel that Williams does not look up to Pound but is pleased by Pound's interest in *him!* Williams has little use for Stevens, but this is consistent with Williams' objections to prettified language.

At the bottom of Williams' specific poetic judgments lies a theory of language, which is practically a mystique. Usually it is referred to as a *prosody*, and in the widest meaning of that term it is. The prosody mystique in Williams is the center of all his prose and must be understood if the nature of Williams' poetry is to be maintained. As my own opinion of Williams' poems puts him over and above Pound and Eliot and Cummings and Marianne Moore, all the theorists and purveyors of sociological opinion, I will attempt to examine Williams' "prosody."

II

At first glance, Williams' remarks about poetic form seem superficial and even inane. One thinks, well, here is a nice man who is sick and tired of sonnets and effeminate poeticising and who would like American poets to have some gusto and originality. On second glance, one thinks the old boy is becoming a bore with his din about prosody and "the line." And all that shrieking about the "language" in *Paterson* is as bad as the precise definition in the *Cantos* or the "way of saying it" in the *Four Quartets*. And because Williams refuses to use the standard terminology of criticism, because he has a sincere interest in an American poetry, and because he is so suggestible, at least in his early years, to the literary politics of his fellow writers, he generally sounds half unintelligible. But there is a lot more to his "prosody" than that, much more, in fact, than exists in the new criticism.

Prosody is the science of verse. In English there is not, and there has never been, such a science. (This is one field of study I feel qualified to pronounce upon: at one time or another I have read every work on English prosody; no two are alike; none is definitive; and all are bad.) English scholars have long since given up prosody studies as a hopeless task. Because prosody and versification have such a justifiably bad name in English literature, no reader is apt to prick up his ears when William Carlos Williams or anyone else introduces the subject. Prosody is a mare's nest. Eliot and Pound took care not to identify themselves as prosodists, even while they were quietly laying down laws for it. In public they always guffawed at the mention of the word.

By prosody Williams does not mean versification. If you examine his own poems or his own remarks about what he calls mysteriously "the line," you will see the following things: He neither preaches nor practices "foot" prosody; he does not preach or practice meters; nor syllabic versification, such as Marianne Moore adopted; nor is his prosody accentual; nor is it "typographical" or what one critic calls grandly "spatial" form; nor does he base versification on rhyme nor on the internal figurations which rhyme may produce, as in Hopkins. The prosody of Pound is based on cadence which runs close to foot prosody —an imitation of Homeric and English trisyllabic. Eliot's prosody is extremely conservative, either a copy of Laforgue, at its most daring, or of Milton's *Samson Agonistes* (though I have never examined this closely), and it degenerates easily into modified "iambic." Williams' prosody is more advanced than any of these: it consciously departs from every intonation of the past. This is also its danger, as it is its advantage.

The thing to remember about Williams' "line" is that it is not a prosodic line at all. The word "prosody" for him is a metaphor for the whole meaning of the poem. Iambics to him mean cottages all in a row: sameness, standardization of things and of lives. His refusal to write iambic is therefore the same thing as Whitman's. It means that the iambic is not a language for the American poet. Pound and Eliot maintained the same doctrine, each in a less convincing way.

A good start for understanding the significance of Williams' belief about prosody and language (they are the same thing) is to consider his contempt for the modern sonnet. The virtue of the sonnet (which is the only "set" form in the English language) is that it prescribes a kind of syllogism. A sonnet in its simplest form makes a statement, develops or contradicts it, then resolves it. It is a game; hence its popularity with lovers and poets. Eliot began by rejecting the sonnet; Pound rejected it after a few acrobatic flops. On the other hand, a poet like Cummings has advanced the sonnet to a new fame. With him it becomes the most ironical sonnet in English literature. What Williams resents about the sonnet form, even in the hands of Cummings, is the neatness of it. That is what the sonnet is for. The "line" (in this case the sonnet line) that builds up to the thrust is a trick poem or a formal exercise. A poem, according to Williams, should not be that closed, should not click like a box (which was Yeats's way of describing his own metrical poetry). The "closed" poem—the poem that clicks like a box—is the type of poem which has lately become a standard in the twentieth century; the most recent models were made by W. H. Auden.

All the appurtenances of the closed poem, especially the stanza, became anathema to Williams from the beginning. Rhyme itself seems to him meretricious; when he uses it (and he uses it as well as anybody), it is with a slur. The poem must not be governed by meters—any meters—nor by periods and paragraphs (stanzas) nor by the figures of speech. What is left? Nothing. The raw material of the poem is all. It is the same process that Whitman went through; a rebirth.

But Williams had even rejected Whitman's line. (We must try to remember that Williams uses the word "line," I think, in the metrical sense and in the linguistic sense at once.) The turning away from Whitman is all but fatal in Williams, but he manages to do pretty well in his own way. Williams grew up in the day when Whitman seemed incorrigibly nineteenth century and Emersonian. How Williams could have missed the lesson of Whitman is beyond me. But Williams started over, too. No ideas, no meters, no forms, no decorations; only the search for the raw poetry of experience.

"No ideas but in things," Williams said over and over, for a time. He became an "objectivist," a man on the search for objects instead of thoughts. But this was just a variation of Pound's imagism; for there could be no object-poetry that would lead anywhere; any more than Imagism could stand on its own legs. Williams dropped the Objectivist idea, just as he dropped the "antipoetic." These were harmful simplifications. Williams' larger conception of poetry is based on the understanding that a thing is neither poetic nor antipoetic, neither prose nor poetry: there is something else which cannot be so bound. To write a poem about a rotten apple is not "antipoetic"; people laugh at such a poem and love it precisely because it is the poetry of the thing. The poetry of the rotten apple lies outside prosody, outside what is proper for apple-poetry, and outside what is called Symbolism. (If you say "apple" to a modern critic you will be pelted with religion, mythology, and Freud before you can duck—but to Williams an apple is an apple.)

As for Williams' versification, it goes entirely by ear, and luckily for him he has a good ear most of the time. It is not cadenced, not accentualized, not syllabified, not metered. It may or may not have a "typographical" form: sometimes it has, sometimes it hasn't. For certain periods Williams will print in "couplets"; at other times in tercets; he is not averse to the single word per line nor the long line. Generally (and this is the significant thing) he accommodates the "line"—that is, the typographic or verse line—to the sense of the whole poem. Thus he is doing approximately what Hopkins did in sprung rhythm, creating a total form rather than a unit form. It was a horror to Williams to see *The Waste Land*, partly because of Eliot's use of the old "unit" forms: an iambic passage here; a trochaic passage there; an image poem here; a long rhetorical build-up there and so on, with no organic principle anywhere.

But Williams himself in his desperate moments does the same thing. *Paterson* is just as artificial as *The Waste Land* when it comes to the "line."

Williams and his contemporaries had been schooled to despise "narrative poetry." To tell a tale in verse seemed to the early modern poets of our century the weakest excuse for writing a poem. They tried to get rid of tale-telling altogether and switch to Ideas, which are much more "masculine" than narratives. There is a large residue of narration in Williams' collected poetry which for years he did not know what to do with. The wonderful episode 17 in *Paterson,* one of the most powerful passages Williams ever wrote, was without a context until he stuck it in *Paterson.* But true to his Modernist upbringing, he could not even then *narrate* it, any more than he could narrate *Paterson.* Williams' "epic" poem is thus just another example of *The Waste Land* technique. He is better when he writes about Sacco and Vanzetti (a theme which could not move the great culture poets to even a single word) or about the death of D. H. Lawrence (which the culture poets also avoided like the plague). An interesting thing about Williams' poems is that they move from one to the next easily. The "secret of that form," as Williams calls it somewhere, is to make poetry natural, not literary. This is, in fact, the secret of his "prosody," the secret of his "antipoetic" line, the secret of his concentration upon objects as ideas. *The "secret of that form" is the eradication of the line between poetry and prose, between life and art.* Eliot speaks of an art emotion, an emotion reserved for the moments when one turns on the esthetic faucet. And it is precisely this attitude toward poetry that Williams condemns.

At the present, at the end of his long struggle with prosody, Williams turns to something very like a "form" but so loose that one can hardly call it a form. Perhaps it began with an admiration of a little quatrain by Byron Vazakas which resembled typographically a toy pistol or the State of Oklahoma. Vazakas managed this thing for speaking in his own voice. Williams hit upon a step-down kind of typography which he has used constantly in recent years. But it is not a be-all and end-all; he may drop it any time he likes. It is not a syllogistic sonnet or ballade at any rate. This style differs from Williams' earlier style only in that it appears to conform to a certain regularity. But there is none, except the regularity of thought as it progresses in the poem.

Had Williams been as good a theoretician as he was a poet he would probably be the most famous American poet today. But Williams cannot explain, fortunately for him, or he explains badly when he does. It is the poem he is after. His kind of poem may be the chief development of the American poem since *Leaves of Grass.* When it is successful, as it is an amazing number of times, it abolishes the dualism of form-content, expression-artistry, and all those other dualisms which get in the way of art. Williams' almost mystical repetitions about "the line" (and somewhat wildly in *Paterson* about *Language*) are a decree against critical speculation about forms. He knows that forms are not predetermined, not inherited, not traditional. He knows, too, that forms do not matter for the honest artist, whether he uses them or not. It is when form becomes a fetish that he draws back and howls.

Speaking of howling, Williams has been the sole example in twentieth-century poetry, along with Lawrence, for hundreds upon hundreds of poets, the majority of whom are Americans who oppose the Eliot "line." Williams knows too much about poetry to set up a critical shop or lay out a curriculum like Pound. He is the godfather, all the same, of nearly all the existent avant-garde poetry, all the free poetry that exists in the English world today. This is recognized by the young poets who long ago branched away from the cultural highway and took to the back streets and bohemias of the land. Williams is no bohemian; he is a serious man of letters (as the stuffy expression goes), but he is closer to the life of the poet than any of his contemporaries. By the life of the poet I mean the man to whom the daily life is the poetry itself, whatever his occupation. Williams may have been trying to do the impossible in taking for granted the unity of expression and artistry in the early years of the century, but he was one of the few who accepted this high premise of the poet. When the "great catastrophe" occurred, most of Williams' friends dropped by the wayside or split into little groups or went over to the enemy, as Williams put it. It is curious that through all the ensuing years Williams remained loyal to Pound and could not perceive that it was Pound who was the lever for the catastrophe and would continue to be.

III

As a critic Williams has no credit whatever. Eliot puts up a full-scale esthetic which anticipates every question and answer. Pound bludgeons his opinions across to a few listeners. Yeats weaves over the crystal ball in a trance of culture sensibility. And poor Williams is haunted by the two spectres of Whitman and Pound, the genius and the crank.

Compared with Pound's prose, which has the tone of the voice from Sinai, Williams' critical style is weak and plaintive. At times it contains a note of hysteria, frequently its shrillness gets in the way of the clarity, but on the whole there is the pervading innocence and warmth of personality, heightened by genuine excitement. But when he intellectualizes he follows in the footsteps of the Eliot-Pound faction. He praises Joyce for his clarity and his great interest in form but his basic liking for Joyce has to do with Joyce's humanity. This is not a virtue that the Joyceans usually single out. And of course Williams is attracted by the banality of subject in *Ulysses.*

His allegiances are unstable and extreme. Williams reacts sharply to the immediate political or literary event. He is as prone to follow Pound (where the politics are not too obviously putrescent) as he is to follow the Left. Extremism seems to him worth a diagnosis. His detestation of Eliot seems to be a hatred for compromise; Williams does not compromise but he veers crazily from side to side. He writes about Lorca with a political passion while clinging with one hand to the coattails of Pound. He follows Pound's admiration of Jefferson while taking a "leftist" position on Jefferson. "Let's have a revolution every ten years," is Williams' view of Jefferson. Whereas Pound would say: A solid aristocracy without hereditary rights. At the end of a stirring, almost scholarly essay on Lorca he ends with a little stab at Whitman, saying that Whitman was a romantic "in a bad sense." Williams is always looking over his shoulder at Pound; in himself he feels no critical authority. Here he mimics the modern classical view of Whitman.

Frequently he takes off into the realm of esthetic speculation, always with a certain desperate gaiety that characterizes his criticism. "The poem alone focuses the world," he says. This pleases the Pound side of Williams. Or in an essay about E. E. Cummings: "We are inclined to forget that cummings has come *from* english to another province having escaped across a well defended border . . . ." [2] This is about the difference between English and American which Williams makes the center of his criticism. But he knows he is on the side of the Romantics, on the side of anyone who is opposed to "lapidary work," anyone who opposes a literary poem. Again he will buckle down to a first-rate piece of criticism in his bitter essay about the failure of Sandburg to continue as a poet. Here he is on safe ground. Williams is as close to Sandburg as twins but he can tell the difference between himself and the professional Americanism of Sandburg. He understands Sandburg because he has been through the same process of handling Americana. But Sandburg's soft-pedaling is to Williams the worst sort of propaganda verse. Sandburg follows the identical course Williams does in his own "formless" poetry; only Sandburg settles for a form and Williams still continues the search. When Williams talks about Auden he can say something as mixed-up and as *true* (reading Williams' criticism one begins to write like him, on both sides of the fence) as: "I wish I could enlist Auden in . . . a basic attack upon the whole realm of structure in the poem . . . . I am sure the attack must be concentrated on the *rigidity of the poetic foot.*" When Williams begins to underline something like "the rigidity of the poetic foot" he sounds even balmier than his friend Ezra. It is as though Williams had reduced all the cultural viciousness of modernism to prosody—which in fact he has done. Marianne Moore seems to him to have taken recourse "to the mathematics of art." He adores her persnickety syllable snipping, but he cannot abide Auden's much more fluid and graceful "feet." The point of argument seems to be British versus American. Puzzling over Dylan Thomas' poems after his death Williams said that they smacked of the divine. But having fallen between the two stools of the "divine" Eliot and the agnostic Pound, one is not sure what *divine* is, except, as Williams says, "drunken." Clinging desperately to the only poetic he knows he cries at last, "Without measure we are lost." *Measure* is used prosodically and abstractly, as the rule, the law—one is not sure how it is used.

IV

Williams is always more or less on the right track, but he never comes to the point in his criticism. He does in the poems.

Williams' poetry is bounded by *Kora in Hell* (1920) at the beginning of Williams' literary life and the epical *Paterson* at the other end. Pound wrote him about *Kora in Hell* and said, "The thing that saves your work is opacity, and don't forget it. Opacity is NOT an American quality." The opaque was something Pound might praise; and there is no telling how deeply influenced Williams might have been by this great literary law of

Pound's. There are three other books preceding *Kora*, but the original preface to *Kora* is a mightily opaque and gossipy monologue
sounding like Pound. More important, Williams announces that
the plan of *Kora* is "somewhat after the A.B.A. formula, that
one may support the other, clarifying or enforcing perhaps the
other's intention." This is the "form" of the *Cantos*, *The Waste
Land*, and other "mythic structures" of the Twenties. The real
precedents for the book, however, are the so-called prose poem,
the *Illuminations* of Rimbaud, the poetic notes of Baudelaire, the
abortive prose experiments of Eliot, and so on. Probably the real
model of the poem was the pretty little French poem, for children perhaps, called *Aucassin and Nicolette*. Williams was
charmed by this piece and evidently kept it in his mind as a form
using verse and prose. And the official precedent for *Kora* is a
book called *Varie Poesie dell'Abate Pietro Metastasio*, Venice,
1795, left by Pound.

Kora in Hell is a series of observations about poetry and the
stance of the poet, full of little psychological asides about our
civilization, not in the Poundian political way but in the surrealist
associational manner. It is not a surrealist poem, however; there
are no "correspondences" between the symbol and the content.
Williams is concerned, like all the avant-garde writers of his
time, with the feasibility of "associations"—the random use of intellectual and personal experience. Williams simply made it his
business to jot down something every night, however nonsensical,
and then make a comment on it. The chief and it may be the only
fact of interest about *Kora* is that *Paterson* coming at the end of
Williams' poetry uses the identical method. The method consists of a free use of poetic languages in various states of excitement, alternating with a free use of prose languages. Eliot, Pound,
and Joyce all attempted the same technique, with varying success.

But in between *Kora* and *Paterson* we have close to a thousand
pages of some of the best or most interesting American poetry in
our history. Almost all of this poetry is in a style which is immediately recognizable as Williams' own; further, it is a workable
style, one which permits him to write a poem almost at random.
(One critic takes pleasure in pointing out that many of Williams' poems are written on the backs of prescriptions.) At its
best, which is a good bit of the time, it is not "experimental"

poetry or crank technique. Naive it certainly is, even what some writers call primitive; it is precisely Williams' innocence of forms that frees him to respond to daily experience as a poet. Williams went on writing, day after day, year after year, losing manuscripts, not finishing them, giving them away, but never letting up. Poetry to him was a daily function of life, a means of seeing. In a sense, he is our first American poet since Whitman. It hardly matters that his counsellors poisoned his mind against Whitman; Whitman is his mentor after all.

Critics and journalists tend to heroize Williams for writing poems late at night after a hard day's work at the hospital. Williams has never felt heroic about being a physician. It is pointless to try to imagine Williams ensconced in some village on the Italian Riviera brooding over the effects of the 1905 nickel on the souls of little children. Williams was a New Jersey doctor and that is that. His poetry is the poetry of a very busy man, as busy, say, as Sir Walter Raleigh or Gerard Manley Hopkins. Not that one can generalize about busy poets and poets of leisure. A poet does pretty much what he likes—that is part of the reason why he is a poet. Williams wanted to be a doctor, have a family, live near New York City, and write poetry. As far as anyone knows he did all these things very admirably.

But the seeming offhandedness of Williams' poems *is* a condition of his life. Obviously the poems would be different had Williams not been a doctor. New Jersey, New York City, Ezra Pound, the delivery room, the back alleys of charity patients, home, the little magazine, the month of March, these are all the elements in which his poetry moves. Poets once accommodated themselves to improvisation at the dinner table of princes; Williams accommodates himself to the brutal round of modern professional life. It does not embitter him; it sweetens him. And the poems are "scrappy," as the critics note, but there is a method to their scrappiness. And they are not astrology or economics or theology. The element of speed in composing the poem is part of the technique of his poetry, just as speed is a factor in certain kinds of painting. There is, in fact, a definite "oriental" tendency in his work, not cultural orientalism like Pound's but an instinct for the work that is as natural as nature herself. And the daily life has a lot to do with it. He survives as a poet even better than his contemporaries, a consequence, perhaps, of his roots in a pedestrian world. Williams never became an "exile"; how can an obstetrician be an exile?

The earliest poems are marked by the ornate imprint of Pound (the use of foreign exclamations and translation-sounding rhetoric and even the "Browning" dramatics which Pound quickly switched away from when he discovered that he could be opaque with impunity). The character of this style is that of a half-biblical, half-Victorian tone which is the quality of all of Pound's early adaptations. In Williams it sounds like:

> Eight days went by, eight days
> Comforted by no nights, until finally:
> "Would you behold yourself old, beloved?" [3]

Actually Pound never rose above this style, either in the *Pisan Cantos* or in the latest additions to his epic. Williams saw through it more quickly. It goes on intermittently through "So art thou broken in upon me, Apollo" and many such imitations of Style but soon it stops abruptly. Where the break comes in Williams is in his break into his own thoughts: where he exclaims or asks:

> Your thighs are appletrees
> whose blossoms touch the sky.

Which is more or less phony Pound, but is followed by

> Which sky? . . .
>   Agh! what
> sort of man was Fragonard?

This is the beginning. Williams sheds figurative language as a snake sheds its skin; henceforth he is naked, a poet without decoration, without metaphor.

> March,
>   you remind me of
> the pyramids, our pyramids—

There is still a lot of mincing Italian, Spanish, Latin quotation, but this falls away also.

> a green truck
> dragging a concrete mixer

```
passes
in the street—
the clatter and true sound
of verse—
    .   .   .   .   .
Moral
    it looses me
Moral
    it supports me
Moral
    it has never ceased
    to flow
```

(through various series of data, menus, signs on walls, and labels on bottles). Then a descent into pure spoken idiom, the rejection of all the devices of poetry for speech, always a sign of the poet's sincerity. Where Eliot ends up snipping philosophy from textbooks, Pound cutting whole chapters from history documents and statistics, Williams dives back into the spoken tongue.

It can never be said of Williams that he writes a well-rounded poem like "Ode on a Grecian Urn" or "The Love Song of J. Alfred Prufrock" or even "my father moved through dooms of love." He loathes the *fait accompli* in poetry or in painting. On the other hand, he does not worship the "fragment" for the fragment's sake. He tries to find the center of his experience in relation to the art of poetry; and he finds it over and over again. His "discoveries" are many more than "The Red Wheelbarrow" or "The Botticellian Trees"—good poems but two of many hundreds which are not repeated in the anthologies.

Williams puts his poetry in a direct relationship with daily experience. With Eliot there is no daily experience: there are "symbols" of the quotidian (empty lots, carbuncular young men, sandwich papers along the Thames, the silence in the subway) and with Pound there are stock market reports, the struggles of artists, and war communiques. Williams tries to accommodate his poetry to what the day brings to a poet in a place like New Jersey, where there is no dazzle of the past or of the cultural present. Williams writes about a piece of paper being blown down the street which he is afraid to run over because it looks like a body; or an apple rotting on the porch rail.

He does not exploit his knowledge. It does not occur to him that what he happens to know as an expert might be turned to the uses of poetry. He is not trying to impress others. He himself is the organizing center of the poem, bringing together around him the untold *disjecta membra* of the day. Without metaphor. This is the challenge. Hence the directness of all his poems and their somewhat shocking physical quality. Williams is like Catullus in his outspokenness and unthinking sensuality and amorality—for there is no bragging or sexual athleticism (or asceticism either) in the poems. Pound is sexless, Eliot ascetic, Yeats roaring with libidinal anguish. Williams includes the physical in the day's work; he meets it at every turn, being a doctor, and is not obsessed.

> The young doctor is dancing with happiness
> in the sparkling wind, alone
> at the prow of the ferry! He notices
> the curdy barnacles and broken ice crusts . . .

or

> I bought a dishmop—
> having no daughter—

There is very little twentieth-century poetry like this except outside the English language. But Williams does not "translate" or "adapt" except infrequently. He refuses to improve upon the language—this is the whole secret of his flatness of style and the inconclusiveness of the forms. He writes in his speaking voice.

A newly published book by Williams serves better than anything I have ever read about him to clarify and sum up his poetry and his poetics. It is a strange and charming work called *I Wanted to Write a Poem.*[4] The book is an informal bibliography which is also a kind of autobiography. The editor, Edith Heal, lists the books chronologically, fifty of them, and gets the poet to discuss their inception. Mrs. Williams, the poet's editor throughout his career, makes additional comments. Throughout this running commentary one can follow the fifty-year search for form which has been Williams' lifelong preoccupation.

His earliest influences, he says, are Keats and Whitman. He would rather be a painter than a poet (his mother is an artist) but cannot because of the medical profession. He finds his contemporaries quickly: Wallace Stevens, Marianne Moore, Hilda Doolittle, Ezra Pound. Pound is the only one of these to whom he feels literary loyalty. Stevens tags him with the label "anti-poetic" which Williams resents ever after. (Mrs. Williams, curiously enough, does not understand the poet's rage over this designation.) He abandons rhyme and meter in his second book (1913). While he is writing *Kora*, "Prufrock" appears; Williams says in *I Wanted to Write a Poem:* "I had a violent feeling that Eliot had betrayed what I believed in. He was looking backward; I was looking forward. He was a conformist, with wit, learning which I did not possess . . . . But I felt he had rejected America and I refused to be rejected . . . . I realized the responsibility I must accept. I knew he would influence all subsequent American poets and take them out of my sphere. I had envisaged a new form of poetic composition, a form for the future. It was a shock to me that he was so tremendously successful; my contemporaries flocked to him—away from what I wanted. It forced me to be successful." He consciously rejects free verse, simultaneously rejecting metered verse. "The greatest problem [he says] was that I didn't know how to divide a poem into what perhaps my lyrical sense wanted." *Paterson* seems to him the answer: he personifies a city and follows its river (the Passaic) and the river-of-history from Paterson down to the sea. Documentary prose breaks the flow of the poetry. Evidently it is the formless form that he has been searching for. In *Paterson Two* he hits upon the step-down form in which all his subsequent poems are written. The line he now refers to as the "variable foot." He has found it and he still has room to admire the prosody of Robert Lowell. "His style should have been repugnant to me—but it wasn't."

What then is the "prosody" of the Williams poem? If we can believe that every good poem ever written in form is good despite the form, and that every formless (free verse) poem that succeeded has succeeded despite its formlessness, then we will be getting close to the idea of Williams' form. It is the purest theory of poetry I have ever heard of and I take it to be the idea of all poets, formalists or vers librists. For meter has nothing to do with it; meter is an aftereffect. Metaphor and simile have nothing to do with it. "The coinage of similes is a pastime of very low order, depending as it does upon a merely vegetable coincidence." Structure has nothing to do with it: you cannot remove the parts from the whole; or rather you cannot find the structure. Beautiful language has nothing to do with it any more than the antipoetic. And finally, poetry is a secular art "free from the smears of mystery."

I am not sure I understand all this (assuming I've got it down accurately) but I know in my bones it is right. It is not theory; it is the laborious explanation of an artist stammering out the reasons why his poem came out the way it did. Each poem is its own form, as it must be. The poem is unique and unrepeatable; it is when you repeat that form arises, for form is imitation, as in Eliot, precedent heaped upon precedent. With Williams the poem is raw, quivering, natural, an *objet trouvé*, something you look at twice before you pick it up. It is the extreme of the original, the condition of poetry which frightens off most poets, a complete breakthrough to his own language. It is the kind of poetry which it may take years to see but once seen remakes all other poetry and conceptions of poetry.

But I do not mean that Williams' works are perfection or even that he has written a score or two of poems which will set him beside Milton or Catullus or Marlowe. It is hard to judge such work comparatively; it is too new, too unlike anything else. But there is one sure sign of its value: it has already penetrated the poetry of a whole generation of American poets, not the ones we read month after month in the apple-pie-order journals of letters or the fat anthologies, but in the less known, less official magazines and pamphlets strewn over the countryside, and which Williams has always lent his hand to. With D. H. Lawrence, Williams is the leader of what authentic American poetry is being written today. Little enough of it is up to the mark, yet the tendency is the right one. The example is there in Williams' poems, not in his criticism. And it is being followed. When I read his poems I feel I am reading a foreign language, my language. After all, there is practically no American poetry to speak of, and nearly all of it has come in the twentieth century, and a good portion of that has been written by William Carlos Williams, as he hoped.

I call him the true contemporary because he saw the challenge from the beginning and saw it whole: to create American poetry out of nothing, out of that which had never lent itself to poetry before. To do this without betraying the present to the past (like Eliot) and without exploiting the present (like Sandburg) and without trying to force the future (like Pound). I call him the true contemporary because he could not resist trying to write the Great American Epic. But in Williams' case this can be overlooked: he has written enough true poetry to show the twentieth century that American and poet are not contradictions in terms.

KARL SHAPIRO

START WITH THE SUN

Start with the Sun

IN all periods when man finds himself alien to the whole, a lost cousin of the universe in which he has been displaced by his own mind's discoveries, he must make some effort to redefine himself. We say it is now that man is in trouble (though "now" may be in the eternal present). "Vitally, the human race is dying," wrote D. H. Lawrence in his 1930 *A Propos of Lady Chatterley's Lover*. "It is like a great uprooted tree, with its roots in the air. We must plant ourselves again in the universe." One solution for man's separateness is the theme of those we call life-writers—principally Walt Whitman, D. H. Lawrence, Hart Crane, Dylan Thomas—those who have a sense of the cosmos and who in their art perform the ritual of union. What they say in their work is a recognized primitive truth, though often expressed with symbolic complexity: that man may find himself both human and divine as he returns to touch the earth with awareness and love, and joins the sun's creative stream. "Start with the sun," said Lawrence as his conclusion to *Apocalypse*, "and the rest will slowly, slowly happen." That is, start with the elements, with the first principle of creation, with the knowing eye of the creative self.

The poetry which starts with the sun—the "life-poetry"— makes two great affirmations: connection and creation, and these squarely in the face of man's increasing terror at the loss of humanity and his bewilderment at the absence of God. The sense of humanity is best realized by *connection*, when man knows his own identity within the circle of the cosmos. The sense of divinity is found in *creation*, in the germinal sun of each beginning. To make these affirmations was Whitman's profound intention in *Leaves of Grass*. How he and other poets after him viewed nature and man and art will indicate more of the unity of their work.

Whitman was a preacher of sorts, and his recurring text was unity, or the theme of cosmic connections. Here the poet may say: I am part of all, or I am like all other forms, or I *am* all. All objects of the universe have reference to the soul, said Whitman. That we are part of the living incarnate cosmos was the great text of D. H. Lawrence to the very end, as he finally wrote in *Apocalypse:* "I am part of the sun as my eye is part of me. That I am part of the earth my feet know perfectly, and my blood is part of the sea." In all life is the "same old law," said Whitman. "The force that through the green fuse drives the flower/Drives my green age," wrote Thomas. One name for all, said Hart Crane:

> I dreamed that all men dropped their names, and sang
> As only they can praise, who build their days
> With fin and hoof, with wing and sweetened fang
> Struck free and holy in one Name always.

In Whitman's vision-poems man is even more wildly identified with every other man and animal and object. "We two, how long we were fool'd," he wrote:

> Now transmuted, we swiftly escape as Nature escapes,
> We are Nature, long have we been absent but now we return,
> We become plants, trunks, foliage, roots, bark,

and we are fishes, hawks, clouds, seas—"We are snow, rain, cold, darkness, we are each product and influence of the globe." This is the incantation of man's union with all of life. But even death has its position. Whitman marveled at the chemistry of the earth which makes spring out of compost. To be the earth and the sea is in the death-life cycle of Thomas's lines on the burning death of a child—death in which one must "enter again the round/Zion of the water bead/And the synagogue of the ear of corn."

The aim of the poetry of connections is outlined in one of Whitman's last poems ("As They Draw to a Close") in which he states the intentions of his songs: to introduce man through the fusion of Space and Time and "the flowing eternal identity" to Nature which encompasses all these and God—"to the joyous electric all," and even to an exultation in Death, which is also part of the scheme. The very bigness of this program did not bother Whitman, for the point was simple: wholeness and unity —or as man we die, and die in ourselves, if we are out of the rhythm of our natural home. The result of conscious and emotional attachment is freedom: "Me imperturbe, standing at ease in Nature." Only the planted tree has the power of the new leaf and the growing branch.

If the theme of life-poetry is first of all the wholeness of man and nature, its characteristic image and symbol will be taken from the archetypal rhythms of birth, death, and renewal; from the elements of water and earth, fire and air; from the alternation of day and night. It will use the old emotionally charged myths of Adam and the ark; of Dionysus and Persephone; of wine, the tree, the phoenix, the fish; of the zodiac and all weathers. Because the poet feels the natural world to be live, though not sentient, man may find his union in the sense of something beyond and before the reason—germ, sea, sun, touch, force, pulse— perhaps Thomas's "elementary town" in "Twenty-Four Years." He goes *in* to night, womb, seed; but he must be prepared to go outward as well as inward. Whitman, for example, sees the universe itself as a road for traveling souls in "Song of the Open Road." He is imaginatively at home in space with sun and stars, exuberantly

Speeding with tail'd meteors, throwing fire-balls like the rest,
Carrying the crescent child that carries its own full mother in its belly,

and, he continues in "Song of Myself," "I tread day and night such roads." In another line of that poem Whitman chants, "I ascend from the moon, I ascend from the night." Lawrence's lines in his last, unfinished "Prayer" are similar:

231

Give me the moon at my feet
Put my feet upon the crescent, like a Lord!

Such images become the sacred objects of man's ritual of celebration in the natural world. They remind him that he, too, is in the rhythmic design.

Another way of preserving the concept of man's cosmic nature is in the ancient dual glass of macrocosm and microcosm, in which the universe is body, and man is a universe compact. Whitman's "Out from Behind this Mask," a poem to confront a portrait, gives the most complete statement of the microcosm:

Out from behind this bending rough-cut mask,

.   .   .   .

This heart's geography's map, this limitless small continent, this sound-
less sea;
Out from the convolutions of this globe,
This subtler astronomic orb than sun or moon, than Jupiter, Venus,
Mars,
This condensation of the universe, (nay here the only universe,
Here the idea, all in this mystic handful wrapt) . . . .

These lines sound Elizabethan. One is reminded therefore that the idea of man as the universe condensed appears in many other times and kinds of poetry. The difference is that what may in some poetics be a manner, or a conceit, is organic metaphor in the Whitman kind of verse. It is almost less metaphor than literal belief. With Dylan Thomas, for example, nature habitually operates in sexual forms, beginning with the implied fecundity of the "torrent salmon sun" of the "Prologue" to his *Collected Poems* (see also "In the Beginning" and "My World is Pyramid"). This is not a mirror of the world, but the world as it is. Conversely, the body of man is made up of natural forces ("Light Breaks Where No Sun Shines"):

Dawn breaks behind the eyes;
From poles of skull and toe the windy blood
Slides like a sea. . . .

In other poems he uses the "seashell flesh," the "other sun" of the blood, "thunderclapping eyes," "weather in the flesh and bone," and reverses the images to those of man in nature, as in the lines from "In Country Sleep":

> the vein of birds in the winged, sloe wrist
> Of the wood! Pastoral beat of blood through the laced leaves!

The complete chain of images to and from man is suggested in elemental terms, as Thomas in "Especially When the October Wind" describes man "caught by the crabbing sun" and walking "on fire," casting his "shadow crab upon the land." But the focus can be reversed: man also throws his shadow shape into the sky. The myth of the man in the stars, the astrological macrocosm, is familiar in cosmic poetry. Thomas's sonnets of "Altarwise by Owl-Light" have their exegesis in the zodiac, according to Elder Olson in *The Poetry of Dylan Thomas*.[1] That Lawrence also used the Kabbalistic myth of the offspring of the stars, the children of Adam, is pointed out in *D. H. Lawrence and the Body Mystical* by Frederick Carter,[2] with whom Lawrence began the work which resulted in *Apocalypse*. And may not Whitman's "Children of Adam" poems refer obliquely to the descent through the body of what Carter calls that great original "Father of Men, the great protoplasm Adam," and the possible journey back to the beginning? The life-poets have generally told a universal story— the saga (in Thomas's phrase) from mermen to seraphim.

To start with the sun means also to start from beginnings. It means, in life-poetry, the theme of creation. And creation begins first of all with direct personal involvement. Out of yourself and nobody else, said Whitman, must come the recognition of life:

Stop this day and night with me and you shall possess the origin of all poems,
You shall possess the good of the earth and sun, (there are millions of suns left,)
You shall no longer take things at second or third hand, nor look through the eyes of the dead, nor feed on the spectres in books,
You shall not look through my eyes either, nor take things from me,
You shall listen to all sides and filter them from your self.

The journey in Time and Space must be a firsthand affair. He is lucky who knows where he is, who absorbs and returns directly, who is "the caresser of life wherever moving." If he senses the mystery ("alive in the waters and singingbirds" as Thomas described in "Poem in October"), he will also find a greater mystery, even a divinity in himself. Whitman suggests in many ways the divinity of man. Visually, he draws the halo—"no head without its nimbus of gold-color'd light" ("To You"). In "A Song for Occupations" he reverses the source of divine knowledge: bibles and religions "have all grown out of you";

It is not they who give the life, it is you who give the life,
Leaves are not more shed from the trees, or trees from the earth, than
they are shed out of you.

But the chief sign of man's divinity is his power to create. In this he is as good as God, and as responsible, Whitman says in "Laws for Creations."

God is sometimes identified with the life-force, and so symbolized by the sun as the pulse or force of creation, the power which orders the cosmos. Whitman's lines in "Passage to India" condense these uses of the sun-symbol:

O Thou transcendent,
Nameless, the fibre and the breath,
Light of the light, shedding forth universes, thou centre of them,

. . . . .

Thou pulse—thou motive of the stars, suns, systems,
That, circling, move in order, safe, harmonious,
Athwart the shapeless vastnesses of space. . . .

Lawrence sometimes thought of the physical sun, or light, as simply a part of the whole process of becoming (perhaps you and I and the sun, in the plasm of life, have created each other). But there is also a greater mystery, an interior light. In "Space," Lawrence speaks of a cosmic, wild heart

that sends pulses even through me;
and I call it the sun;
and I feel aristocratic, noble, when I feel a pulse go through me
from the wild heart of space, that I call the sun of suns.

Both Lawrence and Whitman used images of the revealed and the unknown (or dark) creative forces. Whitman in "Song of Myself" described this mysterious order: "The bright suns I see and the dark suns I cannot see are in their place." The sun finds its human evidence in the creative mind and the creative body; thus the importance of the sexual symbols used so frequently by both Lawrence and Thomas. All signs of power and growth in nature become sacred revelations. Crane thus presents in "Lachrymae Christi" a Dionysian Christ in the resurrection of spring, and Lawrence's terms of the primitive "mana" and "demiurge" emphasize the God-power in nature and the pulse of creative life which is the symbolic sun.

At this point in the literature of physical mysticism there is a turn in the idea of creator and creation. Though it is not unusual to think of God as the life-force, the pulse of creation, it is here that a special significance is given to the object itself. For the *object*, which is the incarnation of the divine impulse, may precede the *idea* of creation and be therefore the god himself. So the mystery is truly alive in the water and the singing birds. Whitman's constant invocations to object and person, to every body and leaf, are not accidents in his poetics. For in "Song of the Open Road," it is "you objects that call from diffusion my meanings and give them shape!" Lawrence's dramatic version of this idea is in "Red Geranium and Godly Mignonette." God did not plan these things; no one could have thought of them.

But imagine, among the mud and the mastodons
god sighing and yearning with tremendous creative yearning, in that
    dark green mess
oh, for some other beauty, some other beauty
that blossomed at last, red geranium, and mignonette.

Thus the creator (God or the poet) is in some great channel of heat and movement and desire, and is seen only in the body of what has appeared. God is both the urge and the object. In some of Lawrence's loveliest lines (in "The Body of God"),

    There is no god
    apart from poppies and the flying fish,
    men singing songs, and women brushing their hair in the sun.

To start with the sun is to start also with the creative, divine object, the physical world of the real poems—"what we call poems being merely pictures," said Whitman in "Spontaneous Me." To him, the real poems were in "The loving day, the mounting sun, the friend I am happy with," and in all human, physical nature. Perhaps the best statement of the intention of the life-poet is in the little-known lines of Whitman's "Debris":

I will take an egg out of the robin's nest in the orchard,
I will take a branch of gooseberries from the old bush in the garden,
    and go and preach to the world;
You shall see I will not meet a single heretic or scorner,
You shall see how I stump clergymen, and confound them,
You shall see me showing a scarlet tomato, and a white pebble from the
    beach.

What kind of poetry will come out of this emphasis on the creativeness and continuity of life? In the first place, man and all other physical forms will be the vocabulary of the poet—a kind of earth-language. Whitman made this very explicit in passages in "A Song of the Rolling Earth":

A song of the rolling earth, and of words according,
Were you thinking that those were the words, those upright lines?
    those curves, angles, dots?
No, those are not the words, the substantial words are in the ground
    and sea,
They are in the air, they are in you.

Human bodies are words, he says—and all the elements:

Air, soil, water, fire—those are words,
I myself am a word with them—my qualities interpenetrate with theirs
    —my name is nothing to them,
Though it were told in the three thousand languages, what would air,
    soil, water, fire, know of my name?

       .   .   .   .   .

I swear I begin to see little or nothing in audible words,
All merges toward the presentation of the unspoken meanings of the
    earth,
Toward him who sings the songs of the body and of the truths of the
    earth,
Toward him who makes the dictionaries of words that print cannot
    touch.

236

Some of the most vivid expressions of earth-language are in Thomas, perhaps because he is closer to the ancient Druidic lore of the first alphabet found in the shapes of twigs and trees. He uses the calligraphy of leaves in "A Winter's Tale," and in "Altarwise by Owl-Light" has one very compact passage:

> Now stamp the Lord's Prayer on a grain of rice,
> A Bible-leaved of all the written woods
> Strip to this tree: a rocking alphabet,
> Genesis in the root, the scarecrow word,
> And one light's language in the book of trees.

"Especially When the October Wind" is a language-poem on the substance of poetry: "syllabic blood," the "wordy shapes of women," the "vowelled beeches," "water's speeches," and the "dark-vowelled birds." The real poem finds the grammar to release the meaning implicit in man and the body of the world.

The poem is another object in a world of forms. The art of its creation is sometimes minimized if one looks at the rolling, seemingly diffuse lines of Whitman and Lawrence, or the density of language in Crane and Thomas. Why is one not more compact? Why is the other not more clear? (Why is Whitman's scarlet tomato not Lawrence's red geranium?) It is true that Lawrence emphasized the pulse and flow of open rhythms; Thomas said that his poems were "hewn." [3] But however the shape of the lines may differ, or the speed of articulation vary (as some poets work faster than others, so imagery may flash on the mind's screen by either slow motion or a high-speed projector), the one principle in common to all the poets who emphasize the life-process is freedom—or spontaneity, movement, scope. Whitman and Lawrence give the effect of a large, open, living flow in their prosody. Crane in his "condensed" and Thomas in his "compressed" poems also give the effect of daring and freedom in the way their images generate and fuse into a sometimes bewildering but actually organic stream. They skyrocket, though in different landscapes. Poetry is an artful earth in either form; it has the effect, not the actuality of freedom and the raw uncolored stuff. Though a poem may seem roughly free and simple on the surface, its sophistication may be in some interior logic—like Whitman's hinge of the hand that puts to scorn all machinery. Lesser poets and imitators of poets are likely to rely on the effect only. They end with exclamation without intention, with a line like a throw-away bottle. The real poem in Whitman's tradition is itself an earth-language. It too is an object, a form, an element. It has order and rhythm like the total cosmos. As life itself is always in movement, this kind of poem leads to unquietness, not completion. The true poems, said Whitman in "Song of the Answerer," are not the finish but the outset:

They bring none to his or her terminus or to be content and full,
Whom they take they take into space to behold the birth of stars, to
    learn one of the meanings,
To launch off with absolute faith, to sweep through the ceaseless rings
    and never be quiet again.

Never to be quiet again—this means that the true poem has in it the spark of creative power, that its physical form is creative as well as created. The poem is a process of creation which is never still in any real imagination.

Start with the sun, said Lawrence. Perhaps one begins and ends with genesis: As Thomas said of his own art, the poet writes "for the lovers, their arms/Round the griefs of the ages." It was Whitman's hope that life would be made evident, incarnate, in his own leaves and that they would transmit the creative sun: "Thou orb aloft full-dazzling!" he began his bardic invocation, "Strike through these chants." Writers in the Whitman tradition make the strongest affirmation possible: that we do not live by either illusion or disillusion; that no life is cheap or need be separate; that in the earth we may grow into possibilities; that we take nothing secondhand. To be absorbed directly out of the self and directly with the earth in the pulse of creation is no mean aim for a writer. Such an ideal, seriously practiced, might change the face of poetry in any period. Start with the sun: Perhaps then we may be absolved from the poetry of mirrors.

BERNICE SLOTE

NOTES AND
BIBLIOGRAPHY

Bibliography of Editions Used

WE have given reference notes only where they might be useful in helping the reader find material from which we quote. With a few exceptions (indicated by notes), the texts of work by Whitman, Lawrence, Crane, and Thomas are taken from the editions listed below. When it is convenient for the reader to find quotations from the shorter works, we have in our text identified only the general source. For the longer works (the novels of Lawrence), we have added page references in parentheses.

WALT WHITMAN

Complete Poetry and Selected Prose. Ed. and with an introd. by James E. Miller, Jr. Riverside ed. Boston: Houghton Mifflin Company, 1959. Including the Prefaces, "A Backward Glance O'er Travel'd Roads," and "Democratic Vistas."

"Specimen Days," in *The Complete Writings of Walt Whitman.* Ed. R. M. Bucke *et al.* 10 vols. New York and London: G. B. Putnam's Sons, 1902. Vol. IV.

Start with the Sun

D. H. LAWRENCE

Poems

The Complete Poems. Phoenix ed. 3 vols. London: William Heinemann Ltd., 1957. Including the author's note to *The Collected Poems* (1928), the original Foreword to *Pansies*, and Richard Aldington's Introduction to *Last Poems*.
Love Poems and Others. New York: Mitchell Kennerly, 1915.
New Poems. New York: B. W. Huebsch, 1920. Including the author's Preface.
Pansies. Limited ed., privately printed. London: P. R. Stephensen, 1929. Lawrence's signed statement in the book reads: "This limited edition [500] is printed complete, following the original manuscript, according to my wish."

Novels

Aaron's Rod. London: William Heinemann Ltd., 1954.
The Boy in the Bush, with M. L. Skinner. London: Martin Secker, 1924.
Kangaroo. New York: Thomas Seltzer, 1923.
Lady Chatterley's Lover. New York: Grove Press Inc., 1959.
The Lost Girl. New York: Thomas Seltzer, 1921.
The Man Who Died. London: Martin Secker, 1931.
The Plumed Serpent. New York: Alfred A. Knopf, 1933.
The Rainbow. New York: B. W. Huebsch, 1916.
St. Mawr. New York: Alfred A. Knopf, 1925.
Sons and Lovers. New York: Random House, "The Modern Library," n.d.
The Trespasser. London: William Heinemann Ltd., 1950.
The White Peacock. London: William Heinemann Ltd., 1950.
Women in Love. London: William Heinemann Ltd., 1954.

Studies

Apocalypse. With an introd. by Richard Aldington. London: Martin Secker, 1932.
A Propos of Lady Chatterley's Lover. London: Mandrake Press Ltd., 1930.
D. H. Lawrence's Unpublished Foreword to "Women in Love." San Francisco: Gelber, Lilienthal, Inc., 1936.
Fantasia of the Unconscious. New York: Thomas Seltzer, 1922.
"On Being a Man," in *Assorted Articles*. New York: Alfred A. Knopf, 1930.

Notes and Bibliography

Phoenix: The Posthumous Papers of D. H. Lawrence. Ed. and with an introd. by Edward D. McDonald. New York: The Viking Press, 1936.
Psychoanalysis and the Unconscious. New York: Thomas Seltzer, 1921.
Sea and Sardinia. London: William Heinemann Ltd., 1950.
Studies in Classic American Literature. New York: Albert & Charles Boni, 1930.

Letters

The Letters of D. H. Lawrence. Ed. and with an introd. by Aldous Huxley. New York: The Viking Press, 1932.

HART CRANE

The Collected Poems of Hart Crane. Ed. and with an introd. by Waldo Frank. Black and Gold ed. New York: Liveright Publishing Corporation, 1946. Including the essay, "Modern Poetry."
The Letters of Hart Crane. Ed. and with a Preface by Brom Weber. New York: Hermitage Press, 1952.

DYLAN THOMAS

The Collected Poems of Dylan Thomas. New York: New Directions, 1953.
Letters to Vernon Watkins. New York: New Directions, 1957.
Quite Early One Morning. New York: New Directions, 1954.

Notes

THE WHITMAN TRADITION

1. Sylvia Beach, in *Shakespeare and Company* (New York: Harcourt, Brace and Company, 1959), p. 128, says that after Eliot pronounced against Whitman, only "Joyce and the French and I" were old-fashioned enough to like him: "I could see with half an eye Whitman's influence on Joyce's work—hadn't he recited some lines to me one day?"

2. "Back to Poetry," in *Collected Criticism of Conrad Aiken from 1916 to the Present: A Reviewer's ABC* (New York: Meridian Books, Inc., 1958), p. 102. First published in the *Atlantic*, CLXVI (Aug. 1940), 217–223.

3. Letter to the author, 9 April 1959.

4. Henry Treece, *Dylan Thomas* (London: Lindsay Drummond Ltd., 1949), pp. 51–53.

5. Letter to an unidentified correspondent (15 Jan. 1932), in *The Letters of Hart Crane* (see bibliography), p. 395.

PART I. WALT WHITMAN AND THE SECRET OF HISTORY

1. Allen Ginsberg, *Howl!* (San Francisco: The City Lights Pocket Bookshop, 1956), pp. 23–24.

2. Federico Garcia Lorca, *Poet in New York*, trans. Ben Belitt (New York: Grove Press, 1955), pp. 118–127.

3. *The Poetry and Prose of Walt Whitman: with a biographical introduc-*

tion and a basic selection of early and recent critical commentary, ed. Louis Untermeyer (New York: Simon and Schuster, 1949), pp. 963–964.

4. Sidney Lanier, *The English Novel*, ed. Clarence Gohdes and Kemp Malone (Baltimore: The Johns Hopkins Press, 1945), p. 39.

5. See note 3, above, p. 996.

6. *Ibid.*, p. 1005.

7. Henry Adams, *The Education of Henry Adams* (Boston: Houghton Mifflin Company, 1918), pp. 384–385.

COSMIC CONSCIOUSNESS

1. Richard M. Bucke, *Cosmic Consciousness: a study in the evolution of the human mind* (New York: E. P. Dutton and Company, Inc., 1923).

2. Foreword by C. G. Jung to the Richard Wilhelm–Cary Baynes translation of the *I Ching* or *Book of Changes*, Bollingen Series XIX, 1950. The page references to Jung's foreword which follow are to the Anchor Books edition of *Psyche and Symbol: A Selection from the Writings of C. G. Jung* (New York: Doubleday and Company, Inc., 1958). Copyright © 1950 by Bollingen Foundation, Inc., New York.

3. *Psyche and Symbol*, p. 226.

4. *Ibid.*, pp. 227–228.

5. *Ibid.*, p. 230.

6. Alan Watts, *The Way of Zen* (New York: Pantheon Books, Inc., 1957), p. 85.

7. Erwin Schrodinger, *Mind and Matter* (Cambridge: Cambridge University Press, 1958).

8. Robert Graves, *The White Goddess* (New York: Farrar, Straus and Cudahy, 1948). Copyright 1948 by Robert Graves. Used by permission of Farrar, Straus and Cudahy. Page references are to the paperbound edition of *The White Goddess* (New York: Vintage Books, Inc., 1958), pp. 475–476.

9. *Ibid.*, p. 455.

THE POETICS OF THE COSMIC POEM

1. Letter to William D. O'Connor (6 Jan. 1865), in *The Poetry and Prose of Walt Whitman*, ed. Louis Untermeyer (New York: Simon and Schuster, 1949), p. 934.

2. T. S. Eliot, *Selected Essays: 1917–1932* (New York: Harcourt Brace & Co., 1932), p. 125, p. 10.

3. Henry Treece, *Dylan Thomas* (London: Lindsay Drummond Ltd., 1949), p. 39.

4. Yvor Winters, "The Significance of The Bridge, by Hart Crane, or What Are We to Think of Professor X?" in *In Defense of Reason* (New York: The Swallow Press and W. Morrow and Company, 1947).

5. D. H. Lawrence, *Psychoanalysis and the Unconscious* (see bibliography), p. 25, p. 50.

6. Brom Weber, *Hart Crane* (New York: The Bodley Press, 1948), p. 153.

7. See note 3, above.

8. John Malcolm Brinnin, *Dylan Thomas in America* (Boston: Little, Brown & Co., 1955), pp. 125–126.

9. See note 3, above, p. 47.

10. Unpublished letter to Mr. Harry Klopper (30 May 1946), used by permission of the Executor of the Dylan Thomas Estate and of the owner of the manuscript, Mr. Charles Feinberg. This passage may not be quoted in whole or in part without permission of Harold Ober Associates Inc.

PART II. THE FIRST WHITE ABORIGINAL

1. All of the prose quotations from Whitman are found in *Democratic Vistas* (see bibliography).

THE *LEAVES* OF D. H. LAWRENCE

1. F. R. Leavis, *D. H. Lawrence* (Cambridge, Eng.: The Minority Press, 1930), pp. 3–4.

2. Harry T. Moore, *The Life and Works of D. H. Lawrence* (New York: Twayne Publishers, 1951), pp. 311–316.

3. E. T. [Jessie Chambers Wood], *D. H. Lawrence: A Personal Record* (London: Jonathan Cape, 1935), p. 122.

4. Glenn Hughes, *Imagism and the Imagists* (Stanford: Stanford University Press, 1931), p. 170.

5. Dallas Kenmare, *Fire-Bird: A Study of D. H. Lawrence* (London: James Barrie, 1951), p. 81.

6. Harry T. Moore, *The Intelligent Heart* (New York: Farrar, Straus and Young, 1954), p. 62. Copyright 1954 by Harry T. Moore. Used by permission of the publisher.

7. Witter Bynner, *Journey with Genius* (New York: The John Day Company, 1951), p. 321.

8. Richard Ellman, "Barbed Wire and Coming Through," and Horace Gregory, "The Poetry of D. H. Lawrence," in *The Achievement of D. H. Lawrence*, ed. and with an introd. by Frederick J. Hoffman and Harry T. Moore (Norman: University of Oklahoma Press, 1953), p. 267, p. 249.

9. See note 3, above.

10. R. P. Blackmur, "D. H. Lawrence and Expressive Form," in *The Double Agent* (New York: Arrow Editions, 1935), pp. 103–120.

11. Letter to Harry T. Moore, in *The Intelligent Heart* (*op. cit.*), p. 79.

12. Letter to Catherine Carswell (11 Jan. 1916), in *The Letters of D. H. Lawrence* (see bibliography), p. 311; and Lawrence's Preface to *New Poems* (see bibliography), p. viii.

13. *D. H. Lawrence's Unpublished Foreword to "Women in Love"* (see bibliography).

14. Aldous Huxley, Introduction to *The Letters of D. H. Lawrence* (see bibliography), p. xx; and James E. Miller, Jr., *A Critical Guide to Leaves of Grass* (Chicago: The University of Chicago Press, 1957), pp. 6 ff.

15. Lady Cynthia Asquith's phrase, quoted by Lawrence in his letter to her (1 Sept. 1916), *Letters*, p. 369.

16. Rebecca West, *D. H. Lawrence* (London: Martin Secker, 1930), pp. 24-25.

17. Dorothy Brett, *Lawrence and Brett: A Friendship* (Philadelphia: Lippincott, 1933), p. 104.

18. The version of MS. "A."

19. Frieda Lawrence, *"Not I, but the Wind . . ."* (New York: The Viking Press, 1934), p. 295.

THE DANCE OF RAPTURE

1. J. Middleton Murry, *Son of Woman* (London: Jonathan Cape, 1936), p. 296.

2. F. R. Leavis, *D. H. Lawrence: Novelist* (New York: Alfred A. Knopf, 1956), p. x.

3. Letter to Godwin Baynes (Summer 1919), in *D. H. Lawrence: A Composite Biography*, ed. Edward Nehls, I (Madison: The University of Wisconsin Press, 1957), pp. 500-501.

4. T. S. Eliot, "Introduction: 1928," in *Ezra Pound: Selected Poems* (London: Faber and Faber, 1948), p. 8; and "Foreword," in Father William Tiverton, *D. H. Lawrence and Human Existence* (New York: Philosophical Library, 1951), p. viii.

PART III. VIEWS OF *THE BRIDGE*

1. Allen Tate, "A Distinguished Poet," *The Hound and Horn*, III (July-Sept. 1930), 580-585, and Yvor Winters, "The Progress of Hart Crane," *Poetry: A Magazine of Verse*, XXXVI (June 1930), 153-165.

2. Two significant articles are Stanley K. Coffman, Jr., "Symbolism in *The Bridge*," *PMLA*, LXVI (March 1951), 65-77, and John R. Willingham, " 'Three Songs' of Hart Crane's *The Bridge*: A Reconsideration," *American Literature*, XXVII (March 1955), 62-68.

3. Comments from letters to Gorham Munson (18 Feb. 1923), p. 125; Herbert Weinstock (22 April 1930), p. 350; Waldo Frank (23 Aug. 1926), p. 275; Selden Rodman (22 May 1930), p. 351; and Waldo Frank (27 Feb. 1923), p. 127, in *The Letters of Hart Crane* (see bibliography). All references to Crane's letters are to pages in this edition.

4. The view of Whitman as a cosmic poet is presented in the recent study by James E. Miller, Jr., *A Critical Guide to Leaves of Grass* (Chicago: The University of Chicago Press, 1957). See particularly Chapter 1, " 'Song of Myself' as Inverted Mystical Experience."

5. Letter to Caresse Crosby (26 Dec. 1929), p. 347.

6. Joseph Stella, "The Brooklyn Bridge," *transition*, 16-17 (June 1929), 87-88; reprinted from a monograph, *New York*, privately issued by Joseph Stella.

7. Waldo Frank, *In the American Jungle* (New York: Farrar & Rinehart, 1937), pp. 123-127.

8. Letter to Charlotte Rychtarik (21 July 1923), p. 140.
9. Letter to Otto H. Kahn (12 Sept. 1927), p. 305.
10. Letter to Caresse Crosby (17 Sept. 1929), p. 346.
11. See note 2, above.
12. Letter to Waldo Frank (23 Aug. 1926), p. 274.
13. Letter to Waldo Frank (12 Aug. 1926), p. 272.
14. Letters to Gorham Munson (18 Feb. 1923), pp. 124-125, and Otto H. Kahn (12 Sept. 1927), p. 305. See also the letter to Waldo Frank (18 Jan. 1926), pp. 232-233.
15. "General Aims and Theories," in Philip Horton, *Hart Crane* (New York: W. W. Norton & Co., 1937), pp. 323-328. See also Crane's letter to Harriet Monroe in *Poetry*, XXIX, 36-38.

PART IV. OF MONKEYS, NUDES, AND THE GOOD GRAY POET

1. Letter to the authors, 19 June 1955.
2. Dylan Thomas, *Letters to Vernon Watkins* (New York: New Directions, 1957), pp. 85-90.
3. See "A Pact," in Ezra Pound, *Selected Poems* (New York: New Directions, 1949), p. 27.
4. Letter to Gorham Munson (2 March 1923), in *The Letters of Hart Crane* (see bibliography), p. 128.
5. Henry Treece, *Dylan Thomas* (London: Lindsay Drummond Ltd., 1949), pp. 47-48.

PART V. THE GREATEST LIVING PATAGONIAN

1. Henry Miller, *Tropic of Cancer* (Paris: Obelisk Press, 1934), p. 167.
2. Henry Miller, *Big Sur and the Oranges of Hieronymus Bosch* (New York: New Directions, 1957), p. 227.
3. *Tropic of Cancer*, p. 232.
4. Henry Miller, *Tropic of Capricorn* (Paris: Obelisk Press, 1939), p. 31.
5. *Ibid.*, p. 10.
6. Henry Miller, *The Books in My Life* (New York: New Directions, 1952), p. 169.
7. *Big Sur and the Oranges of Hieronymus Bosch*, p. 165. The two quotations immediately following are from the same source, p. 166 and p. 230.
8. *Ibid.*, p. 264.
9. Henry Miller, *The Smile at the Foot of the Ladder* (New York: Duell, Sloan and Pearce, 1948), pp. 112-113.

THE TRUE CONTEMPORARY

1. William Carlos Williams, *Autobiography* (New York: Random House, 1951). Copyright 1951 by William Carlos Williams.
2. This quotation and the one which follows are from Williams' *Selected Essays* (New York: Random House, 1954). Copyright 1954 by William Carlos Williams.

3. William Carlos Williams, *The Collected Early Poems* (New York: New Directions, 1951). The quotations which follow also are from this collection.

4. William Carlos Williams, *I Wanted to Write a Poem: The Autobiography of the Works of a Poet*, reported and edited by Edith Heal (Boston: Beacon Press, 1958).

START WITH THE SUN

1. Elder Olson, *The Poetry of Dylan Thomas* (Chicago: The University of Chicago Press, 1955), pp. 64–86.

2. Frederick Carter, *D. H. Lawrence and the Body Mystical* (London: Denis Archer, 1932), pp. 21–25.

3. Henry Treece, *Dylan Thomas* (London: Lindsay Drummond Ltd., 1949), p. 141.

Index

251

Acknowledgments

THE authors wish to thank the following publications in which some of the sections of this book first appeared: *Centennial Review*, *Modern Language Notes*, *The Rising Generation* (Japan), *University of Kansas City Review*, *Western Humanities Review*. For permission to use copyrighted material, we thank the following authors, publishers, and authors' representatives: Curtis Brown, Ltd. and the Estate of D. H. Lawrence; Harold Ober Associates Incorporated; Allen Ginsberg and City Lights Books; Farrar, Straus and Cudahy, Inc.; Houghton Mifflin Company; Grove Press, Inc.; Random House Inc.; Mr. Waldo Frank; Les Éditions du Chêne; Liveright Publishing Corporation; Mr. Brom Weber; New Directions; Alan Watts and Pantheon Books Inc.; Alfred A. Knopf Incorporated; The Viking Press, Inc.; J. B. Lippincott Company; Beacon Press; Mr. Henry Miller; and Bollingen Foundation, Inc.

We are grateful to the Executor of the Dylan Thomas Estate for giving us permission to quote from an unpublished letter of Dylan Thomas.

Many others have helped us in individual ways. Special mention must be made of Mr. Bernard Kreissman, Assistant Director of Libraries for Humanities, the University of Nebraska, for his assistance in getting us the books we needed; Mr. Charles Feinberg, for reading and criticizing the manuscript; Mr. Malcolm Cowley, Mr. Waldo Frank, and Mr. Derek Stanford, for advice by letter and interview; Barbara A. Miller, for making the index; the Research Council of the University of Nebraska, and the American Council of Learned Societies, for grants in support of the project.